A Green Hill Far Away

Joan Vardy

www.gingernutbooks.co.uk

First Published in 2013
By Gingernut Books Ltd

All characters in this publication – other than the obvious
historical characters – are fictitious and any resemblance
to real persons, living or dead, is purely coincidental.

Cataloguing in Publication Data is available from the British Library

ISBN 978-1-907939-35-8

Printed and bound in Great Britain

Gingernut Books Ltd
Head Office
27 Sotheby Ave
Sutton-in-Ashfield NG17 5JU

www.gingernutbooks.co.uk

DEDICATION

I dedicate this book to my mam, for without her it never could have been written. All our family's treasures, gathered in over generations of hard work and honest living were handed down to my mam. These precious gifts she passed on to me in overflowing measures. Mothering love; a forever love which was always there, before the lullabies and beyond the letting go. Mam had a gift of joy, to turn a job into a game, for everyone to join in, sing and be happy. Yet still, mam found time in a busy day to share with me peace and beauty, even in a war-torn world. Mam had patience to teach me well, the hundreds of little tasks that no one has to think about teaching a child who can see and learn by copying, without even thinking for herself.

Each day brought new challenges, but with kindness, mam shared my load with me. Besides bearing her own heavy load of work and war and worry, she shared with me her Christian belief, the goodness of prayers and praise, and told me the stories of Jesus as she got on with her housework. In faith she journeyed on alone. Doctors and nurses could offer no help or advice on which way best to care for me. Mam did all she could for me, the best way she knew how. When the going got too tough for both of us, then mam cherished me with gentleness.

Then came the parting, the day I was taken away to a special school. Then mam found the self-control to say, "Toodle-oo, sunshine," and her deep mothering love was proven in the letting go.

ACKNOWLEDGEMENTS

Thank you to everyone who finds themselves in my book, or in another book like mine. For being there at just the right time, when needed the most, those who would say they needed no thanks, good people; like the ones who stretched out their hands to stop my pram from speeding down the shopping street; like the boy who stayed near me by the water's edge. He would not leave me till I turned away; and the elderly gentleman who led me to safety.

Thank you, all children, for playing with me, and thank you to everyone who treated me as an ordinary child, like the bus conductor who tossed me off the bus as it slowed down at the corner, and the gentleman who caught hold of me for a safe landing.

Thank you to everyone who found themselves helping me to write my book; my family and dearest friends for their encouragement, promptings and suggestions about the queries. I have taken your advice, put things to rights by adding small details, which I did not know at the time, but help the story be followed more easily. I have left out some small details, to tell a story truthfully as it was for me then. I could not always say how old I was – I was too young to know that. Some stories overlap others in time, but I think I have just about got them in the right order.

Thank you my husband, John Bryan, for sharing me with my book, for the five years it has taken me to write it. Thank you dad; for digging me out and prodding me. When self-doubt had stopped me from writing, by saying, "Do you remember the bomb on the park, and how you were locked in?" I had already written about the bomb, but afterwards thought I must have imagined that, and if that, how much more?

Thank you, my sister Beryl Parker. For giving up your time, adding to and confirming some of my memories; for your comments, amusing, reminiscent, from your heart, with an overcoming spirit, surprised at the high quality, powerful, a mixture of moods, creative and very, very funny. The last thing our Beryl said to me before she died was, “Now, how’s the book going? You must get it done.”

Thank you our daughter Aileen for your comments, ‘It was well explained.’ ‘I could tell you were little.’ ‘I really got the feeling when you were in that baby gas mask.’

Sorry Avalon, our granddaughter. My book made you cry. You were still young when you heard it, and I cried when I wrote it.

Thank you to my dearest friend Beryl, my school friend, my long-life friend. One letter from you reads, ‘thank you for the privilege of being chosen to comment on your book. I would like to know what sort of people it will reach. It will be there for future generations and your family. You see how different the war was for you, living in an industrial area rather than an agricultural or a coastal area like me. The thing that impresses me most is how much you can remember, and in what detail you can go into. I could really picture you in that wheelbarrow. I have enjoyed your book so far, and can’t wait for the next bit, when you’ve got time.’

Thank you to everyone in advance, who has a hand in getting my book published into all formats, from shop shelves into homes, into minds, and deep down into hearts. Thank you all, for helping me to achieve my aim; to let everyone know what it is like to be born blind, bear the hardships of wartime, believing in Jesus Christ as saviour.

INTRODUCTION

I have used just easy words to tell what life was like for me, being born blind during the Second World War and living in the East Midlands' coal fields in England. From being woken in the night by the air raid sirens when just a few months old, to going to school on a long train journey to a Sunshine Home for blind babies and young children.

All my memories are here. Some take just a few moments to read, so dip in where you will, and please feel free to have a good laugh along with me. But if you begin at the beginning, as I did, please read through the sad, bad bits with me. You may become more and more confused, as I did, but you will find out what blindness meant for one small child, who learnt to be content with her lot. I do wish that one day you too will find your own green hill, as I do in my second book *Where the Sunshine Shines*.

WHERE THE SUNSHINE SHINES

A pale blue sky filled the caravan window on the first morning of our summer holidays. I had woken early, so I lay quietly, wedged between my husband's bare back and the cold metal wall, with our large dog curled up on my feet. Our little girls breathed softly as they slept close by, whilst from over the field came the countryside sound of a tractor. On the farm, work had already begun.

No work for my man today. He could sleep on. For one whole week, there would be no pit blower to call the colliers to work on the day shift, sounding loud enough to awaken the whole village before daybreak. No pit chimneys to puther out smoke, smothering their wives' clean washing hanging out on the clothes lines to dry, or soot smuts to rain down and settle on their babies, put outside in their prams for the fresh air. Nor even the sound of coal trucks, screeching under their heavy burdens, being dragged along behind the panting engines. Nothing at all to spoil this morning, this pale blue sky. My heart filled with joy. I praised and thanked my Lord. In the stillness He spoke to me clearly. Commandingly He said, "Write a book. Call it, *Where the Sunshine Shines*."

I thought of the coming week spent with buckets and spades on the sands. No, that would not make a very good book. My Lord was asking me to write a book about the Sunshine Home for Blind Babies and Children, my first school, called Sunshine House, the place where I had learned to love Him. I saw the whole story at once, in a great golden globe. I wondered where to make a start.

ENGLAND, 1948

A little girl is five years old now, so she must go to school. She is travelling by train. It is taking her hundreds of miles away from her home. She must learn to be herself. I pictured this little girl, alone in the compartment. She is sitting in the middle of a long seat. The steam from the engine floats past the windows in billowing clouds, turning the pale spring sunshine into shades of gold. They fall on her face. She watches the shines and shadows through her sleepy eyes. She has rosy cheeks. Her hair is dark. It is plaited in pigtails and tied in stiff ribbon bows. They rest on her shoulders. She wears a dark raincoat. The front is spoiled, the sleeves are wet, and they are too long. Her feet just hang over the edge of the seat, showing the soles of her shoes, which are brand new.

Now she is gently stroking the plush seat, tracing the patterns with her fingertips, but she is so still, nobody could know just how happy she feels on the inside. The train sways and talks to her. It says, "far away, far away, far away, far away."

The pale blue sky fills the caravan window. I tell my Lord, "Nobody will know this little girl. If they have never known her past, how will they ever learn her future?"

My Lord says, "There must be an introduction. Yes, write the introduction first. Begin at the beginning."

BOMBERS DOWN MY BED

The eerie wail sounds in the darkness. Again, it comes to awaken me, to dream my sleepless dream. It's always the same. But there is no escape from a sleepless dream. I must live through it to the end.

I see the white light. I do like that white light. When the white light shines, the wall beside me glows a luminous green. The whole wall is a shining light. I know the wall is there when it is black, because then I can stretch out to touch it with the flat of my hand. It is cold and hard and I cannot push it away. But now the wall is shining green. I do not want to stretch out my hand to touch it. It may sink right through the wall and be covered in the green light.

Now there is another light, a line of light. It comes peeping through into this darkened room, through the gap near the hinges on the door. That is not a nice light. The bad thing is coming again. I do not feel it. I do not hear it at first, but it fills my whole being with an inborn fear, and I wait for the sound.

Now I am wet or cold. I know that wet and cold are two things, but I am not sure which one is which. Sound is a solid thing. As the murmur grows into a hum, it gently touches my face as with feathered fingertips. In the bed close beside me, the other one stirs and cries. I know, without knowing any words, she thinks she is alone.

The other one is another one like me. She can be two things, quiet and still, or noisy and jerking about. That is when I stiffen myself, keep still, keep quiet to keep safe. I am like the other one, so I must be two things, but I only know one of them. I do not cry. No use to cry. The sound grows into a throbbing chord. It strokes me from head to toe.

The good one always comes. The voice is soothing, but the hands are shaking. The good one will not stop the bad one. Behind the blackout, the window rattles in its frame, in fury or in fright. Outside the crescendo rises as chilling chords of engines fill the air. They rub me all over with a rough bath towel. Then whining scales come crashing through the green walls, flooding over me in waves. They roll over me to trap me underneath and hold me down, while thunder comes crushing down to beat me like a drum.

Is fear pain? Is sound pain? Or are these three things that come at the same time? Can three things come at the same time?

The bad thing is so strong now; it pushes me right inside myself, where I can shelter in the numbness. From the inside, I hear joyful laughing bells, defying my fears and ringing hope into my heart.

The other one quietens, and the good one makes us comfortable. She turns us over and tucks us in tight, close to each other.

When the good one leaves, the wall is black, and my dream is done, but just for now.

AIR RAID SHELTER

I was being carried by Mammy with the hurrying crowd to the shelter. The grey day was filled with deafening noise. Voices around me were saying, "It will stop soon." Then the siren's summons died down. Then we were sitting on an earth floor. As Mammy tucked my woolly blanket around me, she sing-songed, "You can be good now, because you're still only a baby, so you don't know any better. It's bad for your sister, because she is older."

So there I sat in the half-light, propped up against the wall, and huddled up to my mammy, while she dandled my miserable sister on her lap. I studied the wall, learning that bricks and mortar are not one bit bothered about all this din around us. The wall was quite empty, yet at the same time, the wall was full up. It could keep still and keep calm.

Then a voice with authority called loudly over the commotion, "You cannot stop in the entrance. It is dangerous here. You must go right inside the shelter."

Mammy pulled my blanket tightly around me. I felt my tummy sinking as I was swung and lifted high to be carried through the black gap into what seemed like a bottomless pit. From below me, the heat and stench rose up to meet me and, above the babbling blackness, I heard a scream; a scream of pain that I long time remembered.

"This is no place to be!" shouted my mammy, and, swinging round, she ran with me in her right arm, my sister in her left.

When we reached the fresh air again, there was a sudden cold dampness on my cheeks. The women called after us, "Come back, come back! You'll be bombed."

Mammy turned her head to call over her shoulder. Her wavy brown hair brushed against my face.

"If I've got to die, then I would rather die in my own home." Her young voice sounded determined.

I was still wrapped in a bundle, and I could see the green stripes of my blanket, and the pink stripes of my sister's blanket flapped in my face. Mammy hurried over the rough ground. I could not hold my head up straight and it bumped against her shoulder, so I could see the grey sky, and behind the misty grey sky, I saw the house tops rise and fall like a raging sea.

THE SOLDIER

I could sit up, and was put in my pram out on the backyard most mornings. One morning I had a tasting trial between my sun bonnet strings, a paper bag and some dried things which had been inside it. There were two bags, which had been tucked under my pram covers, and must have been forgotten when we came home from shopping, but I could only reach one bag.

The dry things were square and flat. If I rubbed them on my nose, they felt rough, but then I could see they were a light brown colour. They were far too dry to keep on putting in my mouth, and not very tasty, and they crumbled up in my hands. The white paper bag was better. It tasted sweeter, and made my mouth water. But it went into lumps which were so chewy. In this tasting trial, my bonnet strings came out on top. The taste of starch was not too bad, and they were good for sucking on, right there to pick up again if I dropped them.

I was quite happy in the sunshine, but then I sensed danger. There was nothing I could see but my white covers and clothes, nothing to hear, just the sounds of the morning that I was used to hearing. Nobody had touched me or rocked my pram. This was something new. There was something on my back, not really sharp, not really cold, yet fixed and frozen to me. I could not shrug it off. I looked over my shoulder to face my foe. Whatever it was, it was on top of our pebbledashed wall. I could see a dark shifting shadow against the dazzling blue sky. I screwed up my eyes, turned away and covered my ears with my hands to block it out. I thought it might go away, but it would not go away.

From somewhere far off, I heard screams. It was not me screaming. I was here, inside, in the blackness, all numb and safe. Then I heard my mammy calling, over and over again.

"She's ate the biscuits! She's ate the biscuits!"

A voice from behind me said, "Don't you get biscuits, ma'am?" It sounded so friendly that I felt warm again, and opened my eyes. Mammy's dark sleeves were moving about. She was picking up the broken biscuits and dropping them into the other paper bag. She was talking about me and biscuits. I turned to look over my shoulder again to see who it was that had frightened me so. Now I knew what I was supposed to be seeing, it seemed this young man had, as my mammy would say, a mucky face and a † dotty shot. He was wearing a black hat, or had thick black hair. He spoke straight at me, but his words were for my mammy.

"Sorry, ma'am. I frightened your baby, ma'am," he told her. "But it's been a time since I saw one."

"That's ok," said my mammy. "I can't think why she screamed at you like that. She's never seen a soldier before."

They went on chatting.

"Can't you put your pram somewhere else?" the soldier wondered. "Say in your front garden?"

He sounded sorry when Mammy told him that we had not got a front garden and this being the one and only spot that caught the morning sun I needed.

She said, "I can hardly offer you a biscuit now, but would you come in for a cuppa?"

"No thank you, ma'am, I've not much further to go now," he said. It was just to the next town, and so merrily did he go on his way up the hill. My mammy was still gathering biscuit fragments, murmuring to herself, "and it had to be my baby, it had to be my baby he saw."

† dotty shot – dirty shirt

NEXT TIME YOU'LL WEAR YOUR REINS

I was sitting in my pram outside the baker's shop. My mammy was inside, waiting to be served. My sister was running in and out of the doorway, chirruping and climbing on the pram wheels to come and see me. The baker's sunblind was pulled down. It completely blocked out the sky, making it too dull underneath for me to see anything except the silhouettes of shoppers in a rosy glow.

A group of shoppers stood near me, chatting. As my pram rolled towards them, they parted to let me pass between them, just as though I was being pushed, even though I was travelling handle first. They did not stop chatting; neither did they stop me. I kept on rolling down the street, into the daylight, where my covers looked brilliantly white. My pram picked up speed. The wheels whirred as I left the † coursey and careered on in the road. I put my hands over my face to take cover in the darkness. I heard the everyday noises of the town and my pram wheels squeaking as I travelled faster and faster.

Still, nobody took any notice of me. I knew that this hiding was doing me no good. It did not help. So I screamed. That scream was loud enough to be heard in heaven, and it was. It was my very first prayer, which was immediately answered. The pram came to a halt. I uncovered my eyes and felt happy, and was unharmed.

I could see many outstretched sleeves. One was bright green, and there was one bare forearm. None of the arms had bodies, but they all had hands, and they were all different and all clutching the edges of my pram. From way behind, I heard my mammy's voice. When she reached me, she was panting and so upset.

"You could have been thrown out. Next time, hold on," she told me. That scared me. Mammy sounded quite sure that there would be a next time. She cried and the shoppers gathered around her with comforting words. Mammy sobbed. "If there'd been traffic, if she'd tipped up, if she'd gone that bit further, † int't' square..." Then she turned to me.

"Next time, you'll wear your reins, like 'em or not," she said.

Nobody else spoke to me. I had been forgotten.

† coursey – pavement/sidewalk
† int't' – into the

THE NEXT TIME

The next time, my pram was in the sunny spot at the top

of our yard, near the back gate. I was happily bouncing and rocking myself, enjoying listening to the squeaking springs. They magnified my every movement. It felt like sitting on top of a wobbly jelly. Then without me knowing, my sister took off the pram brake. I lingered on the brink of descent just long enough for Mammy to come running up the yard to catch the pram. She wedged a building brick between the wheels and the spokes and went back into the house.

Then I saw my sister's brown head bobbing about. She warned me that she could remove both the brick and the brake. And by the sound of her voice, she elaborated on what the consequences would be for me. She jarred the pram, giving the brick and the brake a few hard kicks. I felt myself moving forward and grasped the sides of the pram as Mammy had said I must do. I rolled from the warm sunshine down into the shade made by the houses, and hurtled towards the back door. The wheels hit the step and the pram jumped straight through the open doorway, tipping up onto its handle in the back kitchen.

Mammy was talking to herself. She was saying what a mercy it was I had been held in by my reins, and it could have been a washday, and I could have been thrown into a tub of boiling water. I was hanging in the air by my reins pulling tightly round my chest and under my arms. I was hurting and crying.

Mammy picked me up and set the pram on its wheels, saying that she never thought I could be hurt by wearing my reins that were supposed to keep me safe. I had been wearing my thick brown winter coat, and she hoped it had protected me. But if I was hurt, there was not much she thought she could do about it. She would just have to put the pram on the yard again and keep her eye on me to see how I got on.

My resourceful mammy tied the pram to next door's railings with the washing line. She said to me, "Don't worry, it won't happen again."

But the pram had been tied so tightly to the railings that I could no longer make it move. It refused to respond to me. No more would it bounce up and down for me. No more would it rock back and forth. Now my pram stayed still and quiet. The silent springs sang no more. With no resistance from the ground, it seemed to me that there was no ground at all. With no feeling of movement beneath me, it seemed I hung in the air. My image of the world about me had gone. Now all I could do was sit still, tied in my pram, tied to the railings, in my own little world, just being a blind baby.

Tying my pram to the railings had just been a makeshift, Mammy said, for that day. A permanent remedy must be found. So she held a meeting. Present was me, sitting in my pram; my sister, sitting on the dustbin; our line post, and next door's railings. Mammy stood at the front, and she did most of the talking. But next door's railings seemed to have the biggest say.

They were the only railings in the way. The house next door, on the other side of us, had a pebbledashed wall. Some houses in the row had broken-down stone walls, while other houses had nothing, nothing for boundaries at all. But next door's house had railings on both sides. They were the kind of railings you can get your foot stuck in if you tried to climb up them. Mammy dare not hang her peg rugs over those railings to give them a good beating on cleaning-up day. Instead she used her washing line.

So it was left up to the line post to stand firm, Mammy hoped. After a long one-sided debate about me needing to bounce about in my pram, and my sister to be reckoned on, her favourite pastime being to remove the dustbin lid and rummage through its contents. Then Mammy summed up, with a blessing for the Girl Guide movement, and brought the meeting to a close with a victorious giggle.

The meeting was over. Each morning after that, Mammy devised a fine network around the pram wheels with the clothesline, leaving the springs free to move, mastering fancy knots to keep the dustbin lid on tightly, and fastening both securely to the line post.

I can just recall the bother once, when Mammy forgot it was dustbin day.

THE PLAYPEN

I was quite happy to be put on the yard in my pram. I could bounce about and feel the warm sunshine, and if it was windy, Mammy would put up the hood. 'Shed', she called it. Then I could suck the cotton trim. It tasted of soot. Mammy would keep coming out to see me, and spend some time chatting over the gate. But without warning, she might rock the pram. Then she would say, "You'd think she'd be glad to be rocked." I was, but only when I rocked myself.

When I went for a ride in the pram, I was not at all happy. I could not see as far as the pram handle, so I never knew when I might travel backwards, or get tipped back and forth. Mammy might play that game where she pushed me up the hill and let me roll back on my own. That was when I had to cling on more tightly than ever, and at any moment I might be startled by my rattle being shaken close by my face. It hurt my ears, and made me take in a sharp breath. So soon, Mammy made up her mind that I did not like my pram, and it was put away, up in the garret.

So for my morning fresh airing, Mammy put up a playpen on the yard, where it was just about level, near the back gate. But that was in the shadow of the house where there was no sun till teatime. I had a pegged rug to sit on and wore a winter coat to keep me warm. This coat was something new. It was not like the soft white clothes I had been used to wearing. It was rough, and was so stiff it was hard for me to bend my arms. It was heavy and dark. This coat was so long, I could not crawl in it. I caught my knees on it and pulled myself down to the rug. So I moved around the playpen on my bottom, keeping close to the bars. I did not notice the corners, but after some time I knew there was no way I could get out. I gave up trying.

The wind blew fresh on my cheeks. I was not too happy about my fresh airing, but I did not feel alone. Beside me, caught in this cage, was a pillow and a bear. The pillow was soft. It could be pushed and squeezed. It was coloured grey. When I picked it up to give it a cuddle, I saw the grey change to black and white stripes. But the bear was brown. Even when I picked it up, it was still brown. It was hard, even when I hugged it. I knew the bear was like me – it had arms and legs and a body. I knew which way up it went, because it had a head. No face, just like Mammy and Daddy. No face, just a head, and it did not like me, I could tell. But it seemed hardly fair that it should have to be in the cage with me. I might have thrown the poor thing over the playpen bars, but I could not see over the top. For me those bars went up and up forever.

When Mammy came out, she leaned over to reach me. So I formed a new idea about the playpen. In my head I made a picture, not a picture to see or a structure to feel, a vague sense that I cannot name. Mammy helped me to pull myself up with the bars. Holding tightly to keep myself standing was hard work. Then she showed me the wooden beads.

"Blue and green, green and blue," she said.

I saw the beads. I slid them along the rod. They made a clacking sound. But I could not get them off. My arms and legs got so tired; I just had to flop down. Mammy was telling our neighbour over the wall how I did not do anything, because I could not see that anything was there.

When she went back into the kitchen, I tried again to get those beads off the rod. I was surprised to feel a tickle in my throat, and hear my own voice making vowel sounds. My arms and legs hurt so much that I just had to leave go and flop down on the rug again, just sitting there making vowel sounds. I listened and learned that I could move my mouth into different shapes to make the sounds into different shapes.

Soon, Mammy made up her mind that I did not like the playpen, and it was put away, up in the garret. Then Mammy carried me round the house with her from room to room and sat me down on a rug while she got on with her work.

BABY GAS MASK

We were in the back bedroom. Mammy was making the bed. Then she came and sat down on the rug to tell me about this baby gas mask. I did not listen hard to what she was saying, because this thing that she called a gas mask had been laying about on the floor for a few days now, so I had found out about it for myself. It was somewhere for brown bear to stay safely out of sight.

Mammy thought that I was too big for the gas mask, but we had been given it.

"As you are, as you are," she said, and she announced, spiritedly, "We will have a go."

Mammy sat on the edge of the bed with me on her lap, the gas mask beside us. She was always kind to brown bear.

"Come out, teddy, you've had your turn," she said.

So now it must be my turn, I thought. But I did not want to play this game. I sat with a hard bar between my legs on Mammy's lap. There were straps with tinkling bells on the end fluttering about. Then brown bear came to play with me. It bounced closer and closer to me and tickled my nose, then hid itself away. I could not tell that the teddy was held by Mammy's hand. I did not like brown bear or its games. Then I begged in my heart that it might be gone for good.

Next, things happened so quickly, that I did not know how, but I found myself in darkness with just one tiny square of light to see through. I was shut inside a black dome, made more frightening because my legs dangled outside in the fresh air. Mammy was outside. Her voice sounded so muffled, I could not tell what she was saying. I knew that this was a good thing that Mammy was doing for me. There was a great hissing noise in my left ear. As Mammy pumped, she seemed to be counting. It was terrifying. I kicked, I screamed. I did not know the sound of my own voice; it was so near, so loud. I was trapped. The air smelt so bad, so musty. I tried holding my breath.

Then all at once I was back in the cold air in the bedroom, spluttering and trying to swim to the surface. Mammy was trembling as she held me close to her. All over my body I felt a tingling of pins and needles. Now I knew the shape of myself. Now I knew me. Mammy was crying. She shook her head. I felt her hair. It was wet on my face. I clung onto her ringlets.

She hurled that gas mask across the bedroom. I heard it land at the bottom of the stairs. When she had soothed us both, Mammy said to herself, "If the worst comes to it, then that would have to be that." Then to me, she said, "You would like it if we were all together, wouldn't you?"

And we both agreed that we would all like to be together for always. Then Mammy had a thought. Perhaps after all, it was teddy who I did not like. I was grateful that brown bear never came back again after I had wished him away. My sister remembers how serious mam and dad sounded when they talked about it at night, how dad agreed and supported mam, saying she was right. Then he went out in the dark and brought back another gas mask for me.

DOUBLE GRANDDAD, DOUBLE BED

I felt unsure about the new visitor. I was standing on the hearthrug, with my back to the fireplace. In the easy chair sat my granddad, who I had not met before. Mammy and Daddy had both gone upstairs, but they would not take me up there with them. They were making a lot of noise in the bedroom, with heavy bumping and scraping sounds.

Until this evening, I had thought that my eyesight was the same as everybody else's. I did not know that I could not see so well, and even less in the evening with the curtains shut and the light put on. I had put all my trust in my eyes. They told me the truth, the whole truth, and nothing but the truth. So I looked up at my granddad to see him for the first time. No face with eyes and ears, mouth or nose. No hair, just a bald pate. No way for me to share his loving glance. No way for me to return his loving smile. I saw my granddad - just a bright pink pudding plate. It was above the back of the easy chair, so to me, Granddad was just a head, not a whole man wearing dark clothing that I could not see, just a head, hovering like a pink balloon.

I was scared of this bobbing balloon and hid my eyes in my hands and turned my back on him. But things got worse when I opened my eyes. While I had been hiding them, Granddad had moved to the other chair, resting hisself on the back, just a pink pudding plate resting on its edge. I turned away again quickly, but I saw Granddad again, still bobbing about above the first chair. I thought I had only got one granddad, so now he had split hisself into two, and now he was talking to himself. I had a horrible thought. How many more bits might Granddad split hisself into? My tummy rolled over, and I let out one of my 'help me' screams.

Mammy wrapped a comforting arm around me.

Granddad spoke loudly. "This is the first time I've been, but if all she does is scream at me, I shan't be coming again."

Mammy told me that Granddad had bought a double bed for me and my sister, and how grand it would be for us now that we were both growing too big for the single bed. She tried to show me how there were two granddads, who had both come to visit us. To start with, they were both wearing different boots. But my mind was set. I had one mammy, one daddy, one sister, and one granddad. One double granddad.

Mammy said she had not told me things before because she thought I was too young, and I would think the wrong things. So now she tried in vain to tell me things which neither of us knew anything about. But it cleared the way for us to come closer. I could almost feel her sorrows falling from her as I took in the truth; that my eyes could not be trusted.

Daddy had a saying about starting from scratch again and building up, beginning again with nothing. And that was what I had to do.

GROWN-UP GASMASK

By remembering my baby gasmask, I tried very hard to use my grown-up one, although my gasmask was just an ordinary one, not like my sister's. Hers was a Mickey Mouse mask, but she would not let me touch it. Mammy explained to me that my sister was older than me, she knew more, and I was lucky to be so young. Then I was left with a nasty hurt feeling inside. I was as much a part of this family and this war as anybody else, so I had begun to both hate and fear this Mickey Mouse, who I had not seen.

Mammy showed me a picture of him in a book of my sister's, but all I could see of him were those big black ears. My fear and my hatred grew. So I liked my own gasmask all the more, and had no fear of it at all.

Each day, when we went upstairs to make the beds and tidy the rooms, I would practice my breathing with my sister, and it was quite a contest. Mammy taught me with patience and because I was the little one, I made sure that I learnt how to use my mask better than my big sister. But still, we both giggled over blowing raspberries. She seemed to accept me when I could make rude noises, and I grew to love the smell of that rubber.

Before hanging up my gasmask on the bedpost where it lived, Mammy would clear its window with spit and the corner of her pinafore. I liked the concertina part of the mask, but it was the green metallic disk on the base which carried me away. For when I rubbed my nose on it, I could see patterns of moving lights.

Now I squint back through the years to recall them. But they are lost.

THE AUCTION

Mamam was leading the way into the hall. She called for me and Mammy to follow her, saying, "It's all for a good cause." I knew that my mammy had not many pennies to spare. She had told me she did not need anything. That was why she had brought along her big shopping bag, hoping that on the way out, nobody would know whether she had bought anything or not.

Stepping inside the hall was like finding yourself in front of a big busy painting for me. It sounded hollow, yet it was full up. Chairs were noisily being scraped into place over the bare floorboards. Everybody was talking at once, so I could not tell what one of them was saying. When we were sitting down, waiting for a clock to say it was time to start the auction, Mamam made this time a time for just us two to share.

Mamam was my mammy's mam. That was why we called her Mamam. She was quiet on the inside, and quiet on the outside. She was warm on the inside, yet she kept cool on the outside, and I was precious to her. For me she had what nobody else had for me. Or what she had for nobody else but me. It was a sound in her throat which could smile, or it could stop her from crying. It agreed with me instead of saying, 'yes'. It could say, 'God bless you,' or 'I am pleased you are behaving yourself today'.

When the clock said it was time to start, Mamam said the lady at the front was holding things up for people to see, so people were calling out to get them, while others were still chatting. Some people sounded cross when they did not get what they wanted. Yet somehow Mamam kept fetching things. She said, "You have to, if you can. Besides, they only cost coppers."

For me she fetched three gollies on a ribbon, a white one, a pink one, and a blue one. Mammy thought they were for tying on a baby's pram, so Mamam untied them for me to play with. She folded up the ribbon round and round her hand, and she put it neatly into her pocket. She thought she had a good use for it at home. And she bought me some children's plates; thre'p'ny bit shapes with straight edges and corners. From then on, Mammy thought I had better use them for my sandwiches.

My Ruby Rabbit was bought that day at the auction. Mamam thought I was big enough to go up to the front on my own, but I would not, because I could not. So she came with me. I did not know that the lady was holding out a toy for me to take. All around me I heard cries of 'aww' and 'shame'. I am sure it was real heartfelt pity, but I was so hurt that my throat was too tight for me to say 'thank you', when the soft toy was put into my hands. Mamam led me back to our chairs. She said she would not take me up to the front again. I know now she meant it kindly, but I supposed then the reason was that I had not thanked the lady properly.

The smaller things were being auctioned first because it was thought that people would not stay to buy them if they had already bought bigger things. So while the auction carried on, Mammy took me on her lap and we looked at this toy together. She kept calling it a rabbit, and I kept asking her how she knew it was a rabbit. She knew by its long ears. The left one hung down limp and content, while the right one stood alert, ready to listen out for me to tell it my secrets. It had been knitted in grass-green garter stitch. I could feel the ridges running up its back. It was sitting up, showing its white tummy.

That night at home, my daddy named the rabbit Ruby. It was because of her bright red nose, he said.

Ruby Rabbit was my bedtime toy, and she lived to a very great age.

AS BRIGHT AS A PENNY

Christmas morning, my sister switched on the light above our bed. Santa would be leaving our toys downstairs, so we turned back the blankets to play. The sheet was so bright it stung my eyes. I screwed them up tight with the pain. We now slept in the double bed that the granddads had brought. It was very cold in the back bedroom, but we were just about to have what promised to be a good game with Rough and Ruby, our toys, when to spoil it all, a shout came from the front bedroom.

"It's four o' clock. Go back to sleep."

Rough was beloved by, and belonged to, my sister. And as his name suggests, he was a dog. He felt rough to touch, but

Mammy told me his fur had once been silky and a baby blue. But he had now grown grey, either with old age or the dye off his dubious stuffing coming out in the wash, his only mark of distinction being a blue darn on one end where his nose might once have been. Both in size and shape, Rough resembled a building brick, and he was a brick, too. He was hard enough to let me use him as a step, and I valued those few extra inches when I needed them the most.

Downstairs Santa had left two dolls. My sister's was bigger than mine. Hers was dressed. She named it Jean, although Mammy thought it had a boy's face. My dolly had no clothes to put on, and she looked more yellow than pink. She had a flat silver nose. Daddy named her Jenny. "As bright as a penny," he said. I asked him if it was her nose that was as bright as a penny, and his voice sounded upset. He told me that Jenny was not new, but after all, that was how he had named Ruby Rabbit for me.

The baby dolls were made of celluloid, hard plastic. Their arms and legs were held on by elastic threaded through their bodies and it often wore out, so it was quite normal for arms or legs to drop off during play, and a tricky task for Daddy to thread them with new elastic, using Mammy's button hook.

Jean's mouth was open just enough for her to be fed small objects by my sister, so that I could not pinch them from her. When required, they could be shook out through the hole in her body when the leg was pulled away. One day Jean was fed real food, which went bad inside her, and Mammy hunted the house out for days to find the cause of the smell, then doing a first aid act, with a makeshift stomach pump.

When I was old enough to know, I learnt how toys had been hard to come by, how Mam had travelled a long way to buy those two second-hand dolls. She had thought that both the dolls would fit into her large shopping bag, but there was only enough room for my doll. Without any clothes to wear, she must be hidden, while my sister's doll was carried in Mam's arms like a baby. The doll was dressed in a pale blue frock, a green corduroy coat and beret.

As Mam caught the bus to go home, it was getting dark, and beginning to rain. Standing room only inside the bus, and a polite gentleman gave up his seat for mam, with her baby and her groceries, to sit down. She was so tired, that she took the seat offered, with her groceries on her lap, cradling the baby in her arms, hoping, with the bus being so full, nobody would notice. But then she thought that people might think it was odd if she did not speak to the baby. So she spent the long journey caressing and cooing as though it was a real baby she had been nursing.

I did not part with my doll Jenny till years later. On that day, she was wearing a set of baby clothes I had knitted for her myself, and a terry towelling napkin, which mam had found years ago. It was clean, she told me, and folded. It must have fallen from a baby's pram, and it must have been a caring mother, to take a clean napkin. So she had kept it, just in case.

PUT OUT THAT LIGHT

One evening, after dark, I was romping with the cushions on the settee, when a knock came on the window and a gruff voice called out. So I reached up for the curtain, and pulled it open. Then the man growled something, I could not tell what. So I supposed he wanted me to answer the door. I climbed down from the settee and opened the front door to him. It was the air raid warden. He was very angry. I had let show a light, and now I would be the one to blame if we were bombed. Mammy and Daddy joined in with him, and I was told to keep off the settee after dark when the curtains were closed.

When the warden had gone, Mammy and Daddy talked about him. Mammy called him a nuisance, and other things, and Daddy had an idea of a place he could go, and what he might do once he got there.

Every night after that, the curtains were tucked down behind the settee, even for years after the war had ended.

My sister said, "Isn't it funny? I'd often wondered about it, but I never knew the reason why!"

OUR HOUSE, THE BUS STOP

The bus stopped on the front, right outside our door, and our front door opened straight out onto the coursey, so when the bus stopped; it was so close to our window that it blocked out the daylight. So we all had to stop whatever it was we were doing, and wait while the bus moved on. The bus would often stop while we were eating our dinner and Mammy would get upset about it. She knew that the passengers on the top deck could look down over our net curtain, and they could see what we were having. The light would be switched on, because we knew we would be in the dark because of the bus stopping.

Outside on the wall by the door, there was a board for timetables. It was empty. Timetables I knew were taught in school, so I thought that people were meant to know them off pat, like they learned them at school.

Sometimes people would knock on our door to ask when the next bus was due, and Mammy was always helpful. She would tell them how long they may have to wait, but she would not tell them where the bus might go. But once a lady was invited to come in for a drink of water while she waited, and in a roundabout way, while the lady and Mammy chatted, I'm sure she learned where the bus might take her.

Sometimes the passengers would sit on our windowsill while they waited, and on the green electric box at the side just there. Mammy would call them 'cheeky beggars'.

On nice days I might go out and ask people to pick me up and sit me on the windowsill. When the bus came along, they would offer to lift me down, thinking that I was going on the bus with somebody else waiting there, and they would be took aback when I said that, "This is my house. I live here."

Mammy said it was all right with her if that was what I liked to do, and it was my windowsill.

THE REWARD

I knew that I should not tell anybody where the buses went to, and that it was all to do with the war, but still it was all a big mix-up for me. Nobody must know, not even me. But I was often reminded about it, all the same.

One sunny morning, I was out on our front when a man seemed to appear from nowhere. He was wearing a light brown coat or mac, with a dark square on the front, which could have been a belt buckle. His hands were deep down in his pockets, just at my level, so I could see them.

He said, "Good morning to you." His voice was strange and worrying. He asked, "Where does the bus go?"

Now all us kids were brought up to be most polite to grown-ups, but I would not tell him. So we chatted on a while. Then he asked, "If you can't tell me where the bus goes, can you tell me where the road goes?"

I told him, "The road goes to the butcher's shop."

The man sounded cross. "The butcher's? Is that all? All you know, or all you're going to tell me?"

Just then, I heard the garage man calling out from across the road. The man mumbled something, moving off as quick as he had come. The garage man came a sprint over to our house, hammering on the front door. Mammy came quickly, still wiping her hands on her pinafore.

Then Mammy wanted to know about me and the mester, while the garage man, with other men, ran down the road. The man might have wanted the Post Office, I thought, and now I felt sorry that I had forgotten to tell him about that, and he may have wanted to go there.

Soon, I was surrounded on the coursey with a circle of trouser legs. Mammy wanted to know again about me and the mester, now that there was somebody there to listen, but this time I was not sure whether I got it right or not.

I was too occupied with all the trouser legs. To me they looked like dark thick railings. I could see the bright sunlight between them and the men's bodies were all joined up, making one black wall. I tried counting them then, by putting the legs into twos, starting with one leg that sloped towards another, and I called that one man. From there, I went around the ring, but some legs stood alone and some legs stood in threes, and I lost count when all the feet shuffled on the rough ground. Ah, I thought, they've all got their shoes on!

Then I told my story again. This time I forgot some of what I had already told, but I remembered other things, like the big belt buckle. Now it was a new story.

I counted the legs again. I told myself it was silly to start halfway round, so this time I started with the first pair I could see on the left, but now all the legs were moving, and a man's voice was saying that I must be given some sweets.

Mammy said we had used all our coupons, but the man insisted. "There must be a reward, rations or no rations," he said. Then a quiet spoken man volunteered to go to the shop. Voices said, "They won't let you have any," but he said he would dare to go and ask. "They'll have to give me some. They've got to do," he said.

I cannot recall the kind of sweets I was given. I ate one and did not like it, so I gave the rest to Mammy. The paper bag that they came in was all I wanted.

Sometimes when us kids had what we called tuffees, the shop would not give us a paper bag. The ones with just one corner in were for kids. We had to take a cone made from newspaper. But this bag was a white bag with two corners, the sort only given to grown-ups, and it was not at all creased.

That was reward enough for me.

S STANDS FOR SHELTER

Mammy sighed. She said she could not keep me in forever.

I was three now. I should be going out to play like the other kids. But first I must learn about the air raids. Although she did not think there would be one, I must still learn, just in case.

There was a sign about the air raids. It was up high on the jeweller's shop on the corner. Mammy took me there and picked me up to feel it. It was a cold enamel plate, somehow held up there by four big, rough bolts that were sticking out from it. There should have been one in each corner, Mammy said. But one of them was missing, I told her. She was not sure why one of them was missing, but it could be that somebody had found a better use for it.

On the black plate there was a big white arrow. It was like a finger, pointing to the shelter. The letter 'S' was the sign for shelter, and safety, so I thought, if there was an air raid, I would be safe if I came to the safety sign.

Mammy said, "No, oh, no! I shouldn't!" and her voice trailed. So we went around the corner, and stood on the edge of the coursey. I must not cross this road unless I heard the siren, but then this was the place where I must come. Oh, Mammy said that I would know when I heard the siren. There would be no mistaking it. Everybody would be rushing, but I must try not to run. Her voice quavered. "I should think somebody'd take you across wi' 'em. If they don't, you'll 'ave to foller 'em," she said. "But you must go to the shelter, and you must wait there for me."

The back gate shut heavily behind me. I heard Mammy sniffing as she went down the yard. Then the kitchen door banged shut. I realised I was on my own. I took in great gasps of the cold morning air, and shouted to the kids I could hear up the road.

"I can play! I can play!"

The game that morning was 'follow my leader'. I thought the kids were just going up and down the road, enjoying themselves. They were laughing and shouting as they went. I did not see that they were hopping or jumping, or skipping. I was told I must "Foller't marks on't coursey," and warned that if I did not copy, they would not let me play with them. I just followed on behind the others, hearing their happy shouts, straddled along the road.

At the back with me, there was a little one. The kids let him play, because he was just too young to copy them. He helped me by telling me to feel his legs, but his legs could not do what they should, so we did a funny little dance as we followed along. When we both caught up with the leader, the kids told him that I would not join in. They pushed me in the middle of the circle to face him. They gathered around us in silence.

As the leader thought it over, I watched in wonder. He could just move his hand over our gate, making white lines. I begged to know how it was done. Nobody had ever asked him that before. Swollen with pride with my admiration for him, he gave me a little white stick, folding my fingers around it to hold it properly.

"Copy me," he said. I waved my hand about in the air as I thought he had done, but no marks came on the gate. Then I was shown that the stick must touch the gate, but then I pressed on too hard. The stick snapped into two bits. I thought I had broken it, but I was amazed to find that it still worked, so now I understood. I felt I knew about the whole world; and everything in it that there is to be known.

I was wrong. There was a little more learning for me that day. The leader told me, "Learning's like playing, really. Would you like to learn to write, like we do at school?"

Would I just! The white line showed up very well on our dark maroon gate, and using it for a blackboard, my leader made a good teacher. My lesson began.

"Copy me," he said. "Do a snake, like this."

"Like a 's' for shelter?" I asked him.

There was a silence. I thought it said, be quiet, don't interrupt.

But my teacher said, "Not everybody knows about that."

I copied his 's' for shelter.

"Next to it, do a chimdey, with a pot on each side," he said.

So that's what a chimdey looks like, I thought. I could not see them on the house tops. I did not even know that houses had roofs. Next I copied his stick standing up, and lastly a stick with another stick going over the top, like a pick standing on its handle, I was told. I was a girl, so I would not know about that, but his daddy had one, because he worked down the pit. But my daddy only worked on the pit top.

So that was all there was to it. I could write, so why did kids go to school? I wondered. I was handed a new stick, and told I must copy this out properly, or it would not make sense. I was to write it on every house up the road, and everybody will know about the 's' for shelter sign, I thought.

I told my teacher how all the houses looked like one house to me, because they were all joined up, and I could not see if there was a house behind a high gate. It was summed up for me. One doorstep with a windowsill makes one house. Or one gate makes one house. The leader then gave a hooting call for his band to follow him, and they were gone.

I made a start with next door's gate by doing the snake, then running back to our gate to check every part of each picture. The chimdey with a pot on each side, the stick standing up, and the pick, standing on its handle. I did the same on the jeweller's shop doorstep. Then I worked my way up the road, drawing on steps and sills and gates, but I missed out the chip shop's back garden, because they had neither step nor sill, nor gate.

Soon, I managed to write without going back to our gate to

check every time for each little picture. I went on up the road drawing my little pictures, until I came to some steep steps. I crept up, feeling the rises and treads, puzzled to know how many houses there might be at the top. Somehow I thought that there might be a door for each step. I think there were four in all, but at the top, there was just one door, and I could not find a windowsill. I wondered how many steps I should draw on, but after giving it some thought, I climbed down backwards, writing on every step, even though I could not see my white lines against the clean white stones.

By this time, my stick was almost used up. It was so little, that I dropped it. I hunted for it on the rough ground, and I was still groping for the little stick in ashes or slag, when I heard the shouting. I dusted myself down, and ran to see what it was I was missing.

A crowd had gathered on the corner. It seemed like half the road was there, all of them talking at the same time. A woman was shouting at the kids. As I understood it, one of them had used her windowsill for a lavatory.

How could they climb up? I thought. The question was; which one of them would do such a thing?

The kids all said, "It were 'er. It were 'er."

The woman drew in a great breath. "She's got bad eyes. She can't write! Have you had some chalk?" I was asked.

I had not heard the word chalk before, but I had to show my hands. I looked at them. They were black. The woman said, "I don't know where you've been, but it's not chalk on your hands. Mind you wash them, before you sit to t'table."

The jeweller was wanting to know just how many customers did they think he would get coming to his shop, with such a thing as that on his doorstep? And he was wanting to know just who was going to clear it off.

Our neighbour over the wall was elected, because she had

the most kids. "But my kids can't write," she excused herself. So another mummy offered.

"It'll be one o' my little beggars, I'll be bound," she said.

Our road had never seen anything like it, not even on a Friday. It was heads down, bottoms up all along the road. I walked up and down the line inspecting long white skirts, shoes upside down with long heels, bright coloured pinafore strap tails wagging in the wind. There was such a clanking of buckets, such bristling of brushes, such showers of soapsuds wrung out from floorcloths as you never did see before in your life.

And at the house with the steep steps, I am sure I heard more four-letter words slip out than were scrubbed out, till every trace of my war effort was gone.

When Mammy had done, she led me down our back yard. Her hand was still wet and slippery. In her other hand, the bucket made a chirrupy, chirrupy sound. When we were near the back door, she said, "Maybe you'd better come in. 'Appen that's enough for your first day." Her voice was gentle, at the same time excited. I felt sure we shared a secret. My heart was overflowing with joy, but I knew the words must stay stuck inside my chest, so tears filled my eyes as I washed my hands in the bucket of warm water before I sat to table.

My mammy told Daddy all about it that night at dinner, how every gate and every windowsill had shone in the morning sunlight, "even them as 'asn't seen soap and watter for a good long time, and they looked all the better for it. There were folk speaking to folk as 'ent spoke for years!" she told him.

OUR HOUSE, A FIRST AID POST

A man was calling round the houses to see a suitable one for a first aid post. Our house was near the junction of two main roads, with a drill hole nearby. The man thought the house at the end was a better place, but the lady, having five young children, could not be asked to take it on. My mammy only had two young ones to care for, so she would be in most of the time, and she had been a girl guide.

The man asked her if she had ever been in the first aid room when she worked at the tin factory. She had, but he did not give her time to tell him why. She had cut her elbow on a sharp sheet of tin and had gone to ask for a plaster. When she got to the first aid room, it smelt so clean, and everywhere was so bright and shiny. The walls were white tiles from floor to ceiling. Mammy had never seen anything like it before. She was so frightened by it that she fainted.

The man could see that our house was kept clean and tidy. That pleased Mammy. He thought he had found the very place he had been looking for. So he wanted to know, had we a first aid box? We had not, but he supposed that every household had a pair of scissors.

Having young children, he supposed she kept Dettol in the house, cotton wool and pink lint sheets would be nice, and brandy, if it could be spared. And could my mammy tear up a not-so-old sheet into strips? What a cheek, she thought. All these things were to be kept together in the corner cupboard. And we must keep a folded-up blanket ready on the settee. So we were an official first aid post.

And Ruby Rabbit was the first to benefit from it. When

her tummy turned from white to grey, she had been given a wash, and afterwards she could not sit up straight. So her little white scut was unsewn, and cotton wool poked through the hole until she could sit up straight again without flopping over. Mammy thought that nobody would mind if she sneaked a bit of cotton wool from the first aid cupboard.

But it was not just my mammy who was a first aider. I was a little first aider too. She had told me, "It is our house that is the first aid post." I lived in it, so I was a first aider, she said. "It might not be much, but we all have to do what we can do."

So each morning, after breakfast, Mammy talked about it. She taught me that blood was nothing to be frightened of, not to worry about it, just to put a cushion on it, and get the brandy from the cupboard. She told me what to do if somebody came and I was in the house on my own.

When that day did come, I was ready to do my bit for the war effort. Somebody was shouting loudly and banging on our front door, but before I could answer it, a man burst in, protesting, panicking. But then he stopped short and asked quietly if somebody had died, because the curtains were closed in the daytime. I told him that the curtains were closed to protect my eyes because I had got measles. He jumped back, then he sounded angry again.

"They told me this is a first aid post," he said.

We were still near the front door, and I could see, with the light from the fanlight above the door, that he was nursing his hand, wrapped in a large dirty bundle. It was smelling of oil. So I said my lines as I had learnt them, off pat, as Daddy had learnt everything at school.

"Come and sit down by the fire to get warm, if we've got one." I could not see it alight. "Or lie down on the settee if you are bleeding, and I will cover you with the blanket. There is brandy in the cupboard if you need it."

He sat near the fireplace, and said, "No, I don't need it, but you certainly know your stuff." I urged him to lie on the settee.

"You must keep warm," I said. "And if you lie down, I shan't have to."

When I had practised covering Mammy with the blanket, she had wriggled and squealed, but he had lain quite still. Leaving him there lying quietly, I went out the back door to find my mammy. She was at a neighbour's.

She soon had him strapped up properly, but at first he turned down her offer of a cup of tea. But he accepted, after a long "Pleeeeaaase," from me. I could tell we had an understanding, him and me. I thought, now there won't be enough tea ration left for me to have pobs, and I might have to have bread and jam, if I kept quiet about feeling sick.

Pobs was the rule at our house when kids were feeling poorly. Mammy would break bread into pieces in a basin and cover it with a cup of tea. No wonder it was considered as a quick cure.

Both Mammy and Daddy made so much fuss of me, I found it puzzling. I had done everything right, so they wanted to know what was wrong. They were shocked to learn that the brandy bottle and the Dettol bottle seemed the same to me. Mammy said it would be too hard for me to learn about two bottles. If I learned about the Dettol bottle really well, look at it, feel it, smell it, then I would know that I had picked up the brandy bottle.

Joan Vardy

THE GERMAN'S MEASLES

That dose of measles was followed straight after by a second dose. This time it was given to me by the Germans. So I was poorly for what seemed like a very long time. Sometimes I stayed in our bed, sometimes in Mammy's and Daddy's bed. But if Mammy had to go out, she would carry me downstairs and put me on the settee. I was too weak to walk.

One day I was on the settee and my sister was kicking up a fuss about having to go out with mammy in the rain. In her tantrum, she broke the strap of her green pixie rain hood, and Mammy said that she would have to wear my red one, so I cried. Mammy told me that she should be the one to be crying, because now she was going to get wet, as she had thought of wearing the rain hood herself.

Left alone in the house, it was gloomy. I tried opening the curtains, but Mammy had trapped them down the back of the settee. There was only one patch of grey. That was over the other side of the room, the fanlight above the door. That was all I could see.

When Mammy got back, they had brought some chips wrapped up in my rain hood, which my sister would not wear. But the chips were for her dinner, even though they were in my rain hood to keep them warm and dry.

But then our doctor came, Pop Waller, we called him. He talked quietly to Mammy. She sounded so upset. But then Pop said I could have the curtains open, and he said that mammy should try to treat us both alike.

After checking me over, he sat my sister at the place in the settee I had been sitting, and put me on the other end, propped up with cushions, wrapped up in blankets. The sun streamed in, warm on my face, and it seemed like a new world.

And what was more, Pop said if chips was what I wanted, then chips was what I would have, and he took a few from my sister, just about six of them. He told her, "You'll have plenty there," and he put them on my lap in a piece of torn newspaper. Then he sat at the table talking to Mammy.

While Pop and Mammy were talking, I understood some of what they said. When Pop spoke seriously, he spoke so softly, I did not want to know what he meant. I managed to eat just two chips.

"Two will be enough for today," said Pop, taking the others away from me. "And now I've watched you eating your dinner, I will be going."

While I had been so poorly, the kids next door had been kept quiet. But now I could hear them, all round his little car, chatting to him, and they sounded so happy that my spirits rose, and I turned the corner on the road to recovery.

After that, we all seemed to know where we were, with new strength to go forward; until Mammy tried to put my shoes on. I would not have it. After such a long time, they seemed so hard and heavy. So she went out and spent a lot of money on a new pair to encourage me. The new shoes fastened with buckles, not with shoelaces, strings like my old shoes. Around the edges were bright white daisies, Mammy said, although she knew they would not stop clean for long. The money was well spent, if I would walk again.

The shoes were shiny. I could see them. They were bright red, just like my pillar box moneybox, I thought. I could feel the daisies' stitched petals around the edges, but when I tried to walk in the new shoes, I fell down, hitting my head on the sideboard.

Maybe I had just slipped on the lino, but an auntie had

come to help Mammy with me that day, and it was her who picked me up and put me back on the settee. Mammy was weeping, saying that I would never be well. Auntie comforted her, saying that I would have to learn to walk again, and of course that would take time, but I had walked once, so I would walk again.

This gave new hope for me. Auntie was so happy, full of life. I caught the spirit that Mamam had given her, just as I had caught the measles from the Germans. So I tried again. Auntie showed me how to put my hand out to find bits of furniture to hold onto, and I was soon walking round the house again.

VICTORY IN EUROPE DAY

My dad has told me that this could have been VE day, but he cannot clearly remember. But it was not the end of the war. That day, he said, was like any other day. He was on the night shift at the pit, and that night he went to work. You had to do, he said.

We could not have a seaside holiday in the war, but we did have a break in the countryside. But that valley where we stayed now lies beneath dam water. The surrounding hills still stand on guard duty, defending forever that place, which can only be revisited as it is in my treasured memories. It still lies sleeping peacefully, as it did in those days, years ago.

The children paddled in the brook, romped in the fields, where their happy voices were carried far on the air, from all those years gone by. Daddy's friend needed a holiday too, and he had nowhere to go, so he was invited to come and join us. So now there were two families to share the four-berth trailer. I felt stifled inside. I crawled underneath to where Daddy had to sleep with his friend, because there was not enough room inside the trailer. They laid one either side the big brown trunk to guard the food. I pleaded with them without success to let me sleep under there with them, where there was more room.

How beautiful it must have been for them to stroll along, with fields replacing the factories, the hills replacing the pit tips of our own home town. But for me, being no higher than a dry stone wall, I had a different view. For me there were no distant hills with whitewashed cottages dotted about here and there. Not even a blade of grass to see, just the blue paint of the pushchair.

Pram riding had been stressful enough, but this pushchair had no springs. It lurched about over cart ruts and tree roots. I got so tired of hanging on the side to steady myself to keep my balance. So I begged to walk. I could hear my sister's lament as she lagged behind. So she rode and I walked.

At first dad took just tiny footsteps over the rough ground. Then Mammy said it would be best if I held the handle of the pushchair low down and walked behind the wheel, as she was trying to find good ground and miss most of the stones. I toiled along, earning for myself my nickname of 'trudger'. My sister did not feel at all upset about riding in the pushchair. She lay back with her sparrow legs sprawled out. Could this be how she came by her name of 'spadger'?

At the whitewashed pub, chairs and tables were set out on the grass. One grey afternoon, most of them were occupied with people having a leisurely drink. I had had a bottle of mineral water, and drunk it too quickly, Mammy said, when I asked for a second bottle. She told me that the landlord let everybody have just one drink at dinnertime. That was why folk had to take their time over it.

It was so quiet, so still. This was a new thing for me, to be able to hear all sounds; everybody talking just quietly, without the sounds of the town blocking out their voices. I heard the other children playing below, in the brook. They splashed and giggled. Up on the hillside they called to one another. These sounds were carried to me on the air, but I could not hear the whole picture. It was like seeing stars shining, and in between, the space of the black sky, so quiet, so still.

Then all at once, the landlord rushed out of the pub. He was cheering and running round the tables, swinging a big white towel around and around his head. Then everybody together jumped up, all hugging everybody they could reach. Some were laughing, some were crying, and others joined hands and skipped around in circles. Others picked up chairs and danced with those. It was bedlam. The pub dog was barking; he was so frightened. He darted for cover under our table. I joined him. I remembered that Daddy said that under the table is a safe place to be when the Jerries come over.

So me and Chummy the dog sat and comforted each other under the table, forgotten in the uproar above our heads. I had heard dogs barking before, but I had never seen or touched one. This one may have had big brown appealing eyes, but all I could see were three black patches on his white fur. Two of the black patches I found out were his ears, but the other patch was just flat. It felt just the same as the rest of his fur. This dog was not just one solid block like our Spadger's dog, Rough. Chummy had bones that were all packed in at random, not at all joined onto one another. He jumped at me and he bounced about. His warm tongue licked me so lovingly.

Then the landlord came, pulling Chummy out from under the table by the scruff of his neck. He was saying that the dog might go and bite somebody, and it must be locked up. Poor

Chummy was put behind a big black door. I heard the catch shut firmly. He yelped and scratched all that long day.

I thought that I might be taken along with him, and I waited for the landlord to come back and get me. From there, under the table, I watched a young woman. She lifted up her skirt, showing her white petticoat. I saw her high-heeled silver shoes slip from her feet as she hopped and kicked her legs. I thought, when I tell my mammy about her, she'll go tut-tut. Then cheers went up around me as crates of bottles were noisily bumped about.

It took quite some persuading to get me to come out from underneath that table, and at first I refused to drink the bottle of fizzy orange I was given, and for a long time I tried very hard not to drink any of it. My daddy had gone for a drink with the other men, so Mammy and me were left together. We sat talking. Mammy said she thought I was too young to listen, but she knew that I did listen, so she talked. I listened because she talked to me, not at me. So we grew closer to each other.

I told Mammy about that young woman showing her petticoats, but she did not tut-tut. Instead she forgave the young lady, saying that she was a very young lady, although she had thought herself that she was not dressed quite right. But people had to wear what they had, and it didn't matter really. The war was hard on young people. Mammy had had her younger life, and she was sorry that they had missed those years.

Later on the sun broke through the clouds and everybody went for a walk, being far too restless to sit still. They all stopped to talk to us. They all seemed to be on their way back. They were all saying the same thing. Perhaps we were the last ones to go! The place, which just a short time ago had been so quiet and still, now buzzed with excitement.

I was glad not to have to be mixed up with all this muddle. It was not my muddle. As I trudged along, I gazed at the trees as we passed. The sunshine had turned the black and white scene into colour for me. It had lit up the tree trunks and turned them nearly white. The leaves were a pale green, and the sky a clear blue. Yet I could not say what it was I could see. Nobody noticed, not even our Spadger, fast asleep in the pushchair as the world passed her by.

We stopped when we came to a wall with a bike leaning up against it. There was green creeper growing over and into the wall. When I pulled at it, it clung on firmly. It tasted bitter, and was most unfriendly, although it felt soft. But I could grate the gravel under my feet here, and gravel was hard.

Two youths had both ridden this strange bike to bring us the great news. Mammy said it had taken the youths a long time, and it had been hard work for them to get here. Daddy was going to offer the youths a drink, but Mammy said she thought perhaps better not, as they were talking nineteen to the dozen, drinking down pint pots of reward, sitting on the wall there. Daddy wanted to show me how this machine worked, but Mammy said, "No, let her sort it out for herself."

When I looked at it, I thought I could see two bikes, but when I felt it all over, I could only find two wheels. This baffled me, made me wobble inside. Then Daddy told me all about this bike, but my mind refused to take it in, even though I tried very hard. He was telling me that two could ride one bike. I ended up in tears.

There were some things in the world I could not make my mind up about, but I could just wonder at. And there were other things in the world that I could not make my mind up about, that I worried over. This black metal puzzle was one of those things.

That night, lying awake in the trailer, Spadger and I looked up through the window at what we now agreed was an unbelievably bright Wedgewood blue sky, and we fell asleep listening to the merrymakers.

That holiday had been a good break for us all, but my heart sank when we first got back home. Our house felt so strange. It felt empty. The clock had stopped ticking. It was bare. There was no cloth spread over the table and it was cold. There had been no fire in the grate for some time. But in the days and weeks that followed, it was quite clear to me that Mammy and Daddy were happier now, and bit by bit, things seemed to change.

CHUMMY

Spadger and I shared a money box. It was in the shape of a pillar box. On the side of it, so Daddy told me, there was a picture of Chummy, the pub dog. Each time I posted my savings through the letterbox slot, I remembered Chummy. I could think of him still locked up and whining behind the big black door.

I had met him just that once, that day under the table, but how clearly I could see him, when Daddy told me about him, with a studded collar and a bright pink tongue hanging from the corner of his mouth.

At one time I had saved a total of sixpence, all in ha'pennies and farthings, but our Spadger only had fourpence ha'penny. I kept a jealous guard over things if she took out money to spend it. So while I watched, Daddy made her take out one of those big whole pennies, so that I would know she had not taken any of mine.

Joan Vardy

THE CRICKETERS

Our leader had plans. Now that the nights were lighter, our mams and dads would be glad to get us out of the house in the evening. So we were to go home, on some lucky chance that we might have an early dinner and get out on the street again wearing shoes. It would be a long walk, but we would all be going. The bigger kids questioned him.

"Yes," he said, "even the little ones. Or the plan won't work."

Trailing after the big kids, it seemed a long climb up the hill. My little friend did not like to be so far from home. He held my hand, and I was glad of that, because although he did not know, he was leading me. I could see nothing but the evening sun. I had never seen it so low in the sky before.

At last we reached the cricket ground. We were not supposed to go on it, but there was a gap in the fence on top of the wall. The leader said to me, "If you go through, and straight on, you will find some swings. He's too small, so they won't shout at him; or you either. They might let you have a go."

The little one and I were shoved through the gap, the idea being that the big kids would come looking for us later, and then the cricketers might let them stay to watch the match.

We had not reached the swings before one of the players called out, "Oy! You littl'uns! You can't come on here! Go back, now." And he came over to put us through the fence. He spoke so kindly, and he was shocked to see two littl'uns out on their own so late. Then he heard the big kids running off, and he soon changed his tune. "So that's your game, is it?" he shouted, and struggled and squeezed to get himself through the gap to be after them. But he gave up the chase and came back to lift us up and over the wall, through the gap onto the coursey. "Go straight home now," he said.

My little friend could not see the kids, and we stood a while, making our minds up which way to go. He wailed for his mam. I thought it might be best if she did not hear him so far from home. Then I worked it out. We had climbed up the hill with the sun in my eyes. So now we must turn our backs on it, and go down the hill. So it was me who led the way. I took my little friend's hand, and just followed my shadow. He was still wailing. I cheered him by showing him his shadow, and he played with it as we went along. But my shadow had grown so tall in the late evening sun, that I could not see to the top of its legs.

Then the sun went down, and there was nothing to guide me. On and on we went, and it was my turn to want my mammy. My little friend, I thought, might be frightened of the dark. He was dragging his feet now, with his trousers hanging heavy. All I could see was grey, and neither of us spoke. Then we heard his mam call him.

"Aah, look," she said. "She's † 'owding 'is 'and, and she's brought 'im 'ome."

She told us that all the other kids had been sent to bed a while ago for leaving us, and the mams and dads had all gone different roads to look for us. When we got home, we were both made such a fuss of, that just for once, it felt good to be a littl'un.

† 'owding 'is 'and – holding his hand

Joan Vardy

OUR HOUSE, A SHOP

Most evenings, after the dinner table had been cleared, we got ready to open our house shop. Mammy's balance scales were wiped clean and put on the table, and I could play with the weights. But I must be careful with them, because if they got damaged, they might weigh light. Every so often a man came round to check them. There were dints in the bottom of the weights, to pour in a little more metal if it was needed. Once when the man came round, he had taken a little of the metal out, and Mammy was pleased about that.

On the weights, there was raised numbers: a quarter, a half, one, two, four, eight, and a great big one. Mammy and Daddy thought I could either see or feel these numbers, but I knew the weights by their sizes and I could hold them in my hands and judge their weight accurately. So I got the right idea in a physical way to add up and take away. In such a way I really understood, without knowing about the numbers at all.

We sold sweets in our shop, and big boxes of them were stored in the wardrobes upstairs, and when Mammy and I went upstairs to make the beds in the daylight, she would find out the blue liquorice allsorts and give me one.

She said, "If anyone says anything, say, 'they can't get the blue to make them'. They'll believe it if you say it."

All evening, people would come in, letting in the cold air. They came for other things besides sweets. Daddy and Mammy ran two twenty-week catalogue clubs, John Noble's and Samuel Driver's, but they did not make people wait their turn for things that they needed right away.

Some people came to sell us things; fruit, which Daddy

had made into jam. That was stored in big stone jars. One lady made pegged rugs from new materials, and she could make one rug every week, and bring it for Daddy to sell. We also sold lino. A giant roll of it would stand in the kitchen in the corner of the chimney breast behind the door. When a roll first came, we would not want anybody to know about it, and the open door would hide it. But Daddy had to keep unrolling the lino just a little, bit by bit. He did not want to crack it, and bit by bit, the roll got fatter and fatter. Then we all had to take care not to crack the lino as we came through the door.

The roll soon grew so fat, until the kitchen door would not open much at all. Then it was a job and a half to get this fat roll through the back door and on to the yard, unroll it until it was flat and it completely covered the whole back yard, blocking off the † lav and the back gate. And do all this without cracking it! Then it had to be measured and cut into different sizes for different folks. Even the gipsies would come and buy it. They would find out about it because they could smell it.

The unsold lino would be put back in its place in the corner. Then it would be easier to get in and out of the back kitchen, and Mammy would not have to shout every time I came in from the house,

"Don't crack the lino!"

We sold vegetables that Daddy grew on his allotment. You could only have one allotment garden, he said. But his was 1200 yards long.

Then there were the plaster plaques that Daddy made. At first these plaques looked like white plates and Daddy would let me stand by him to watch him as he painted the flowers on them. I could not see the paintbrush or the paint pot, but Daddy could just wave his hand slowly over the plaques, and red petals appeared one by one. In the same way, Daddy could waft his hand and turn the plaques into real gold. To me, that was real magic! Yet more still, he could put those plaques high up on the bedroom wall to let them dry, and although they rang like bells, they did not fall down. Now that was a miracle.

When the plaques were brought downstairs to be sold, those flowers were as fresh as before, not like the ones that Daddy grew on the allotment and brought home for Mammy, which she loved so much. They saddened her when they faded away at last.

To really know just how beautiful those plaques were, I could only rely on the sound of people's voices. My daddy did not have a stick of chalk. Somehow he put the flowers that he brought home for Mammy on to the plaques. That was magic.

† lav – lavvie, lavatory, toilet.

UP THE APPLES AND PEARS

At bedtime, Daddy would say, in a cheery voice, "Up the apples and pears!"

There was no light on the stairs, so I climbed up behind our Spadger in the dark, holding on to a piece of string, which was tied on to a handrail, but I did not know anything about the handrail.

Every night Mammy would put Golden Eye ointment in my eyes and sprinkle my other end with boracic powder. That made me smart, but not enough to remind me to visit the lavatory in the daytime. Then Mammy would sit on our bed to hear us say our prayers. We were taught to ask God to bless each member of the family. Granddad, being the oldest, came first, and I, being the very youngest, came last. Then we always asked God to make my peepers better. I just said it night after night, not thinking. Then one night I asked Mammy, "What are peepers?"

She told me how my eyes did not see like other children's eyes did. I did not need telling; I knew that. It was just that I did not know what peepers were. I did not want to change me. I was me. I thought like me, I felt like me on the inside, and God had made me me, so I told my mammy I would not ask God any more because I did not want my peepers to be made better.

That made Mammy cry, and every night after that, she said the last line of our prayer for me. I grew to realise that, although everybody loved *me,* they only loved part of me. Everybody wanted me to change; I could feel their feelings come pouring out of their spirits. It was anger from Granddad, grief from Mamam, worry from Dad, and strife from Mammy, concern from aunties and uncles, and pity from strangers. None of them loved my eyes.

I should have to go down this road alone.

RATIONING

It became a lifetime's habit for Mammy to write down the items in her shopping list in the order that she found the coupons in the ration book. Sugar, butter, margarine, lard, tea.

"Ha ha," she'd say, "jam, and eggs."

The sugar came in a thick dark blue paper bag, just folded in neatly at the top. The butter was cut from a large block, and carefully weighed out onto a sheet of greaseproof paper. To me, margarine and lard were the same colour. They were wrapped up together to save on that precious greaseproof paper. Tea came in a neat little parcel, tied up with string, and the art of doing this still remains a mystery to me.

The string would be patiently unknotted and saved in the shoelace tin, which was kept on one end of the shelf. When the tea had been put into the matching tea caddy on the other end of the shelf, Mammy could make a fan for me with the red paper, by folding it back and forth, back and forth into pleats.

Shop-bought jam was made in the factory at Bolsover. I could spend half a morning cleaning out a jam pot with a spoon, after Mammy had agreed with me that at last the pot was empty. Once, in the grocer's, I had shouted out, my daddy did not smoke. So each time before we went in, I had to be warned, because Mammy thought that she might be stopped from buying Woodbines and Park Drives for her dad. That was my granddad.

THE GARRET STORE

It must have been Saturday evenings that Daddy and I might go up to the garret together, taking up with us some rations to store, and bringing down with us some rations for the week ahead, but I did not know why that was done.

The stairs to the garret led up from out of the back bedroom. Daddy, going first, would be carrying a lamp if it was dark. I could not see anything by the lamplight at all, but Daddy would always remind me to be careful. It was a steep climb for me on hands and feet, feeling my way, as there was no handrail, and the railings round the top of the stairs were unsafe, too wobbly for me to cling on to.

The garret was an L-shaped room with a very dirty window at one end. The roof sloped in parts, where everybody but me had to bend down. Also an electric wire hung low, from one side to the other. I liked it when people had to duck double to get under it. People's voices were always high above me. Coming down to my level, we felt like chums together.

I knew where things were stored in the garret. Behind the railings in the corner, stood my cot, my playpen and my green and cream pram, with its end dropped down and its hood shed – my mammy called it 'put up'.

All kinds of things were laid out neatly round the walls. In the winter there were sheets of glass from Daddy's allotment garden cloches, and a number of empty preserving jars, which grew as the weeks went by. Daddy took great care that I did not go too close to the glass. I might cut myself, or break it, but breaking the glass seemed more important. There were Daddy's plastering tools. He would lovingly pick them up, dusting them off before making believe to plaster the walls, swinging his arm, making the trowel ring and glint in the lamplight.

Mammy told me, "Plasterers have made a good living in the city before the war", when my daddy stayed in digs. But he had to have pyjamas. They would not let you stay, so you had to keep them on under your clothes all day, so that they did not get pinched, because if you could not get digs, you could not get work. Mammy told me all about this, and more.

The Irishmen would buy a bottle of milk, drink some, crack two eggs into it, then drink it all down raw. You could buy hot doughnuts and potatoes from men that came round the building sites too.

Then the war started, and the building sites closed down, so Daddy went to try and find work with his two pals. They had one motorbike between them, with a suitcase-come-toolbox on the back, so they had to take turns to walk and ride. They got a job plastering the barracks of the soldiers who had just joined up. The soldiers had tablecloths on their table, and vases of flowers, while Daddy and his pals slept on straw and washed themselves under running water from a tap in the middle of the yard.

Daddy talked a lot in the garret, but he could not bring himself to tell me all that. He said he would use his tools one day, when the war was over. I thought, *you're just dreaming, Daddy.* I asked him, "How long will the war last?" He thought it would last for about ten years. That's how long wars lasted, he thought, and he clung on to the hope that the war would end as I started to grow up.

There was a large oval fish kettle, which had once been used for preserving eggs in water glass. That was at the beginning of the war, when Granddad had had a lot of fowls, but we did not have eggs now. There were two large oval plates with crimped edges, with green and blue designs on them. They matched the jug that Mammy's chrysanthemums used.

I would listen in wonder as Daddy talked of how once a plate would have been full of meat. Holding one plate in the crook of his arm, he would show me how heavy it would have been by bouncing it and grunting, weighing it up and down. The joint, he called it. He would trace with his finger where the roasties would have surrounded the joint. There were two white enamel buckets, which Mammy said she could do with, but daren't for what folks might say. Daddy spoke of the dancing days, in the years before the war, when there was plenty of everything for everybody.

There was a very large, light blue kettle, and we brought it down with us one night.

"What shall I tell 'em all?" Mammy asked.

"Tell 'em nowt, an' let 'em think," said Daddy.

The kettle was too heavy to be used safely when it was full, but mammy soon learned just how much water to put in it to make the kettle sing sweetly by the fire in the evenings.

In the garret, Daddy talked a lot. He told me things, knowing that I could not tell, and now I cannot tell, only of his feelings that I felt that he felt then: of hope and despair, contentment and terror, of joy, determination, tiredness, up there in the dark and the cold.

Turning the corner in the garret, there were two low wooden chests, with very little food stored inside them. Spreading things out to make it look more only made it look less. Daddy would set his lamp down in a chest to see. In the front corner of the first one, there might be a parcel of tea and a bag of sugar over in the far corner. And if we were lucky, at the front there might be a small box, like a toy building block. Daddy would trace an alphabet letter with his finger on it, and I would just listen patiently.

Inside the box, there were jelly crystals, and if we were lucky, we might take one down with us. For some reason jelly crystals had to be stirred in boiling water to let them go cold. The kitchen mantelpiece was cold and up there, Mammy reckoned, we did not get thumbprints in it, made by testers over-eager for it to set. Jelly was always red and it seemed to take days and days before it was declared ready. Then it was served with hot custard, which immediately melted it again.

With jelly and custard, or fruit, we were expected to eat

some bread and butter. It was no good saying politely, "I have had a piece, thank you." You must be seen to take a piece from the bread and butter plate, and take a bite of it, so that it could not be put back again.

In the second chest, there might be a few tins. There was one tin, which I now know by its shape was corned beef, but I do not recall that tin ever being taken downstairs. There might be bottles of pears or tomatoes that Mammy had preserved herself and we might bring down pears for Sunday tea, or the tomatoes for Sunday breakfast. Putting the lids on the bottling jars was very easy for Mammy. She was very quick. But it was a hard job, 'a job and a half,' he said to get those lids off again. First, the bottles were warmed by the fire for a while. That was why we brought them down on Saturday night, when we had a good fire for cooking the meat for Sunday dinner.

At the far end of the garret near the window were some of Daddy's tools, which were too big to fit in the wooden tool chest on top of the chest of drawers in the back bedroom. I loved to hear the sound of the saw, that sound it made when he picked it up to dust it. He knew all his tools by name. There was one named the plane brace, the King, and for a crown it wore a broad top made of wood which Daddy kept highly polished and oiled.

The King was the whole idea behind me climbing up to the garret, because I was allowed to bore a hole with it. Daddy would find a block of wood for me to stand the tip of the brace on. Then I would lean forward, holding the broad top against my shoulder, to wind the handle around and around. How I managed this without knocking my legs from underneath me, Daddy said he couldn't make out. Despite this hazard, the King was an experience not to be missed. That tingling in my fingers, that shivering in my knees, the shuddering in my shoulder. It makes senses of sounds and feelings together.

After a while I would be satisfied, straighten my back and mop my brow, like I had seen Daddy do. Daddy would assure me that I had drilled a hole.

As I climbed down the garret stairs backwards, my arms would be shaking with the effort and excitement. That super sound made by the King vibrating on the wooden block can best be summed up by the neighbour's enquiry, beginning,

"What in hell's name...?"

OUR WIRELESS SET

Although we did not want anybody to know about it, there we all were, standing outside our back gate, pretending to enjoy the beautiful summer evening. Folk might just think that, even though they had never seen us standing there before. Whatever it was, we were not waiting for it to come.

But when the car drew up, our Spadger was so excited. She thought our daddy had bought it, and when the door opened, she jumped in. She thought we were all going for a ride. But 'it' was on the car floor. I looked, while Mammy fetched a blanket to wrap it in. It was just like a wooden toolbox.

Covered with the woollen blanket, it was carried down the yard and into the house. Mammy † chuntered about that. It was worse for folk to see the blanket. Now in the morning they would all be asking about blankets.

The box was unwrapped and put on the house table. I was told, "No, it can't be opened, and there's nothing inside it for you. Just you wait and see." So I waited, and looked to see.

After some time, the box gave out a shrill whistle, not soft and gentle like the kettle on the hob in the evenings. Then the box spoke. They were words I did not know. It was unearthly, how it made a noise like an air raid siren going up and down. So I hid in the corner near the gas meter cupboard.

The box was put on a stand near where we came in at the front door. But there was not enough room for it there, so it was moved to the wall opposite the window. Daddy said he would have to do something about the wires. Later on, Mamam came. She reassured me by calling the box a wireless set. Now the box had a name, I was not so frightened, and we found out about it together, like chums, me and Mamam.

She thought it was like a little house, with a glass door in the middle at the front, and windows, one on either side. They had bars, and I could put my fingers through to feel the cloth curtains on the inside. There were two knobs, one on either side of the doorstep. One was to switch the wireless set on, and when you did, a light came on inside. I never did like that light. On the day it broke I was happy. On that day, Daddy was not happy. Now he could not see a needle inside that told him what he was listening to. Three times I switched the wireless set up too high and three times Mamam turned it down again. Then she said I was getting fretful, and I should not, because now I was three years old.

The man on the wireless set talked again, and I copied him. Mammy called out, "She's speaking German! Switch it off. We didn't buy a wireless set for her to learn to speak German!" Then the man talked to me again and I answered him, and Mammy said I was not old enough to know what he had said to me.

The wireless set soon became part of our lives, a yardstick for me to measure each day by. I had not thought about the rhythm of a day before, even though our clock chimed the quarters and counted the hours. So far, I had not noticed. Early in the morning I would be woken by the sounds in the dark; the bus at half past four went around so quickly to pick up all the other drivers; the colliers on the day shift walked to work in their pit boots. I heard these sounds, and Mammy had told me what they were. There was no need for me to worry about them, just to fall back to sleep again. When I woke again it would be broad daylight. I would go downstairs.

Each night my mammy would fold up my clothes neatly and take them back down the stairs with her to keep them aired. She thought it might be warmer for me to get dressed downstairs. Now that I could dress myself, I missed those lovely cuddles from Mammy, so she would often find herself sorting out armholes from head holes, maybe giving up the struggle, taking off the muddled garment, and if I was lucky she might pop it on again for me.

Daddy's sandwiches were cut up for work and wrapped in a damp glass cloth and a newspaper parcel, to keep them fresh. Mammy complained about how quickly the cheese went mouldy. It was my idea to cut one thin slice from each side of the cheese wedge. Then it would always be fresh, I said. It was made quite plain to me that my mammy did not like to think that I could have an idea she had not thought of herself. Daddy took tea and sugar to work for mashing. When we brought the rations home, Mammy would count out spoonfuls of tea and sugar, putting them together in a Vaseline jar. Then, when she knew that Daddy had enough for work, we could use what was left for home.

Before the fire got going in the morning, Mammy would wear her long green dressing gown, maybe over her clothes, but she thought she had to take it off when it was light enough to open the curtains. She had to push the curtains open bit by bit with a long cane, which stood ready in the corner. Mammy told me how she used to get up very early in the morning to do exercises with the wireless set, thinking that it was a live broadcast. Then one morning, the record got stuck. So she never got up extra early ever again.

Every morning the clock had to be put right with the eight o' clock pips off the wireless set. We heard the radio doctor and program parade when Daddy had gone to work and we had our breakfast. One of my favourite breakfasts was a thick slice of fried bread, cut up into squares for me. I could easily stab them with my tiny fork. It had been one of Mammy's favourite breakfasts too, when she was young. Then I might have a cup of cocoa. Mammy would cool it by pouring it to and fro from a little cracked jug that she loved and felt she could keep as long as she could find a use for it.

Then it was my job to put out breadcrumbs for the sparrows. Mammy always sliced the loaf up on a sheet of newspaper on the table. She said it was not her fault if the bread was so crumbly. She could not help wasting it. But I must bring the newspaper back. She could find another use for that. I must have a wash before going out to play. Mammy would get a ladle full of warm water for me out of the boiler at the side of the fire. After I had had a wash, she would get a big bucket of cold water to fill the boiler again.

We called our lunch 'little dinner'. Sometimes we would have hot polony sandwiches. Spadger and I would be shown across the road to the Co-op stores to fetch it. We might have to wait a long time with all the other kids, waiting for it to be delivered. When the polony came, it would be so hot, that I could only carry it by its string. When I grumbled that it hurt my fingers, our Spadger said that I was the youngest, so I could not carry the loaf. While the polony was still hot, it could be squeezed out of its red skin and spread on the still warm bread. When polony had gone cold, it could be sliced into rings, but the red skin was always thrown away.

Another little dinner might be smoked haddock. That was if the fishmonger dropped the price of it early enough for Mammy. We would walk around the market place, waiting for the fishmonger to call out. But she did not always drop the price of her fish before it was time for us to fetch Spadger out of school. So sometimes we went home without any. Then we might have a slice of bread and † 'maggie-ann', and half a fresh orange each, while we listened to Workers' Playtime on the wireless set. That was a show that came from different factories. They always ended by singing 'Five Minutes More', and 'You are my sunshine', and I knew it would soon be time for the news at one o' clock. I knew the King's voice and that if he spoke, it was serious, and there must be hush, but I need not be told.

Mammy was always concerned about the missing persons' announcements. The man on the wireless set might say, "Could so-and-so go to such-and-such hospital, where his mother is dangerously ill."

But it was the shipping forecast which most held me by its charms; all those faraway places, poetic-sounding names. I could string them together for the joy of their beauty, made more beautiful for me by my unknowing. I could gaze in wonder from the inside.

Later in the afternoon, I would hear the ripples of Mrs Dale's Diary's harp, and Mammy would bring a bowl of water in from the kitchen to peel the potatoes on a sheet of newspaper on the house table, while she listened to Mrs Dale. Then I knew that Daddy would soon be home. There would be a kettle boiling ready for him on the fire, and it would be his turn to have a wash. More water would be put on to boil for the potatoes for our dinner.

Dinner was always potatoes with vegetables swimming

around in a brown gravy pond in my soup plate. It was not easy to fish them out with my spoon. For pudding, there could be caramel blancmange, Creamola Rice, or golden syrup dumplings. When I had finished, I had been taught to say, "Thank you, Mammy, for a good dinner," and ask if I could leave the table.

With the wireless set, I also learned the rhythm of the week. I got to know what we would do on each day. On Sunday mornings, Daddy took charge of cooking the breakfast. If it was tomatoes, he would cut up spoon-sized pieces of bread for me in my soup plate with the wide edge. I enjoyed this breakfast because I could see some colour, and it was an easy dish for me to eat with a spoon. But to keep me out of the way of the frying pan, it became my little job to switch on the wireless set and find Bing Crosby whistling and singing.

The wireless set was made of a type of plastic that attracted a lot of dust. On bright mornings, with the sun streaming down through the fanlight above the door, I could see dust on the wireless set as grey. I could not stop myself from drawing in it with my finger. This did not please Mammy, but I just had to keep doing it. I had to know why it should work one morning and not another morning, and never in an afternoon. So Mammy left a dusting cloth behind the wireless set for me to do another little job when I had done my drawings, and I did learn that I could only see the dust a few days after dusting day, in the bright sunlight.

So me and the wireless set became friends for life.

† chuntered - grumbled

† 'maggie-ann' - margarine

MAMAM'S AND GRANDDAD'S.

My mammy's mam and dad lived in the next town, where my Granddad worked in the fire halls at the pit. Sometimes we went to their house for tea on Sundays. Mammy always took a big shopping bag with her, not the one she used for carrying back rations from the shop with. She said it was a good bag. Folks would think that she had just not got a handbag. Besides, she needed it for later.

At the bottom of the big bag, there would be a little something for our teas, wrapped up in newspaper, and my daddy's Woodbine ration, which he let my Granddad have, the ones with the pretty roses on the packet. It made me sad when I could not see those roses.

It was a good long walk to Mamam's and Granddad's, by lanes and along roads, with Spadger and me taking it in turns in the pushchair. It could be a bumpy ride, so I liked best to walk, holding the pushchair handle to steady myself with and guide myself. But when Daddy took his turn to push, I might say I was tired and put up with the pushchair's jolts and jerks.

It was a sad street where Mamam and Granddad lived. On both sides there were long rows of terraced houses, each row robbing the other of sunshine and daylight. The colliers had coal to burn and the smell of smoke and soot hung in the air. Sometimes the smoke rolled down the housetops in yellow clouds and floated in the street.

Yet all the women took great pride with their houses. Mammy told me that on Saturday morning they scrubbed their steps and windowsills and rubbed them afresh with rubbing stones, she said. From what I overheard, those who made light work of it were frowned upon, but for those who could not kneel; there was a neighbour only too willing to do her job for her. Some whitened the whole step, and some just the ends. Mamam drew lines on the edges of her steps. All the steps stuck out over the coursey, so during the blackout, folks did not fall over them if they were whitened. And with each house having its own fashion, they knew their own house in the dark.

All the houses just looked the same to me. The steps were too high for me to climb, so Daddy would lift me up, and I would land in the front parlour, but everybody else had to climb the steps without spoiling Mamam's handiwork by standing on part of the step not whitened. But to get round to the back door we could use the long, dark entrance, like a tunnel through the houses. In there, sounds were all made louder, ringing with echoes. A spot of daylight at the other end grew bigger and bigger until we came out and it went all quiet again. We passed along the houses until we came to Mamam's.

It was a puzzle to Mammy how I could find Mamam's house at the back and not at the front. She was annoyed with herself when I told her, "At the back we have to go along till we come to a high brick wall. You can't go any further." That was how I knew.

My auntie, that was my mammy's sister, would be there before us, and before tea, our Spadger would play games with our three cousins in the front parlour. These were always games suitable for Sunday, but games that you need to see to play, like Tiddlywinks or Snobs. Snobs was a set of coloured dice which were thrown in the air and caught in different ways, while other Snobs were picked up or dropped.

It was cold and dull in the front parlour. Through the window, all I could see were red bricks, no sky. And through the window in the † house-place at the back there was that high wall and another street of terraced houses, just as sad as I was. But I would go and sit in there with Daddy. He said that no kids would play out on Sundays, and I would be sitting in the house at home anyway.

My mammy might do jobs for Mamam, because she was getting a bit old and tired now, so she needed help with the work, and my mammy needed me to help her. We might go upstairs to change the bed. The stairs led up through a door from the front parlour. We had to shut it behind us to keep the downstairs warm, then feel our way up in the dark. In the front bedroom there were large scary pictures round the walls. My mammy had grown up with them. She said she loved them, but while she dusted the room she described the pictures and I was happy to listen to her. I do not remember the pictures themselves, but I could tell that Mammy was tenderly attached to them, and I learned that all things are not what they seemed to be, and when two people look at the same picture, they do not see the same one; that people can stand right inside a picture, like standing in a room. It did not matter that I could not understand all I was told. I learned a little, and wondered at the world.

Mamam and Granddad slept in the back bedroom. It was warmer in there with the fire from downstairs always burning, and sometimes the sun shone through the window. The feather bed was fun. It seemed alive to me. If I lay down in it, it folded itself around me. “Like a mother hen,” said Mammy. I thought that Granddad’s fowls must feel soft and warm because they were made of feathers, I knew. A washstand stood in the recess by the window. It had fancy dark green tiles on the splashback. On the top was a set of Mamam’s old green glass trays. They were precious, so I was always very careful near the window.

Going downstairs was always more frightening than going up. It got darker and darker as I flopped down them one by one on my bottom, with a tight feeling growing inside my chest, because near the bottom twisted, and they were uneven there, so I was never quite sure where the next one would be. I had to feel for them with my hands and feet. But when we opened the front parlour door, I would heave a great sigh of relief as I stood up. Then the parlour looked bright and friendly.

Our Spadger and the three cousins would be playing their games on the floor, but they were often squabbling, so it was a good feeling I had inside me then, not having to join in, but go through into the house-place, where Mamam did all her cooking on an open fire in a big black fireplace, just like my mammy did.

Granddad's rocking chair stood on one side of the fireplace, from where he could reach the teapot warming on the top, tipping the kettle to top it up. Every so often he would stir in a few fresh tealeaves. But before tea at Mamam's suggestion, he might scoop out a whole teaspoonful of tealeaves and throw them on the fire, then shake the tea caddy to judge just how much more fresh tea he might add to the pot.

On the other side of the fireplace was the † sofie, for Mamam. It was under the window, where my mammy would sit, using the daylight to do her embroidery, with Auntie beside her, learning the new stitches with the pretty names. A heavy old table stood in the middle of the room. It had big balls for feet, which were fun to feel, and tucked underneath the table there were extra stools in readiness for our tea.

Four o' clock was the highlight of the afternoon for me; teatime for the fowls. Granddad kept them on the back garden in a wire netting run. But one fowl stayed in a tea chest. Her name was Broody. She just liked to sit quietly. Mamam bought the fowls' rations from the Co-op when she ordered her own rations. My cousins were allowed to scatter the corn, but it was my privilege, with Mammy's help, to scatter the grit for the fowls. I could see them, brown and white blotches, no heads, no legs, but they made jerky movements, with low, friendly, contented clucking sounds, and I thought that they must feel like Granddad's feather bed.

Mamam nipped about like a busy hen while she got the tea ready. She had a long, long pantry, which reached from out of the scullery to under the stairs at the front of the house. It had a door made of metal, a meat safe door with holes in it. It was hard to blow through those holes. They were very small. They were for the flies, said Mammy. I thought she meant for the flies to get through. If I put my ear to the door, it was weird how it still sounded open when it was shut.

Even though there was a light about half way down the pantry, it looked dark to me in there, and I would rather not go in. As I got further and further down, it made my ears feel tight. Mammy made all sorts of excuses for me. She put herself in my place and thought what it might be like to be blind. She said that I was frightened of the things hanging up. Until she said that, I had not known that there was anything hanging up. She said that I was frightened of tumbling over things on the floor. Until she said that, I had not known that there was anything on the floor for tumbling over. But it was true; I thought I might break something.

But what I was really frightened of was the unknown. My mammy often tried to help people understand me, making it very clear to them, and even clear to me, that being blind is much more than not seeing. Being blind is being odd. She was right. I asked odd questions. I did odd things. But I thought that other people were odd. They would not answer all my questions, like: why does Granddad hang his cap on that picture of the pretty little girl? Why does Mamam hide her pennies under the table legs? I just stopped asking questions.

People got weary of me.

Tea time was a quiet time when kiddies were seen and not heard, and we were expected to eat up the food on our plates, being reminded to use our best table manners. So this was a very peaceful time for me, when I did not have to try and keep up with the chatter of my cousins, or answer questions in a polite way from my Granddad. I could not always tell what he said, and I was always frightened of saying the wrong thing. But if I did not answer him, he would say something like,

"Why dost thee nay answer thy granfaither? 'As thee nay tongue in thy 'ead?" But he said it very, very quickly.

It was my privilege to sit next to Mamam, near the warm fire. She would give me a hand to eat my tea, even when I thought I was doing quite well by myself. She would make humming, smiling noises, putting my cup in my hands, making soothing sounds as I drank.

In the darker evenings I got very miserable. When the light was switched on, it was such a deep, eerie orange colour. It did not help me to see at all. I got very clingy and whiny. One day, while I was on my own with Daddy, he asked me why it was. He did not like the light either. He thought he understood. It made his eyes ache, so he knew how it must make my eyes ache too. He talked it over with Mammy, and they decided to buy a new light bulb. They thought a 60 watt light bulb would be nice, but it would be just too much for Mamam. A 40 watt light bulb might do, and Daddy would put one in on our next visit, telling Granddad not to worry about the light bill, because he would pay it for them, when it came.

Mamam gasped at the brightness of the new light bulb, recalling her days while working as a maid in service. She said, "Forty candle power? We never did burn forty candles, not even in the great hall, not even when..." and she told the story that I am sorry, but I have now forgotten.

After tea, while the table was being cleared, my mammy put the orange dim light bulb in the empty socket in the scullery, and switched it on. That was too much for Mamam. She took it out again. Recalling her days in service, she said, "I had to wash the pans without one candle, and get them clean. Only the maid who washed the bone china was allowed one candle".

And now, what with forty candle power burning in the house-place, shining in through the scullery door, Mamam thought that my mammy had more light than she needed. She tut-tutted. Mammy chuckled to herself, and washed the pots in the dark.

Their lavatory was outside on the yard. Mammy and I always went together. It was a much bigger place than ours, too long for Mammy to sit on the lav and hold out her leg to keep the door shut if somebody tried to come in. So I would stand with my back to the door when it was Mammy's turn. There was a big pegged rug on the floor and enough space for buckets and ladders, the clothes prop, brushes and mops, and things that my mammy could not put a name to.

Before going home, all the grandchildren had to kiss Mamam and Granddad goodnight. It was expected of us as a sign of respect. But now, with the new forty candle power bulb burning, I could make out Granddad's vest and the shiny fastenings of his braces. He sat forward in his rocking chair, and I tried to judge where to kiss him. Granddad was a bright pink colour from the top of his white vest to the top of his balding head. I wished him goodnight and he growled a question, which I could not answer. He said something like,

"'As thee nay been learned thy manners?" But he said it so quickly.

A thre'p'ny bit, which had been laid on the table for me to pick up, was picked up and thrown into the sideboard drawer. My mammy said quietly, "Don't be too hard on her, father," and she made excuses for me. He made a loud noise, between a spit, a cough and a sneeze. That was like a prayer answered for me. I had not seen that thre'p'ny bit. Besides, a thre'p'ny bit was not much use for me. There were no extra sweet coupons for me to buy tuffees. I could not see comics like our Spadger. I should never try to kiss my Granddad again, as Granddad was so severe. So Mamam was tender and kind. She would lovingly take my hands in hers, holding them in her lap, calling me her precious one, smiling in her voice, saying a prayer and blessing me. Then she would take my face between her hands and give me a kiss.

On light evenings, we took the path home which led past the pit tip. One or two families would gather there, the mammies and daddies would chat while they kept a lookout, just in case. And the kids went coal picking on the tip. One daddy said to mine,

"I've told him to come down, but he takes no notice. You can't do a thing wi' kids these days."

I could not see the pieces of coal, so our Spadger would pick them up and hand them to me to take and put in Mammy's big shopping bag in the pushchair.

"I think nobody'd look in my shopping bag," Mammy said. Somehow it did not seem right to me. We had been put in the tub on Saturday night, had all clean clothes on that very morning and not been allowed to play out on the street all day long. Now it did not matter that the kids were dirty. Mammy reasoned, weren't kids expected to get dirty? Folks wouldn't think twice about dirty kids. She knew it was wrong to steal, but she reasoned, whyever should you not take something from somebody who has thrown it away? That might not be the same as stealing, if you really needed it for yourself. She admitted, it was wrong to be there but we were just to forget about that, she told us, and think about warm potatoes and cabbage, which she could cook for Monday's dinner.

† house-place – back kitchen
† sofie - sofa

THE BLACKOUTS

Mammy was so happy, skipping round the house from room to room, clapping her hands and chanting, "We can take the blackouts down now, we can take the blackouts down. Everybody's doing it today."

But when it came to the bedrooms, I watched her folding the big sheet with the white paint marks on it, and I cried bitterly. Every night of my life, Mammy had put the blackout up to the window. It stopped the Jerries from getting in. Without it, I would not be able to sleep. It had been part of my life.

And then there was my gasmask that she wanted to throw away. It had always been hung on my bedpost. I had never known anything different. Things had always been that way. Next door they had five kids, and through the wall we could hear them crying with me. So my mammy went round to have a chat with their mammy, and they both agreed to keep putting up the blackouts for a while longer.

My mammy said to me that folk would think we were on the side of the Germans, because everybody had taken their blackouts down now. My gas mask was put on the basket chair by the bed, and I would know where it was, just in case I wanted it, said Mammy.

Sometimes I did take myself off upstairs for a quick practice, blowing raspberries, smelling the rubber, and seeing the blue-green patterns on the bottom. Sometime later, when the blackout was taken down again, our Spadger was frightened. There were cars and buses and as they went by, their lights swept around the room, making weird shapes and shadows on the wall. She had not seen those before, and they made her have bad dreams. So the blackout was put up once again, but now we were in the dark once again, and our Spadger still had bad dreams. So one night Mammy lit a candle. I could not see the flame of the candle, but it soothed our Spadger to sleep.

Yet again I was woken by the screams once more. But now I could see, there was quite a nice glow in the room, and as I watched, it grew brighter until the walls shone nice and orange, and it was quite pleasant, I thought, apart from the screaming.

I heard Mammy's footsteps come running up the stairs, and when she came in through the bedroom door, she began screaming herself. I heard her pick up her shamrock plants and throw the water at the blackouts. I lay calmly as she tugged at the curtains, grunting with the effort, asking God to help her, and thanking him that they were so old, that she could rip them down. Then there was a nasty smell, so Mammy opened the sash window, letting in the cold night air.

As she carried the big bundle away with her, she said, "They've got to come down now."

This memory is blurred and I often wonder if it was true, but throughout my life it has come to me again and again, so much so that I had even written it into this book twice without realising it.

THE CHIP SHOP

The chip shop was in our row, just a few doors up from our house. On a Friday, a row of kids might be seen perched on the kerb, with their feet in the gutter, sharing chips, two to a bag. Kids were forbidden to sit on the shop doorstep, or on the form at the back of the shop, not even with scrubbed hands, waiting while their chips were cooked.

I enjoyed waiting in the chip shop. There were fascinating sounds, telling the story, one on from another. The clanking of the fire door opening, the roar of the fire being fed with coal, the crunch crunch of the chip chopper chopping whole potatoes into chips, the shwoosh of the chips lowering into the hot fat, and the newspaper being cut up into squares with a sharp knife.

These sounds were all above my head, but if I pressed an ear to the counter, it sounded as though I was in there, deep down, frying with the chips, with the hot fat bubbling all about me far above my head.

WOT, NO SPUDS?

Once, there were no potatoes anywhere to be bought, but all afternoon tell-tale rumblings came from the peeling shed on the chip shop backyard. Word soon got about that they were frying that night.

"Crafty," said my mammy, "buying up all the potatoes. Now we will all have to buy chips, and that will cost us more money. But after all," she reasoned, "a man has to make a living for himself." And frying chips was his livelihood. Then there was the fat and the coal he had to buy.

That night, all us kids were sent along together with faces flannelled, hands scrubbed, tingling pink, hair wetted and combed down flat, and noses wiped.

The chip shop mester asked everybody to let the kids get to the front to be served first. He said, "Their mams'll want 'em in bed out of t'road." And he reckoned, by the looks of us, we'd been got ready and wouldn't be long.

A man at the back of the shop grumbled that he had been to work all day, and he wanted his supper. The kids could wait. But the chip shop mester said, "The kids will be satisfied with a few pennyworth, and anyway, the fish won't be ready yet."

The chip shop was packed full by now and I was squashed up against the counter, and it was dark down there. Somebody picked me up to see over the top, and the chip shop lady chatted to me. I could see the green gas light now. She said it was above the till, so that she could see she was getting and giving the right change. But it was not enough light to see by, so she stood a candle by the pile of newspapers and two more candles on the back of the chip fryer, to see when the chips were cooked.

I could have told her that. I could hear when they cooked. Then she put down the fryer's lids while the fryer door was opened, to be stoked up, and I saw the lovely bright sparks flying up in the air, but not coming back down again. But the fire glowed brightly. The chip shop mester called out loudly, "Now everybody move back. The back row get out. These kids down at front here won't stand a chance if owt were t'appen."

RETURN TO SENDER

Now that the blackouts had been taken down, at dusk I could see the lights in the houses. Now the kids could play out on the street after dark, and people had all left their curtains wide open. Our leader was going to make sure that we all had a good game.

I was told that because my daddy ran a twenty-week catalogue club, he would have a lot of used brown envelopes, so I was sent home to fetch some. It surprised me that Daddy did have some envelopes, and what's more, he let me have them.

My little friend had been given a box, something like a shoe box, and he was sent to get soil from the chips shop's garden. They had no gate or fence, so it would be easy for him, and with him being so small, he would not be in much trouble if he got caught.

Our leader put the soil into the envelopes and took us round the houses, allowing us to post the packages through folks's letterboxes. It was a good feeling, being with the kids.

But my daddy sounded sharp when he caught up with us. The envelopes had all been addressed to him, so folks had gone to our house, and some had been very rude. So this time it was my daddy's turn to sort the kids out. So now I really did feel like one of the kids. Daddy said we must take the soil back where it came from and only we knew where that was.

By now it had got really dark. My little friend was frightened. My knees were shivering, but I would have to go with him. To add to our lot, the chip shop was frying that night, and the chip shop mester would be in and out of his back door for scuttles of coal and buckets of potatoes from his peeling shed.

But our leader was clever. He stood outside the front of the shop, and when he saw the mester coming in from the back, he gave us a hoot to be off. My little friend and I were waiting at the end of the row, because it was too far for us to run all the way there, and we might not have enough time to empty all those envelopes. When we got to the chip shop garden, the envelopes were too damp to be opened, so we ripped them all up and scattered them.

Next morning, when I returned to the scene of the crime, the chip shop folks were clearing away the evidence, both of them bobbing up and down like Granddad's fowl at feeding time, patiently picking up every last scrap, both amused and puzzled, not having received any post themselves the previous evening. They were none the wiser.

CARTERS

Carters came along the back of the houses with fruit, vegetables and other things for sale. When Mammy was in the kitchen, she could keep an eye out for them, but if she had a job to do in another room, she might ask me to listen out for a cart she did not want to miss. Even from inside the house, I could say which cart was coming in good time for Mammy to find her purse and go out to it. If I heard a cart coming that I did not know, Mammy was always eager to go out and see it. Such carts were often worthy of a small gathering of mammies, each with something to say about it.

It might be that somebody was moving house; flitting, Mammy would say. Every piece of furniture would be graded, with opinions added and bits of vital information passed around the group, till the sound of the cartwheels rumbled away.

Once, a cart came and stopped on the front, right outside our front door. But Mammy said she was too busy to come, so I went out on my own to find out all about it. The garage man had come over the road to sort out some trouble. The new noise I had heard was the trumbling, rumbling sound of a broken cart. I was surprised to see a horse standing there. Not a whole horse, just the huge white feet and the blaze of his white face. The rest was just a blurred shadow.

"It's a gee-gee," I told the man standing nearby.

He sounded cross, saying, "You're too big to say gee-gee. You must be about four now. It's not a gee-gee, and it's not a bobbo either. Its proper name is a horse."

That hurt me. For a start, I was just three years old, not four, but I did wish that I was being brought up more grown-up. I had thought that gee-gees, bobbos and horses were three different kinds of animals. I walked along the coursey, passing a horse, a cart, and another horse, and another cart! Then I came back again saying, "Cart and horse, cart and horse." By saying it, just that one time, I learned what one hundred times of hearing and as many questions to Mammy had not taught me.

I had thought that carts were just brought round by the carters, because when I went with Mammy to buy greengroceries, we stood by the cart wheel. As high as the hub, was as high as I was. The spokes were painted yellow, and the rim was painted red. And I thought that was because of the paint shortage for the war. But I never once saw a horse. It had puzzled me, how the wheels should make that 'blump blump' noise. Mammy thought it must be the bumps in the road that made the carts jolt.

THE MILKMAN

Every morning, the milkman brought our milk with his cart. The back door was kept open ready for him to come straight in. He would set his churn down in the middle of the floor, gently swirl it around, saying, "Fair shares of the cream for all." Our milk jug was washed and ready waiting. It would be carefully inspected by the milkman because he would not put his milk into a chipped or cracked or dirty jug.

One morning, our jug was found to be chipped, so the milkman chose a pudding basin, which Mammy was asked to wash and wipe first. It would do for a few days, he said, but we must get a new jug. My mammy did not throw the old jug away. She said, "It'll do for custard."

The new jug was bigger than the old one, and Mammy complained when it was not filled. The milkman demonstrated how she had bought a measure of milk, not a jugful. The measures were hung on the inside of the churn, and the milkman knew all of their names. One of them he called Gill. I understood when he ladled out the milk, but Mammy was not convinced until after he had gone, when she poured the milk back into her old jug. But she poured it straight back into the new one again.

A neighbour had fetched me some orange juice from the baby clinic. The empty bottle had been put on the kitchen table, ready for her to take back the next time she went down. Beside the bottle stood the jug of milk. I just wanted a drink of milk, so I poured myself a bottleful. I poured carefully, copying how I thought I had seen Mammy doing it, and I did not spill one drop. I drank it down quickly, and when our neighbour called for the bottle, my mammy could somehow see that it had had milk in it. I did not know how. But she did not know how I could manage to do something that she could not manage to do herself.

After that the milk was put out of my way on the high mantelpiece. It kept cool up there. If milk did go sour in the summertime, it could be made into what Mammy called cream cheese, cottage cheese.

SOMETHING AND NOTHING

Once a cart came to our neighbour; when it had gone, my mammy rushed out with the shovel and a coal bucket. I followed her. There they stood in the road, Mammy and the neighbour, arguing.

Mammy, "You haven't got an allotment garden."

Neighbour, "It was my cart."

Mammy, "It's on my part."

Then both together, they shovelled. Mammy stabbed at the road with her shovel, like cutting a line. Our neighbour began banging with her bucket. Each one of them still insisted that they were in the right. When they had both gone in, I stayed outside to look at the road, but there was nothing I could see, no coal, no snow, nothing.

Our bucket was put in the coal house. That night after dinner, Daddy had to make a special trip up to his allotment. I heard him telling Mammy that somebody would give our neighbour a copper or two for a bucket. He said folks with gardens were always on the lookout for a bit to dig in.

I thought he meant dib in like kids did, not dig in like gardeners did. That is not the same, and my hopes of finding out what it was all about faded, when Daddy went to dig in all on his own.

WASH DAY

Monday was the usual wash day for housewives to do their weekly wash. Not my mammy; and she had her good reasons. With everybody drawing water at the same time, there was not enough force coming through the tap, so the whole job took longer to do, and when all the clothes lines in the road were full of washing, the wind blew wet, she said, and it could not catch her clothes to dry them. So Tuesday was wash day at our house.

Mammy liked to make an early start, so by the time I got up, the washing would be all sorted into different heaps around the house floor. I could mark the time of day by their disappearance. The first load was put to soak while we had our breakfast. Mammy could remember how, when she was a small child, her mammy had stood her on the copper's side, to see it being filled, and how much she had enjoyed that. So each week, I was stood on our copper's side to see.

The copper was built into the recess in the corner of the kitchen. There was quite a large space at the back for me to stand, so each week I looked, while Mammy tipped in the buckets of cold water. But each week I felt my heart sink right down into my tummy when I did not see.

So I would let out my feelings on the oval bathtub which hung on the wall beside me. When I banged it, it made a beautiful booming sound. If I put my ear to it, it sent waves going through me. Mammy would shout, "Don't bang the bathtub." It had been galvanised, I knew, to stop it from going rusty. Mammy thought that I might damage it. I would say that I had not bumped against it on purpose, but in the lovely din, as the bathtub danced on its hook on the wall, I could yell away my sorrows.

Mammy would shout, "You rowdy article!" That way I knew she enjoyed me enjoying myself. Each week she would repeat her polite apology to the neighbour.

Then Mammy would light the fire under the copper, which Daddy would have laid before he went to work, and after, she would put potatoes underneath to bake for later. Before the clothes were boiled, they were washed in the ponch tub, or the dirt would be boiled in.

A ponch tub was like a small corrugated dustbin, and a ponch had a wooden handle like a garden spade, with an upside down copper colander on the bottom. Mammy did not like this new-fashioned ponch. 'Posher', she called it. She had preferred her old one, the one with the wooden three-legged stool on the bottom. One of Mammy's sayings was, "Every little helps," so she had two ponch tubs and two ponches.

Our Spadger and I were encouraged to make a game of the work, and I did work willingly, although it made my arms ache. It was fun to ram the ponch down into the soapsuds and try to make the foam jump out over the side and land with a 'flup' on the floor. I would listen while the deep gurgling noise stopped, then heaving up the ponch again with that squelching sound, straining the suds through the colander, showering the clothes. Mammy called me a good little worker.

But one day I ponched too hard, making patterns of holes in Daddy's best white shirt. Ever after I was downgraded to towels and underwear.

Beside the clothes, the pegs were boiled in the washer. It softened them, so they did not split, and the wooden copper stick which Mammy used to hook out the clothes with, was almost as white as they were.

When Mammy mangled the clothes, she had to take great care or she might break the buttons. She knew all sorts of tricks, like winding back and forth, and folding and refolding the clothes. But this mangle, she said, did not do as good a job as her mam's did when it came to the heavier things.

The kitchen would get so steamed up that Mammy could not see the clock. To keep an eye on the time, she would keep its glass door open.

Washday held many marvels and mysteries for me. To make shirt collars come white, they were rubbed with a bar of green soap. Some of the same soap was grated with a cheese grater, into a basin of hot water. Then the soap turned into bubbles. There were hard lumps of soda to soften the water and there was starch to stiffen the best tablecloth and pillowcases, and Mammy's pinafore, in that order. Starch was a white powder which had to be whisked with the egg whisk into cold water in the bread pancheon. I had never known my mammy to grate cheese, whisk eggs, or knead bread. I just supposed that these were the proper names for the utensils.

In the bathtub, now on the floor behind the back door, there would be a blue rinse to make those whites even whiter.

A dolly blue bag was a little lump of something special tied up in a muslin bag, and if I could manage to get my hands on it, it could turn my fingers a vivid blue. For the cream net curtains, there was a dolly cream bag rinse. That was in a big white enamel bucket, but I never did manage to turn my fingers bright yellow with that.

Then there was the magic of rolling up wet woollens in dry towels, then unrolling wet towels to find dry woollens inside.

The washing was pegged out on two lines, with the smaller things on the windy side. The bed sheets were pegged out in such a way that the wind could catch hold of them and then blow them up like big balloons. Old things were pegged out near the road, then it would not be too bad, Mammy thought, if they were pinched by the gipsies. Daddy's unworn pyjama trousers were respectfully hung next to their jacket. Mammy taught me by telling me never to peg things up by their collars, as collars were stitched on with only one row of stitching, so that they could be easily turned if they got worn out.

"And remember," she said, "When cotton is wet, it is weak."

On windy days, it was so exciting to stand under the washing and hear it flapping and snapping in the wind. But if it looked like rain, I had to keep clean, because if it did rain, it was my job to help carry in the washing quickly. Then I would hold my arms out straight in front of me to have the washing draped over them, and carry it like that into the house.

In the house, a newspaper path would be laid from the stairs door over to the window, crossing over the table, and the washing would be draped over the line above it. I could hear the drips getting quieter and slower as the washing dried.

Our neighbour through the railings had her washing done for her, so she never had hot water. Each week she would ask me if my mammy might spare her a bucket of water from her last wash. It was for swilling out her lavatory with. This made extra work for my mammy, because the water from her last wash would be far too dirty to clean out a lavatory, so she had to pass clean water over the railings. "It gets the job done," she said, but not quite like she would have it done herself.

Then Mammy would cut the tops off the baked potatoes and put dripping inside, and Spadger and I would eat them like boiled eggs, with spoons, out on the back yard, if it was not raining, while Mammy got on with scrubbing the back kitchen floor. She used the same bar of soap. This soap, when it was new, had a picture on that I could feel. It was of a baby wearing a napkin and trying to walk.

Before the peg rugs were put down again on the kitchen floor, I liked to stand on the blue and red tiles and make them rock with my feet. They made a flip flop, flip flop sound, like the horse trotting down the road.

On frosty days, when the clothes were fetched in from the line, they could stand up on the back kitchen table all by themselves, and they smelled so fresh, they made me breathe in deeply their ice-cold air.

By four o' clock, Mammy would be getting in the washing line by holding one end in her hand and winding the rope around and around to her elbow as she walked down the yard. Then she would rear up the clothes prop in the lav, and let me know that everything was back in its place, so it was safe again now for me. I liked to know that it was safe again for me, after Mammy's long, hard day.

THE COALMAN

We did not get miner's coal any more, now that my daddy worked on the buildings again, so we had to buy our coal; and bagged-up coal was more money than having it tipped up loose in the road. It was wash day when the coalman came with his horse and cart and he tipped the load of coal up in the road outside our back gate.

He said that Monday was wash day, and he would not dream of coming then, that he was sorry, but what could he do about it now? His horse could not go up the hill with a full load. That was why he had come to us first and he could not take it back, and there was somebody waiting for coal who he could not let down, and he *was* sorry.

I was surprised. Mammy did an unknown thing. She made a pot of tea. There was a cup for her and a cup for me, with biscuits. Then she got on with her washing, while I guarded the coal heap. I felt like the king of the castle, sitting on the top, but I heard people passing by, saying, "That poor kid."

I did not feel poor. Mammy had cut me a fresh crust of bread with jam, spread thick enough for me to see it, and not factory jam, neither. It was real jam, with skins to chew and stones to suck.

A bobby came by on his beat and asked why the coal was not being got in. I told him that my daddy was at work, and Mammy was doing her washing. He said, "The coal must be being got in." And he was sorry, but if it was not in before dark, we would be summonsed. The bobby watched the coal heap for me while I went to tell Mammy.

In the kitchen, clouds of white steam rose from the

copper in the corner. I found my mammy crying like a child, surrounded by the ponch tubs, the basins, the buckets, the bathtub. On seeing the bobby, she had thought that we were to be summonsed there and then.

"We can hardly afford the load o' coal, nay mind a summons," she wept. And "oh," she wailed, when I told her that the coal must be being got in. Without another word, she got those clothes in off the line and without my help, and quicker than if it had been raining.

I had watched the coal being tipped up. To me, it looked like one big lump. I did not know how my mammy, or anybody, could get it through the back gate, down the yard, through the kitchen and put it in the coal house. But Mammy showed me how I could help her. I was happy to use her little shovel, which she made the copper fire up with. She taught me that if I pushed the shovel along the road to the edge of the heap, some coal fell onto it, and it fell apart into lumps. I could hear them go bumpity-bump into the metal bucket.

Mammy and I worked all afternoon getting that load of coal in, me filling the buckets with the little lumps, Mammy carrying them down the yard. The bigger lumps she picked up and carried in in her arms, like babies, but one lump was so huge that it had to be rolled over and over down the yard, and turned to get it through the kitchen door. It made a mess, and Mammy made deep grunting noises, like it hurt her.

Then it began to get dark. Mammy said I must go into the house. It had been safe enough in the light, when the coal heap had been bigger and the buses had had to go right round it, but now it was too dangerous for me. By the time Daddy got home it was nearly dark, and the bobby came by again. But he told Daddy that he need not worry, as it was still yet dusk, and he was sure that we could manage to get the coal in before it was dark. And anyhow, he would not be back.

I heard Daddy say to Mammy, "'ow good it were o' 'im to come back early." Daddy packed and stacked the coal in the coal house by building a wall at the front with the lumps, putting the smaller lumps behind it. Mammy mangled the washing and Daddy draped it over the lines in the house for it to drip, drip, drip down onto the newspapers, like on wet washing days. But tonight we had a good fire to get it dry, Mammy chuckled, because the washing had had a good long soak. So dinner was a little late that night.

While Mammy was cooking it on the fire, I was surprised to see Daddy get down on his hands and knees to scrub that kitchen floor until it came up like new.

THE TOY DRAWER

On wet wash days, for some reason, it seemed to be my mam's job to look after other folks's kids, and that was when we might most likely be delving into our toy drawer. It was the bottom drawer in the corner, next to the gas meter cupboard.

Some toys were simple homemade ones like the aeroplanes the kids could make from wooden clothes pegs by pushing one inside another to make the wings. Sometimes the kids could make them with two sets of wings and they knew all their names and their shapes. I did not like aeroplanes. I never could tell by the sound they made, which were ours and which were theirs. Nor could I believe Mammy when she said, "They're all ours now."

Then there were hand-me-down toys. One I enjoyed

playing with was passed down to me by an older cousin. She had finished with it, and besides, it was broken. It was a wooden horse she had named Dante, after a famous Derby winner, I was told. I had heard of that place called Derby. Daddy had a job to mend Dante. All his bits and pieces had to be threaded through onto elastic; his blue hooves, his black legs, his pink and red body that was shaped like a barrel, even his little rounded, pointed ears. To make him perform, I had to turn him all about in my hands, put him down on the table, call out, "Dante," then he would do all sorts of tricks, with flicks and snapping sounds until he was standing still again.

There were the woollen gollywogs that Mamam had bought me from the auction. I enjoyed playing with those so much that Mammy made me quite a few more in different bright colours. It is easy to make woollen gollywogs. You wind the wool around your fingers until the bundle is fat enough for the body. Then you slip it off your fingers and tie the bundle twice, very tightly, to make three parts, for the legs, the body and the head. You split the leg part into two bundles, tying tightly round the ankles and tying tightly near the top of the head for making the hair later. You make a shorter bundle on less fingers, and not so fat for the arms. Then you tie it tightly round the wrists, and thread it through the body. Next you clip all the ends to make hands and feet and the fuzzy hair. You can make a few stitches for the eyes and a smiley mouth, and to make a really smart golly, you can tie a ribbon bow around his neck, if you've got one.

I had four cardboard boxes with lids, which fitted one inside another. They felt shiny on the outside, so maybe they had pictures or patterns on, but I could not tell. We would sometimes play at building houses with those. I liked that game.

There were two rag dolls, which Daddy's younger sister had

bought for me and our Spadger. Auntie and Uncle had called in with them on their way back from a holiday. They were wanting to get home, so said they were not stopping. They just stood in the back kitchen doorway. Our Spadger spun round and round in circles, swinging her doll round with one of its long legs. Then she put it down on the kitchen table and went through into the house. I did not think the dolls were very nice either.

I did think that was wrong, what our Spadger had done, and I felt sorry for Auntie, so I picked up both of the dolls and said that I would love both of them. I knew which was my dolly. She had a bright green pixie hood. Both of the dolls must have been very much played with, for when they were worn, Mammy bought new faces for them and stitched them on over the top of the old ones.

In the toy drawer there were books, a rope, and a ball, pencils and paper, all belonging to our Spadger, and I could not manage to play with those toys with the other kids.

IN MY PUSHCHAIR

We were just about ready to set off down the street to fetch the rations one cold morning, with me and our Spadger wrapped up snugly together in the pushchair by the back door, when the seat sank slowly to the ground and the wheels came up at the side. Our Spadger wailed on one long, knowing note.

Mammy said, "I told you so. I knew it would happen one day, and it has. I said you would have to walk, and now you will."

I tried to comfort her. I knew it would be all right. The seat was very low, but it was not broken. That made Mammy chuckle. We all had to go back into the house. I couldn't understand that. She explained why. It was too cold for walking and I would soon know about that, she thought. She hunted out my old leggings from the rug clippings bag. It was lucky, she thought, that they had not already been cut up into small pieces for the new hearthrug that Daddy was pegging for us.

I loved those fawn leggings. I was so pleased to be wearing them just once more, even though the bottom three buttons on the leg could not reach to be fastened up. I would have to make do, just for that once, said Mammy.

It was not the cold that made me so miserable. It was holding up my arm to hold Mammy's hand. It was so tiring, made my arm ache. I grumbled. It was our Spadger's fault that the pushchair had broken. She was too big for it, and it was my pushchair now.

Mammy knew why I was crying. She felt like crying herself, and that cheered me up.

ON MY REINS

The nurse down at the clinic had said how sorry she was that she could not be more help for my mammy, but she did find her a friend who had a little girl about the same age as me, and she hoped that we all might find ways of helping one another.

The little girl and her mammy called for us as we were all

going for a walk together one morning. On our table there were some crusts in baking trays, which Mammy was going to dry out later, when the oven was not too hot.

The little girl picked up one crust and started eating it hungrily. I could hear the saliva bubbling round her mouth. It sounded like she was really enjoying it. She hummed when she chewed. So I picked up the other crust and copied her, to find out why it was so good to eat in that way. But Mammy stopped me. She fetched fresh bread from the pantry and spread it with jam, the idea being that if I ate nicely, the little girl might copy me. What a treat that was! And her mammy did sound pleased with her.

The nurse at the clinic had said that the little girl should be walking more by now and that morning she had come in her pushchair, but as mine had collapsed, the mammies both agreed to leave the little girl's pushchair at our house and we would both wear our reins. The little girl might run off without wearing hers. Her mammy sounded upset by my mammy saying that I would not run off.

My reins were made of thick brown leather, fleecy on the inside; and on the front there were tiny bells to jingle. Out we went on the front, tense and nervous. I felt very lost without a hand to guide me, so I would not move. The little girl beside me sprang about, shouting noisily. Then I felt my reins pull tight, and I did feel safe to go forward then with the little girl, but not sideways or up and down like she did. I did try it, it was fun, but it did not feel safe.

So off we went, but I did not like it. I would rather hold Mammy's hand and put up with the arm ache. I hated this walk. I could see shadows, but I did not know if they were in the air or on the ground. I had to feel for steps with my feet, but there was nothing to feel with my hands.

It began to rain, and the little girl's mammy said she would take her home on the bus and call round at our house for the pushchair some time later.

When they had gone, my mammy thought that I might get on better on my own. So she made a game of it, and now that there were no shadows to frighten me, it was better, and we pretended I was a horse. Mammy gave my reins two shakes and said, “Clip clip.” I stretched them tight, jingled my bells and set off at a trot.

“Gee up, gee up,” called Mammy from behind me. I pulled harder, and I pranced about a bit, but I still did not like this game. After a while, Mammy was feeling tired, calling, “Whoa, whoa.” She could not keep up with me. I was getting tired too, but I thought, if I can keep this up, I might not have to wear my reins ever again. I broke out into a gallop, Mammy clinging on tight, her high heels going clip-clop, clip-clop. She was either laughing or crying, as though she was having a ride on the merry-go-round. I tried doing more tricks than I’m sure my Dante’s elastic could ever allow him to perform.

When we got home, Mammy flopped down in an easy chair, her legs stretched out straight on the hearth, her shoes kicked off, with her high heels pointing upwards. I could see her big glasses shining, reflecting the light from the window as she lay back, mopping her forehead with her coat sleeve, breathlessly repeating,

“Never again, never again.”

It had worked. I had won. I felt exhilarated with all that fresh air inside my lungs. And that exercise, it had done me good. Out on our back yard, I did several laps of honour, still jingling my bells, to make quite sure that Mammy knew I still had plenty of energy left inside me. Being a horse had done me better than anybody could have guessed. Cantering round on the back yard I felt safe, because I was still wearing my reins. Then I realised I was on my own, and I could even do this without my reins, I thought. I had learned to run.

In the house Mammy had fetched herself a tumbler of cold water and was sitting in the easy chair again, sipping slowly, still groaning. Then she took off my reins, and as I liked them so much, she said I could keep them in my toy drawer, just in case I should ever feel like being a horse again.

That was my only memory of the little girl, but forty years on, dad tells me that her mam says that she sits silently in a chair, all day long.

OVER THE WALL

The house next door to us, over the wall, was much the same to me as all the other houses in the row, on the inside, I mean. They all had a back kitchen and another room that everybody called 'the house'. I felt quite at home in them all, as the furniture was usually set out in the same way as our house was.

In the middle of each house stood a square table, which might be covered by a chenille tablecloth in some houses, or in others by newspapers. At weekend it might be covered by a best white starched tablecloth. Two chairs tucked under the side, and two chairs on the hearth near the fire, and on the back wall, opposite the fireplace there might be a sideboard. Under the window there might be a long, leather-like settee. Some had soft cushions. Some had lace or embroidered covers on the arms and back. Each house had its own identity by its own family, and the way the families varied, but there were some set rules for all the houses; knocking on the door, wiping your feet before you go in; once in, being polite, and leaving if they had company, or if it was meal time.

These sorts of rules were taught to me by Mammy. But Daddy laid down one very strict rule. He said, "What goes off in other folk's houses is their business, and nowt to do wi' anybody else." If my tongue did slip when I got back home again, it might be caught by a minute's noisy silence.

Just three slips I can remember; pink kali, white nylon stockings – that caused Mammy to draw in her breath, and something brown that I told Mammy about. It was cut up with a bread knife, carved, she thought. I had been offered a slice of this to eat in my hand. They said it would do me good, but I didn't know what it was, because we did not have it at our house. The brown slice was thinner than bread and it did not have much taste. It needed a lot of chewing and we were all laughing together about this joke while we chewed.

"There y'are, what did I tell you?" said one to another. "Kids don't like it. That's why they don't gi' 'em rations."

The house with the pebbledashed wall was the last house in the row. It had an extra bedroom over the two lock-up shops at the end of the row. On their back yard, they had, not what could be called a privy, but what could truly be called a convenience. Theirs was a two-holer, a wooden board with two round holes cut in it, built to accommodate two to sit side by side. I remember how safe I felt, sitting in the dark with a little friend. One thing I had to remember at this house was that they had a step between the kitchen and the house. The daddy asked me, "If you know the step's there, then why do you fall?"

The answer seemed quite clear to me, so surely everybody knew that sometimes the step was a going up step, and sometimes it was a going down step. To show him what I meant, I got down to check that as I was going out of the house into the kitchen, it was a going up step. But coming back into the house again, I got down to feel, and the step had changed itself. This time it was a going down step. I thought, everybody else can see if the step has changed or not. But their daddy said the step hadn't changed. "Well, where did the up step go to, then?" I asked him. He did not know. And he asked his wife when she came in, and she was sure that she did not know either. Poor woman, I thought. The step is a trouble to her and to me.

A gypsy was made very welcome, and asked to spread out her things on the table. They were pleased to see the things, I could hear, with their voices. But I was just pleased to see over the table top. Maybe their table was lower than ours. This was the first time that I could see by pulling myself up and standing on tiptoe. I felt a gentle shower, like rain, falling over me as I knew that there could be no end to the knowing of new things. Being tall enough to see over table tops put a new dimension into my life.

Tables were not only for mealtimes. The table was the hub of family life. One day, Mammy had bought me a plastic pinafore. It was white with a blue frill round the edge. She was not sure how long it would last, but I was happy to wear it, because as she said, it will keep me clean for going out later. I went round to next door's over the wall to show off with it. Their daddy was trying to interest the kids in something on their table.

He said to me, "Here, you may as well have a look. They don't want to know." So I climbed up to stand on the chair like his kids did. I just looked, but I could not see anything at all. He sounded excited.

"Go on, feel it! Feel it all over," he urged me on. I would not have thought of touching things before being asked. All the kids watched me feeling, as I found bits one at a time with my fingers. What I found was, I was told, a big wheel. He said it was like you get on a fairground. I had never heard of one before. Perhaps it stood eighteen inches - two foot high, and it could go round by winding a small handle. As it spun, it made soft, slow grunting click-clack knocking noises. My hands were gently taken and placed on the wooden seats that I had not found.

"It's a ferris wheel," he said. "Made entirely of wood, it is." Then we took turns on working it, so that I could feel the big wheel going round with both hands. At first it bothered me. I could not think how the handle at the bottom could make the wheel move.

"I don't know either," said the kid's daddy. "And you don't have to understand to appreciate a thing. It's a marvel. It's a work of art. It's a masterpiece!"

He was right. When I stopped trying to solve the mystery, I opened up to the full wonder before me.

When they had a new baby delivered to their house, I was invited to go round and help at bath time. Mammy sat near the fire with a little bath on a stand. She patted the baby dry in a towel on her lap. It was a bright pink baby. I was told that they were all like that. But when his mammy powdered him, it made him look not quite so sore.

I did little jobs, fetched and carried things, feeling very grown up, with just a gentle word now and then, not to knock the bath, and mind the step. I fetched the feeding bottle, which was cooling in the kitchen sink. It was a clinic orange juice bottle, I found, filled to the top with milk. I had been in trouble for drinking that much milk. We could only have one jugful a day at our house.

Baby's mammy tested the milk by sprinkling it on her hand.

"I don't know," she said. "Here, you try it. You'll know best." I sucked on the rubber teat and choked. It was far too hot. I took it back to the sink to hold it under the tap. The tap was always left dripping for their kids to wash their hands or get themselves a drink of water.

Their daddy came home and asked lovingly how his wife felt now. She told him how I had been more help than the nurse. He put the kettle on the fire to boil, emptied the baby's bath water. Then I knew it was time for me to go home.

SCARLET FEVER

Their little girl caught scarlet fever. Her mammy was telling my mammy over the wall what she was to look out for on me. She was saying that I was in quarantine. The men came to take the little girl away to the fever hospital, her mammy wailing from inside their house, and mine crying softly because, as she told me, when you're took to the fever hospital, they don't know if they'll bring you back home.

On the yard, the man asked to talk to me. I saw him like a shadow over the wall. He spoke sternly.

"Quarantine means staying on your yard, and do not move off." He barked so fiercely, he rooted me to the spot with fear. I dare not move, even to lift one foot, so I stood there all the morning, rubbing my hands over the rough pebbledash wall. I thought I had to stay out there to see if they would bring the little girl back from the fever hospital. Both mammies reckoned that I was pining, and it would not hurt to pass all the kids to and fro over the wall, just as long as we did not go through the gates and round on the coursey. We had played together every day.

One day, when we had all been passed over their wall, the mammies stood the kids in two rows on their back yard and gave each one of us a glass. Not a cup like at our house. Then she came along the rows, measuring out clinic orange juice. Then she went into the kitchen for some water. I did not want a drink of water, so I swallowed down my measure of concentrated juice, making myself cough and splutter. But when all the other kids had their glasses filled up with water, they enjoyed their drinks, and I felt ashamed, not knowing, as their mammies said, "It has to be let dahn."

Another time over the wall, the kids were given plastic scissors to cut out pictures from the newspaper. I knew that sharp scissors were dangerous. But these were toy scissors, I was told, for cutting paper, not children. I could not join in that game, but I was given a turn to snip, and I knew if I was cutting by the sound I made.

On other days we were all at our house, with pencils and paper, and books to read, because my mammy said she had to do the best she could at a time like this. She showed me how to write the shapes of the letters, but then decided this was a waste of time. But she made quite sure I was not left out all the time. There would be a nice warm fire in the grate, and biscuits and buns during the afternoon.

At last they did bring the little girl home from the fever hospital, and the scarlet fever scare was over. That day, Mammy told me what she had been thinking, but dare not put into words while we were all in quarantine. She had been thinking of a little girl, not like me, one who could run and play, lying in the hospital, and here was I, how I was.

How was I? I was much cherished by all the family and all who knew me. That's how I was. Mammy was not sure what she should think. What would our neighbour be thinking?

She prayed aloud every day for the little girl, I knew that. But also Mammy had been praying that I might be spared. She could not think how she could go on without me, but for one thought; that if the Lord had have wanted it, we would have been friends together forever. So what a wonderful thing it was that not one child had been taken.

That day when we were out of quarantine, Mammy sang praises again. She had had to stop herself from singing while she got on with her work. She could hear our neighbour weeping as she got on with hers. Mammy had been doing all she could to help and comfort. When I had been out on the yard, and our neighbour working at her kitchen sink, my mammy had thought how it might upset her, to see me playing from her window. So that was why, at times, she had come out, taken my hand, going back inside the house for me to play.

But that day we were out of quarantine, the kids had scattered, and now my mammy would like me to go out onto our back yard and make as much racket as I could.

DRIED PEAS

Being in quarantine had brought all the kids much closer together. We had been told, "There's nothing we can do about it, so stop squabbling. Learn to live together."

So we had, and now we still played together in each others' houses if it was raining. One wet afternoon we were playing in their extra bedroom, the one above the barber's lock-up shop on the end of the row.

The room was quite empty, with bare floorboards. I soon got used to the noise, joining in their running up and down game. This game put me on the same level as the other kids, as it was a sound-making game. By the sound of their leather-soled shoes, I could tell where each kid was running, and by the sound of my own shoes, it put me in the middle of the picture. I weaved in and out, or followed their footsteps until we were all tired.

The kids helped me to join in the next game. We were leaning out of the open window above the barber's shop doorway, dropping dried peas as the patrons emerged, newly shorn before putting on their hats. The kids told me when to drop the dried peas.

"Aw!" they all gasped. "You've hit him! And he's nearly bald on top."

I was summoned to the shop to account for my actions. I knew that girls should not go in the barber's shop, so I just stood in the doorway. From inside a man was shouting, but he thought that I should be saying something. But I did not know what he was shouting, so I did not know what I should be saying. There was a loud buzzing noise, sounding like a big bluebottle fly, and a white sheet flowing through the air. It frightened me.

PIGTAILS

We were often playing outside the barber's shop. There was a wide coursey there on the end of the row. When the men came out dressed in their Sunday best, carrying their canes, they were always polite to one another, lifting their big-brimmed hats to show off their new haircuts, I thought.

The kids seemed to think that a lot of the men were nearly bald on top. I thought they came out of the barber's that way. I did not know that some men go bald as they do later. I thought that they had rubbed their hair away by lifting their hats every time they said good morning.

One day, when business was rather slack, the barber says, "All the kids' hairs is in need of a good cut."

It was not looking right for them to be playing outside his shop, so he said he would do all the kids for a few coppers each. They were to go in a few at a time. Mammy sorted through her purse. She found a few coppers for me and our Spadger. Spadger went first while I stayed at home waiting my turn. But when she came back, Mammy sounded pleased. She thought she had had her money's worth. But I noticed how Spadger was quiet. She did not need to wear her hairslide any more. She silently placed it on the table, and I was sent out, clutching my coppers in my hand, with a big knot tied inside my tummy.

In the barber's shop doorway, I stopped to listen. I could not hear that big bluebottle fly, or see the big white flowing sheet, so I stepped inside and handed over my coppers. By invisible hands I was scooped up, and landed on a high chair. I could not find anywhere to rest my feet, so my legs were left dangling in the air.

Then I caught sight of that white sheet floating about, and I froze stiff. The sheet flew in front of me for a second or two, then it blocked out the daylight before settling itself down over me, wrapping itself round my shoulders, pinning down my arms. In fear I shrank down into the chair. As the air escaped from under the sheet, it tucked me in tight, folding itself up into pleats. Its weight hung heavy, pulling my feet down. Silent tears ran down my face. I was trapped.

Next the sheet gripped hold of my neck. It was trying to strangle me! Somehow I slipped from its grasp, landing in a heap on the shop floor. Now the sheet had me in a bag. It had pulled its drawstrings tight above my head. Somehow I fought myself free, making for the light of the open doorway, tripping over the threshold, running for home, shivering with fright, dripping wet.

From round the corner I could still hear the barber yelling, "Don't you come here again! Never did like kids!"

Mammy said it did not look like she would ever get me in a shop again to get my hair cut, so I would have to learn to sit still, and she would have to learn to plait my hair. She soon got the hang of it. So my hair kept tidy and out of my eyes. Later Mammy gave lessons to a neighbour and I earned some tuffees.

On Saturday nights I had to sit still for a long time, while my hair was wound up in rags and tied tightly. Sunday mornings my hair hung down in ringlets that bobbed around my face. They got in my way, but everybody liked them, and because they liked my ringlets, they liked me, speaking pleasantly, praising Mammy, whereas before they might not even have spoken. It made all that tugging and tying and sleeping on knots worthwhile. It made me feel good about myself. And Mammy got her reward too.

The barber thought if he stopped doing kids hairs, their dads would stop coming, so he made a rule: in future he would not do the kids hairs, only if they came with their dads, in the week.

CLEANING UP DAY

On Friday mornings, my mammy cleaned the room we called 'the house'. Her first job was to carry the peg rugs out on to the backyard to give them an airing, hiking them over the clothes line or the wall. On her way back through the kitchen, she would take down her black lead box from the shelf. Then while she took the fireplace to pieces, and spread them about her on sheets of newspaper on the floor, I would have to sit on the settee, as there would be no other place for me, and I was always reminded not to touch. Each piece had to be cleaned. The black lead had to be put on with a brush, then after it was brushed off again. Mammy wanted her fireplace to have a shiny finish, so she would give each piece a jolly good rubbing over with a soft cloth.

Then the fireplace itself had to be cleaned. The oven was on the left of the grate. Its shelf was missing. On the right of the fire grate was the boiler, but its tap did not turn. To fill the boiler, the lid had to be lifted and the water poured in, then the warm water scooped out again with a ladle, being careful not to draw too deep, or to scrape the ladle on the edge, or some soot might drop in. Then all the pieces could be put back in their places again.

There was a hearth plate, the front of the ash box, the kerb and the screen. The screen lived on top of the oven or on the front of the fireplace for safety at night or if we went out shopping. Or it could be stood over a lazy fire to get it to come back to life. Then there was another metal plate, which was hidden away up the chimney. It seemed spare to me, and I thought perhaps Mammy could not find anywhere else to put it.

All the chrome trimmings were rubbed up to make them shine like silver. Mammy thought it was a waste of time to do the boiler tap, with it not working, but she rubbed it up anyway.

I loved black lead days, because all the time Mammy worked, she told me stories. There were stories about when she was a girl, how when they moved for her dad to find work, at first they had to live in somebody's front room. They had to keep the saucepans under the bed, and the mice would rattle the lids at night. On Mammy's first day at the school, she had to stand up in class and say her mam's and dad's names. She had to shout out, Taima and Elijah. She got teased and did not like it. She was rapped over her knuckles for taking too long with her writing. In the school holidays Mammy went camping with the Girl Guides.

"We couldn't go far, just to the rec at the top of the street," she said. "But if any girl guide went home, even to fetch something she had forgotten, she weren't allowed back in camp again. But you could say, 'Hello maam,' if you went down the street when you were shopping."

When Mammy was older, they would go on their bikes to the seaside for the weekend, just wearing their shorts and shirts, with a spare set in their saddlebags, staying in a fisherman's hut overnight and going to a farmhouse for their breakfast next morning.

There was not much work in those days, but at last Mammy got a job at the tin factory. Every morning people would queue up outside the gates at the factory. The boss would come out and look at them, and say, "I'll take you, and you, and you". One rainy morning Mammy and Auntie thought there would not be many in the queue, so they dressed up in their best clothes. It was Auntie who was picked out by the boss, but she said, "We're together,' so they were both told to go back home. They thought they had not got a job, but then the boss added that they should get out of their best clothes and come back again.

At first my mammy worked on a machine that rolled the edges of tins over to stop people from cutting themselves. Later she worked in the printing shop. It was exciting to watch the pictures coming, she said, as the colours were put on one by one. It was like magic paintings. All kinds of tins were made at the tin factory. Some girls took tins home with them, even though they might be searched. One girl wanted a tall tower, so all her mates took pieces of it, then she built it up when she'd got it home. It was hard work at the factory, but they did have some good times. Mammy learnt her dance steps by using two fingers on the canteen table.

After work they went skating or dancing. Mammy met Daddy at a dance. They had looked at a lot of houses for rent. Then they found our house. The rent was a bit more, but it had electric lights and a flush lavatory. Daddy grew some beautiful bronze chrysanthemums for Mammy to carry on her wedding day.

"They looked good with my brown suit," she said. They had a lot of lovely wedding presents, enough furniture to fill the house, besides things for the kitchen.

Some girls tried going to work after they were married, but when you got caught you were sacked, Mammy told me. She said she would never marry a collier. My daddy was a plasterer, but by Christmas time all building work had stopped because of the war, and the weather. My daddy was loading wagons on the pit top.

When our Spadger was coming, my mammy went to her mammy. She lay on the settee to have a rest, and our doctor, Pop Waller came to see her. Our Spadger was a hungry baby.

She cried all night.

When I came, Daddy made a little cot for me. He had to wedge it in the chimney breast recess with a hammer. Before bedtime, Mammy would make me up a feeding bottle, wrap it in a towel and put it under her pillow. It would still be warm enough when I got hungry in the night. My cot was near enough for Mammy to reach out her hand and hold mine through the bars while I went back to sleep again.

When Mammy took me down to the clinic, I was wearing the angora bonnet she had knitted for me. The nurse said, "There's nothing wrong with her eyes. It's only that bonnet. It's irritating them."

I had a real silk crocheted frock; it was green and a great trouble to wash, but so beautiful, thought Mammy. When I was older, about six months or more, I had a highchair. I liked to rattle pennies in a matchbox. One by one they would drop out, but Mammy would find them on cleaning up day and put them in a new matchbox for me.

My first word was 'shoe'. My first pair were blue because Mammy could not find pink ones anywhere. The shoes fastened with stud buttons, which Mammy had saved in her cotton tin. I told Mammy that I could remember going to the air raid shelter. She thought I was too young to remember that. I told her about the lady screaming, who they thought was having a baby. That shocked Mammy into silence.

That day, when we had finished the cleaning up, we went upstairs and we found that green crocheted frock in the bottom of the wardrobe. I felt the patterns. It was rough and hard, and so heavy. I thought that would not be very comfy to wear, but I could not remember it, or sitting in my highchair or wearing my blue shoes.

Between us, we worked out how old I was when I could first remember. It was in months, but I've forgotten how many Mammy said. She said, "I never would tell you anything bad, like that day in the air raid shelter".

On cleaning up days, there were stories about Jesus. I learned that I came from Jesus, and one day would go back to him. Some people thought that in Heaven there was a marble slab with goats sitting on one side, and sheep on the other. It was a beautiful place, and there were not even any tuffee papers up there to spoil it.

"No," I said. "They've thrown 'em all down 'ere." I liked to see those tuffee papers in the gutters. There were heaps of them, and fag packets. They let me know that I was on the coursey, and would not get run down by motors.

And we sang hymns. The one I liked the best was the one about the green hill, with God on the top, the hill without a wall. In our town there were walls, all the way up the road to fetch the meat, walls all the way down the hill to the marketplace, a wall round the Lammas with giant crocodile teeth on top, and a wall round the cemetery, with sawn-off railing stumps on the top. There was even a wall round the football ground on the way to Auntie's that had a wooden fence on the top. It was so high that even by sitting on Daddy's shoulders, I could not see over it. The only way to see the green grass was to peep through a knothole. Daddy said it was criminal. I told myself that someday, somehow, I would go far away, to find that green hill with God on the top.

Mammy would answer all my questions if she could, but she could not say how it was that even though I had poorly peepers, I could see the dust motes dancing in the sunlight. But it was not the dust I could see. It was the sun, shining through our heavy net curtains that made pictures on my face when I moved.

The next job was to sweep the lino. Then it would have to be gone over with a damp cloth. So Mammy would get a bucket of water and some Dettol from the first aid cupboard. She would be so careful to measure out just one spoonful of Dettol. But then, if there was plenty left in the bottle, she would pour in a few spots more.

And I loved the next job, too. That was to go out on the back yard and beat the rugs with a brush till they bounced about. Mammy could shake the rugs and make them go into waves. We had four rugs. One laid at each side of the table, which was in the middle of the room. Each rug was turned about in its own place, so it would wear evenly. As the rugs wore out, new ones were made, and the old ones put at the side of the table, where they might not be noticed so much.

Making pegged rugs was a family hobby that we all joined in, Mammy cutting old clothes up into bits that looked like glove fingers, Daddy drawing designs on brown sacks, then pulling the clippings through the sacking with his sharp pegger. He always edged the rugs with a dark border. Our Spadger enjoyed sorting out the colours for him, and I learned to name colours, those I could see. The rug at the back of the table was good, Mammy said. Folks could see it there when the door was open. It had been made from a long brown coat. “It were a good coat,” she said. “It wore well, and it weren’t half warm.”

Daddy had worked pale green quarter circles into opposite corners on it, but we needed a new rug so badly, that the rug on the hearth had to go down before it was finished. It had two blue and two red diamonds pointing to the centre, making a star and that was also edged with that pale green. I knew how Mammy felt about that coat because it made me sad to watch my fawn leggings being cut up into clippings for this new rug. I would sometimes lie on the rug, rubbing my nose to try and find my leggings. The old rug had to stay at the back of the table because of the bare sacking patches in the new rug where not enough clippings could be found to finish it.

Daddy would feel my velvet frock that Mammy had made me, to see if it was wearing thin, and beg a yard of the bottom of Mammy's long green dressing gown. She thought that the rug would be worn out before any more clothes were worn out.

That bucket of Dettol water went a long way. It was used for cleaning the lavatory, and the kitchen windowsill and the doorstep, and then swilled down the yard into the grate. Then the mansion polish and the dusters were brought down from the kitchen shelf.

Before Mammy did the polishing, she put all the things on the table, things that people see every day, made special for me just to see them once a week. Above the fireplace lived a pair of Bakelite ashtrays for company who smoked. There were two tins. Mammy had a set of three of these tins, but the biggest tin she kept her curling pins in. It lived in the cupboard, near the Dettol. But the one that lived high up on the right hand side of the fireplace was used as a tea caddy, and the little one that lived high up on the left, was used for strings and shoelaces and so on.

So I could see this shoelace tin. It was black with pictures of boats on it. They had bright red and green sails on, and floated on shiny golden waves, and there were birds flying about. This picture was so cheerful, I would gaze for a long time, and through the week, in an empty moment, or when I heard Mammy spooning tea into the teapot, it pleased me to think of the boat. If I had have heard waves lapping on the seashore, or seagulls calling, I could have said, "I'm sure I heard them." But even without seeing clearly, I could go right into the picture, and almost feel the breeze on my cheeks.

A little clock lived up there, above the fire. My mammy's mam had brought it her from the seaside. Every morning it had to be wound up and put right about five minutes. That was with the eight o' clock pips. After polishing, I could see Mammy pick the clock up with both hands and raise her arms to put it back. I thought the clock could somehow stick on the wall. I asked if it would fall. "Not if we're careful," said Mammy.

Next, Mammy had a little job for a little person to do. Under the table there was a forest of furniture legs, chunks and branches growing all ways around me, and I enjoyed dusting the crisscross staves. I did not even have to bend down under there, and Mammy played peep-o as she polished the chairs that tucked underneath the table.

The legs on the wireless stand hung down in spirals, just like my hair on Monday mornings when the ringlets were falling out. When I was a baby, I used to pull myself up with those wireless stand legs, Mammy said.

Then there was the sideboard. There was always a clean runner for the sideboard, which Mammy had embroidered herself, and a space was left clear near the door for her handiwork to be seen by people who were going past if the door was left open. I could see the dirty runner that was taken off. I could trace the trellis work with my fingers and find the flowers, trying to sort out which were the knobbly knots on the wrong side.

On the left side of the sideboard lived the Westminster clock. I knew everything there was to know about the clock, except, how could people look at it and tell me the time? The clock was like a little house. The front door was round and made of glass, but I could not look in there. Inside there were three holes that Mammy could put in the key to wind him up. I thought she scraped the key, because it sounded like rattling sticks along railings. It seemed an odd thing to me that the key could not live in this front room. It had to go round the back, and live in the kitchen. The kitchen door was square and wooden. Inside there was a spoon hanging up. I could see it moving, because it was shiny. I could put my small hand inside and gently feel the padded hammers as they lifted up to tap the rods, making that sound that summed up home. I could lean my ear on the roof and sometimes hear the clock's tummy talking. I could listen to his ticking till I got tired, but the ticking did not change at all. But when the clock chimed, it chimed. After the last note had been struck, I would listen for seconds, and wonder, *where is the chime now? Is it still inside the clock, in my ears, or just inside my head?*

Then there was Diane. Diane was a poor hungry lady who lived in the middle of the sideboard. If I knocked on her tummy, she sounded empty, and she had no clothes to put on. I could feel her all over. She sat with her right leg stretched out, leaning back on her right hand, with her left hand resting on her left bent knee. All Diane had was a piece of old curtain round her shoulders. But it did match our curtains and our cushions. I told Mammy, "If all I had to wear was that old curtain, I would wrap it right round me." She chuckled. I could put my fingers deep into the hard folds of Diane's old curtain. She must have needed a lot of dusting. Mammy always had a few words to say to Diane.

Then lastly, the settee was polished. The cushions were fluffed up; their green velvet stroked all one way. Our Spadger could draw pictures in that velvet. Mammy did not mind really. It was a shame to rub them out. Then the curtains would be tugged down, to make them hang in neat folds.

And so the cleaning up was all done, with a few minutes to spare before little dinner time. Mammy would stand back and look. She said it would never look quite as nice as it did for this few moments. Even when Daddy got home, he would not see it at its best. I could take in the mixed scents of black lead, Dettol, mansion polish, and sometimes DDT that might be sprayed on the high window ledge.

The ticking clocks, the crackling fire and the kettle singing softly, this was my home. Mammy always used these few minutes to reward herself for a morning's hard work well done.

A WHEELBARROW FROM SANTA

I was three years old now, and could go out and play on the street, so this Christmas I had asked Santa if he could please bring me a garden wheelbarrow, and on Christmas morning, there it was on our hearthrug, so shiny and black, made of metal. At first I thought it was a part from off of the black lead fireplace, which each Friday morning Mammy took to pieces to clean. But that strong smell of new paint told me that *this is my wheelbarrow!* But I could hear Mammy chattering away in the background. She was saying, "It is not a wheelbarrow. A wheelbarrow has only one wheel. A dolly pram has four wheels with spokes. A wheelbarrow has two handles. A dolly pram has only one handle."

I could not tell what all the fuss was about. Four wheels must be better than one, and I should manage to push the barrow much easier. I told Mammy, "It not cock over, then." I thought, *for the job I have in mind, it will do very well.*

It was a murky morning. I still wanted to go out, and it was just as well that my dolly Jenny, as bright as a penny, with her flat silver nose, was still far too precious for me to take out.

She still had no clothes to wear, so she must stay warm in the house, wrapped in her new blankets.

Outside our back gate, my little friend was waiting for me. In his hands he held his toy. It was not what he had asked Santa to bring him either. Neither did he want it, but his big brother did, he told me, but he was not going to let him have it.

I asked my little friend if he would help me to fill my garden barrow with soil. He thought, like my mammy, that it was a dolly pram, and if he had a lovely pram like mine, he said, he would not fill it with soil. But when I had made it clear to him how it was really a barrow, he agreed willingly.

I wanted a garden just like our neighbour's through the railings. Mammy often talked about it. Like a picture, she said it was. I was sure that all I needed was a few barrow loads of soil, tipped up on our back yard, and patted down flat, in a square. Surely very soon flowers would spring up, neat rows around the edges, filled in with pretty patterns of colours, so bold and bright. But I knew I might only see them in my head, but at least I would have a garden of my own.

The chip shop had a garden, but it had no fence or gate. We just walked straight on for the soil. While we were filling the barrow, my little friend put his toy on the ground beside him, and we were so busy, we did not hear his big brother creeping up to steal it. But we did hear the chip shop woman. Out she came from her back kitchen. Her voice grew louder and louder as she came up her garden to us, shouting, "Shoo! Shoo!"

I thought she was shouting at us and I was going to tell her all about my new garden, when I heard big brother say we were pinching her soil.

"Who cares? So what's a bit of soil?" she shouted. "They're not thieves like you. Shoo off! Shoo off!" Then in a quiet voice, she said to herself maybe, what my mam would have to say about it, she could not say.

We had just got the first load of soil patted down flat on my back yard. There was such a to-do. I tried telling Mammy how Santa knew I wanted a wheelbarrow. "'Appen he couldn't get one," I said. "That's why he sent me a dolly pram. He wouldn't mind I've filled it wi' soil."

Mammy did not say anything. The pram was taken away and cleaned out, then once again I was shown how to put Jenny to bed, with covers on her to keep her warm. But I would have none of it. Although at first Mammy was loving, she changed her tune, as Daddy might say. I was warned the pram would go to a little girl who would take good care of it. *Then let it go,* I thought, or did I say that?

As the pram was lifted up above my head, I watched the wheels whirring round and round as it went out of my sight forever. I had not wanted a dolly pram, so let the little girl take good care of it.

Out on the back yard, the soil had gone, our neighbour over the wall told me. Toys had always caused arguments, she had found, and as like as not, her kids would break each other's toys before dinner time. "We all want things we can't have," she said. "But things don't matter that much."

That made me think a lot, and feel a bit better.

THE DESERT ISLAND

On the traffic island at the end of our row of houses, there were concrete turrets and sand dugouts, made ready for the Germans coming. "Just in case they get that far," said my mammy. "But they'll 'ave to get past me first!"

But now the Germans would not be coming, and it had been decided that we kids might make better use of the island. Some of us kids had not been taken to the seaside. A beach was something new for us. Sand is not like soil. We did not know how to play with it. We tried digging it with sticks, but the holes we made quickly filled themselves in again. It was just too dry, so we all went home for a drink of water. The big kids carried mine back to the island for me. All our precious liquid was poured on the dry sand, but it just disappeared. I was escorted back home, and Mammy was surprised that I should need a second drink of water. She made me promise to drink it.

Now promises must not be broken, I knew that, but the kids said, "Don't worry. We can still use it after you've drunk it." To show me how this would work, a public demonstration was given by one of the lads. But the gentlemen who were gathered outside the barber's shop did not like to see that. So they brought buckets of water over for us. One said, "Give us your stick."

Taking my stick, he stirred the sand. I could only see his white cuffs showing below his dark sleeves, so I knew he was dressed up, ready for the barber's. He should not have been digging. From then, all our water supply was bucketed over from the barber's shop when needed, even without us having to ask for it. The patrons were pleased to see something good come out of it, and they agreed with one another that the island was a safe place for the kids to play, and no mischief, neither.

Many happy hours were passed on our desert island.

Joan Vardy

UNDER THE STAIRS

But Daddy could remember the night that Sheffield was bombed. He said, "That night when Sheffield were bombed, everybody thought that that were it." He often retold the story how our tanks had rolled past our front door all night long. "They kept coming and coming, too big for the road." They had driven straight over the island, knocking down those turrets, throwing the sand in the air. He said, "By morning, it looked like a beach outside."

Nobody had slept, but the men shovelled up the sand and put it back on the island, so that the factory buses could get through. Then they all went to work just the same, having had no sleep. And the women got to work with sweeping brushes. The sand had even come inside the houses. I told Daddy I knew about it, but he would not believe me. The sand had sounded all grit under Mammy's feet. She did not grumble when she had to sweep it up.

I *did* remember that night when Sheffield was bombed. Mammy took some of the things out of the pantry for me and our Spadger to play under there, because under the stairs was the safest place to be. There were some shelves on one side of the pantry, but they were way above my head. Underneath there was a big breadbin. I could feel the raised letters on the side. They said, 'bread'. Further in, where the ceiling came down to meet the floor, there was a beer crate for Mammy's baking tins, and a green bottle for rolling out the pastry.

I was having a rattling good game. Mammy shouted, "If Jerry knew he'd got you to contend with, he'd turn round and go back!" She sat on a cushion on the pantry step to watch my game, and she wanted Daddy to come and watch me with her, but Daddy was dancing about, wiping his face with a rag and shivering in his shirt sleeves. I was not shivering. I was wearing my coat.

Later some eiderdowns were laid on the pantry floor. Our Spadger was already curled up on a cushion on the breadbin, with the lid put on upside down to make a dint instead of a hump with the big handle. I wanted to use my chamber pot. It was kept under the kitchen table, hidden behind the long green blanket which came to the floor. Mammy supposed that I must have to go, but she thought it would be best if I sat on my chamber pot under the table, and she would tell me the best time to go. She told me, "There's a shovel under then there, and you know 'ow to use the sash thing. I've told you 'ow to get coal in, an't I?"

When I got back under the stairs, our Spadger was needing nursing, so I had a turn on the breadbin. The noise outside was non-stop, and we all had to shout to make ourselves heard. After a while, Mammy shouted, "She's ate the bread!" Now there was none for my daddy to take to work with him. It was so cuddly, so cosy and my tummy was podged. Besides the bread in the breadbin, I had been really surprised to find half a loaf of bread under the kitchen table.

Now that the concrete turrets had been knocked down by our tanks, they became anything our imaginations could think of. We could all play games together, games of let's pretend, where even I could take an equal part. Those stories that children love were brought to life for me, even before I found them in books. I followed footprints, dug for buried treasure; I walked the plank, rode to the beat of the drum. At last I had been accepted as one of the kids. It felt so strange when I got back home, standing in our kitchen. I used to think the island was more real, and so far away.

Joan Vardy

FUNERALS

On mornings when the big cemetery gates stood open wide, we knew we could look forward to a good funeral later. Mammy would remind me to come back and fetch her, if it was a big one. The kids would take turns to be sent up aloft to keep a lookout for the cars coming up the Lammas Road, with orders to call out, "Land ahoy!" or "There she blows!" at first sight of them, at which we would all brush ourselves down and go to make a quiet, tidy line standing on the kerbstones at the end of the island, staring down at our toes.

But one morning I had been sent to gather pretend sticks to make a fire and when the call came from the crow's nest, I was pretend tied up to a post, watching the Indians rubbing the sticks together to light a fire to cook me, and I would not leave that post until that pretend rope was untied. Our leader had to wrap his arms around me again and again, from top to toe to unwind that rope and set me free. I was praised for taking such a good part in the game.

If there were ten or even more funeral cars, they would bring the traffic to a standstill and I could get back across the road safely to fetch my mammy. She would hurriedly wipe her hands on her pinafore and slip it off over her head, pull on her coat, snatch a hankie from the sideboard drawer, then together we would go to watch with the other mammies. A hush would fall on the morning. No garage hollow hammering, no carters calling. All there was to be heard was the soft murmur of the engines, and Mammy's loud sniffs as she dabbed her cheeks with her hankie, being careful not to crease it too much. Then it could be popped back in the drawer again, without being washed.

Then there followed a time of respectful silence before the mammies stirred and the morning moved on again, at a steadier pace. Mammy would thank me and say how good it had been. She would see me safely over on to the island before joining the gossiping group by the barber's shop. She said, "You have to, or you don't learn nowt."

DADDY'S GARDEN

Sometimes on Sunday mornings, Daddy would take me up to his allotment garden. There, in the peace and quiet, I could relax. I could feel myself shrinking inside my coat. On three sides of the garden tall hedges grew, and the air was filled with birdsong. The garden was lower than street level, and iron railings ran along the fourth side. Through the gap under the railings I got a worm's eye view of the outside world passing by that I might never have known about otherwise. There were snuffling dog noses that barked at you, "Come to heel!" and small shoes shouted at for rubbing their hands along the railings. I could see the flashing spokes of pram wheels, which caught the morning sunlight as they passed by, smart shoes on their way to church, sounding as though they might be late. Walking sticks took long, leaping strides, and slow shuffling boots stopped and started along their journey.

Daddy said they would only let you have one allotment, and he did only have one allotment, but his was twelve hundred yards long, that was all. They said you needed a permit to build a greenhouse, but Daddy had managed quite well without one. The glass did arrive. The crates themselves were used to make the bottom boards, and the greenhouse went up, and it had not fallen down yet, without a permit, Daddy said.

In the greenhouse we grew tomatoes. Daddy said eight to a pound, because that was how ladies liked them, and they liked them with three sections on each tomato too, so we tried to grow some. We tried setting the seeds from one of those three sectioned tomatoes. It was one that Mammy had cut up on a salad for me that we saved. Daddy and I were so excited about it. The seeds were set, the plants grew, but it made no difference. Some tomatoes had three sections, but some grew with only two.

Apart from carrots, cucumbers were my favourite crop. We grew them trailing along the ground under a row of cloches. 'Clotches,' Daddy called them. I never went near them without him, and he was surprised at that, but when he opened the lights for fresh air, the metal clips made a grating sound on the glass. That was more than enough to remind me that glass can be dangerous. So we would go together to find the cucumbers. We put slates on the ground to keep them clean, and they stretched out long and straight.

In those days you needed both a male and a female flower to make a cucumber, and once we had five or more females, and just before it was too late, it was me who found the male flower for Daddy to fertilise them with.

Sometimes Mammy would take me and our Spadger up to the allotment while Daddy was at work, and that day I found the male flower, I could not wait to tell Daddy about it when he got home, and he could not wait to go straight up to the garden. Mammy used to pick the fresh fruit and vegetables, and do a bit for Daddy, and if there was a shower of rain while we were up there, she would pick me a big rhubarb stick umbrella. I loved to look up through the leaf and see the veins. It made the sky go green, and it tickled me to hear the raindrops pattering so loud on my head. Yet there I was; quite dry underneath.

On Sunday mornings, visitors often came into the garden and I could hear the gate latch, and I knew before Daddy that somebody had come in. I can just remember meeting a pair of brown boots on the path. But Daddy told me later that this was his dad, my granddad Young. He would be calling on his way for a jar. At one time, Granddad Young's garden had been one of the best. He could tell if somebody had just touched a peapod to find out if the peas were ready, never mind to pick one. He had won cups at shows, and his dad, my great-granddad William, had grown his own variety of pinks. Not one weed had been allowed to grow on their gardens. Granddad Young had a saying, "A weed gone to seed is a weed for seven years."

But these days, my daddy did not have time to do the weeding. He thought it was more important to get some food growing, so some weeds could not be helped.

Another visitor, who often came to see us, was a girl who was a bit older than me, who wore glasses because she had had an eye operation, and it made her glad, now that she could see better. She asked me if I would be having an operation when I was a bit older. I told her I did not want one if it meant wearing the glasses, "Even if I can't find the right strawberries," I lied.

I might meet another visitor to our garden behind the runner bean row. This visitor would call softly to me through the thick hedge, and I could not make up my mind whether this visitor was a person like Jesus, or a person like my mammy and daddy. Daddy thought he had sorted it out for me when he said that it was Mrs Wright. She was a good lady, and she lived in the big house next to the garden. But she only had one arm. I could not picture that in my mind. "How does she manage to walk?" I asked him.

"She walks very well," said Daddy.

I did not know how she managed to walk, because I really did think that Mrs Wright was just one right arm with a head on the top. I would stand by the runner beans and measure them against myself until they grew as tall as me, then as tall as I could reach, then they were out of my sight. As I did not see them stop growing, up and up they went, so thick, so dark, until they reached the sky.

Behind the runner bean row was where I could crouch down when I needed to. But I was wary for if Mrs Wright called softly to me, with her being only one arm with a head at the top. She would make shushing sounds, to guide me to the hole in the hedge behind the bean row. Her one arm would come through the gap and give me nice things to eat. Once, Daddy asked me if I had been eating chocolate. I said no, because I had never heard that word before. From the other side the hedge, Mrs Wright chuckled. "If you don't know, you can't tell him, can you?"

One day, Mrs Wright handed me lots of brown squares stuck together, and she urged, "Eat it up quick."

Too late, Daddy had seen it. I had to take it home, to share it with our Spadger. Then I know that somehow I had lied to him, and felt wrong about it. Mammy knew now why it was that I did not want to eat my Sunday dinners which she cooked for me. Daddy had told me that Mrs Wright was a good lady. Now he was saying that she should not have given me things to eat. I needed a few quiet moments by myself to sort this one out, and made up my mind that right did not mean right as in good, it meant right, as in clever. So it must mean that Mrs Wright Arm was a clever lady, to come through the hedge.

I thank you, Mrs Wright.

CHRYSANTHS

Daddy grew flowers, but he had mixed feelings about those, because they took up space, and you could not eat them, but ladies would always buy flowers, even if there was no food to put on the table, he knew. They bought them on Sunday mornings to take up to the cemetery, but they liked them wrapped up in paper for everybody to see them, and take note.

I did not go near the flowers, because ladies would not buy them if they were damaged or spoiled. My mammy loved all flowers, but chrysanthemums were her favourites. Daddy had grown some bronze ones for her, when they got married. They made Mammy's voice sound so happy, every time she looked at them. I was allowed to go near those. I could find them by their strong smell and I loved to feel the shapes of the leaves.

When the time was right, under Daddy's watchful eye, it was my job to disbud them, because my fingers were so small, I did not do so much damage as Daddy might do. But of the flowers themselves, I knew nothing of how the tight green button buds grew, bit by bit, into beautiful blooms. Just like the runner beans, they climbed way above my head, admired by everybody who came to see them.

One day I took hold of a support cane in each hand and pulled myself up. But still, all I could see was dark green. Daddy said that was because there was nothing to be seen yet. He would pick me up and show me when there was. I waited and waited.

At last the day came when I was lifted up to see over the whole garden. I can imagine now blooms of pale pink, soft yellows, pompoms of pure white and deep red, sprays of rose and mauve. All the shades of autumn, canary and gold to tawny and bronze. But on that misty day, my spirits were dampened. All I could see then was straw-yellow patches, smudged with brown and dirty white daub, as if somebody had taken a huge wooden spoon to stir up the whole allotment.

Daddy spoke sharply. He had picked me up to show me, and now I was just not interested. He put me down quickly, and I stared hard at the brown soil. I would not bother asking again. It had not been worth waiting for. I would give up trying to see what grown-ups could see. Besides, grown-ups never tried to see the things more lovely, like I tried to see. While they searched for bright redcurrants, I saw the golden dandelions shining in the sun. When they reached up for the runner beans, I gazed up at the bright white summer sky. They saw only red tomatoes. I saw the green spiders on the top. Grown-ups never bothered to see the things more lovely, like the shape of the chrysanthemum leaves with their rows of crocodile teeth, or the blue haze of the bonfire smoke, drifting over the garden, like I tried to see. And then they said that I was blind!

PRECIOUS STONES

The potato crop grew near the railings. Daddy would dig them up with the fork, and let me have the fun of finding them on top of the soil. He would tap them with the fork so that I could hear where they were. Then he would chuckle and stand by, finding pleasure in my joy. It was fun to feel the cold, damp, earthy spuds. Then the ground would be dug over and cleaned, and I could hear the chink if the garden fork hit a stone. It would be taken out and thrown away with the stalks and leaves. Daddy liked to see his ground made ready for the winter.

One morning, a lady came by. I saw her under the railings. Her flowers were trying to jump out of their basket. She set it down on the ground and took out two stones. She had to stoop down to pass them to me through the railings. I took one in each hand and thanked her so much. This would be really something to tell the kids about.

One of the stones was blue, but so big that I could hardly hold it in one hand. The other stone was smaller and brown, but more marvellous for me, because it was as warm as new bread. Stones should not be warm like that. It should have been as cold as the spuds. These stones were much better than the little boulders that the kids saved in their pockets, because they said you could see the sky through them. These big stones must be precious.

But I was helpless, stuck fast. I would need two hands to twist and turn one stone to find out about it, and two hands to put one stone safely down on the ground. My hands were just not big enough, so I called for Daddy's help. He threw down his fork and tried to run over his newly-dug ground to help me, with his arms out at the side to balance himself. I was going to bang the stones together to hear them crack. It had puzzled me how sometimes when I banged stones together once, they seemed to crack twice.

Daddy drew in his breath. He said, "Oh, no, don't! Oh don't, drop, don't!"

That day on the way home, Daddy carried the precious stones and I carried the flowers for Mammy. How proud I was, carrying those flowers, stalks up, heads down. That was the proper way, said Daddy. I told him about the flowers in the lady's basket, how I thought they were still alive because they were springing up and down. But Daddy said he had thought they looked half dead.

"No," he said. "Mammy's flowers are not dead."

That did not seem right to me, because Mammy's flowers just hung straight down, with their heads almost touching the coursey when I carried them.

At first Mammy said I could have a blue stone. Then she said that I must share it with our Spadger, and I could not keep it. I supposed it was like our money box, which we kept on the high shelf in the cupboard and not in our toy drawer. Then a string of strange things happened, one after another. First a pan of water was put to boil on the fire, and the big blue stone gently lowered into it. Mammy checked the clock to see what time it said. Then she cut off a slice of bread from the loaf and spread it with margarine, cut it up into fingers for me and our Spadger. Then I was helped up to the table to sit and wait. But Mammy did not know just how long I ought to wait. Next the stone was taken out of the boiling water and by magic my mammy cut it into two with a breadknife.

"Double yoked, that's lucky," she said.

I was shown how to dip a finger of bread into my stone. So boiling stones makes them go soft, I thought. Daddy thought that Mammy was enjoying it just as much as I was, and she was not eating it. Our Spadger would not eat her half of the stone, and she was allowed to leave. Now that was a first! Daddy ate it up for her. He wanted Mammy to have the small brown stone, but she did not put it in the pan. Instead she went rummaging through her baking tins in the pantry under the stairs, making a great din, coming out with her little loaf tin. It was just the right size, she said, to hold half a dozen.

I did not know what half a dozen was, but that was what she used to use it for. She just wanted to see that warm brown stone in the tin. She kept putting it in, taking it out again. Then she leaned with her back on the sideboard, twisting and turning the stone in her hand, like I had wanted to do. I knew because it clinked on her wedding rings. She wondered whether to make a cake with the stone. She said she really would love a cake. I thought Mammy could just put the stone in the boiling water, and it would come out like a cake.

The brown stone stayed in the loaf tin on the sideboard for a whole week, before it was made into a Yorkshire pudding, because it seems you really need two stones to make one good cake. But we could all share a Yorkshire pudding.

FIZZY POP

While the Sunday dinner was cooking, Spadger and I might be sent to a house up the road to buy what Mammy called 'minerals' and we called 'pop'. Pop came in half-pint bottles and we all had one each. I loved to hear the bottles rattling in the bag. It was my job to carry the empties there and Spadger's job to carry the money, and carry the full bottles back home again.

Dandelion and Burdock was Daddy's favourite. It looked black in the bottle, but the top changed to light brown when it was poured into his glass. Lemonade was Mammy's choice. It just looked like water, but when she poured it into her glass, it looked like snow on the top. Our Spadger just had orange, and you could not even see through that, like I could see through my yellow pop. That was if I held it up to the light of the window. Then I could see my fingers, like thick black lines round the other side of the bottle. The colour was so bright that if I gazed too long, it made my eyes sting. Then when I looked away, I could see purple. I supposed that was something to do with my bad eyes.

I would hold the open bottle to my ear to hear the bubbles popping inside, sounding like a sizzling frying pan. Spadger and I drank our pop straight out of our bottles, but once I put the whole of the neck of the bottle inside my mouth instead of just putting my top lip inside. I lifted the bottle for a good guzzle, but when I had had enough, I could not take the bottle out of my mouth again, so I just kept on swallowing. My ears ached. I could hear the fizzy pop bubbling out of them. My eyes streamed tears, tears of yellow pop, I thought. So I let out one of my 'help!' screams, which solved the problem.

After that happening, I chose to go without my minerals for three weeks.

A CLEAN SPOON FOR MY PUDDING

My place at the table was facing the window, sitting near Mammy. I asked her if I could sit at the back of the table, facing the fireplace. There it would be better for me, with the window at my side, I knew. But Mammy thought I would get the best light facing the light of the window, near to her, where she could give me a hand if I needed it. I needed a cushion on my chair to be high enough to reach the table comfortably. I delighted in swinging my legs vigorously, till I could slide off the chair with the cushion, and have to climb back on again. It was my very own pink cushion, and our Spadger did not have one. So it was a rare time, when it was better to be littlest.

On Sundays we had rice or macaroni for pudding. All milk puddings were white, the same colour as my plate. I did not like it if I could not see it, so sometimes Daddy might let me share some of his brown skin from off the top with him. I liked it then, just because I could see the skin.

One Sunday dinner, I dropped my pudding spoon. So I slid down off my cushion and under the table to find it. Mammy came to join in the hunt with me, or so I thought. But she had taken this opportunity to test my eyesight. She said to Daddy, "There, I told you so. She can't see it on the left."

Maybe Mammy moved the spoon then, because I caught sight of it, not the spoon itself, just the shine in the bowl of the spoon when it moved. Realising that I was being tested, I tried to act as though I had not even seen that much. Instead, I said, "That spoon will be dirty. I'll go and fetch a clean one."

The spoons were kept in the knife and fork box on the kitchen table. I stood there for a while with clenched fists, gritting my teeth, gulping down the hurt and anger. By now I had learned to use my brains, not just to find things by their shines and shadows. Nobody liked me as I was. The kids were always playing tricks on me because I could not see. Even grown-ups wanted me to be better.

Mammy sometimes asked me if I could see the firelight. If I said no, it upset her, so that was why I said yes, sometimes. But other times I would say yes to please her, even if I had not seen the fire. Then she would say that my eyes were getting better. That pleased her, and it could have seemed that way for Mammy and everybody else, because I was learning to manage better now. I was using my other senses, even without realising. I was listening, not just to people talking and the wireless set; I heard every single sound that was made and I used it to tell me where I was, to tell me what people were doing, to tell me the time of day or night. These were small sounds that other people do not notice. I did not need to know what made each sound.

And I learned to feel – not just with my fingers – with my whole hands. My feet felt for the floor, my cheeks felt things that were soft. I used my tongue to both feel and taste. If my fingers failed to tell a button from a farthing, then my tongue could taste the difference. I had found my own way of managing without my eyes, and making the best use of the little sight I had.

All my swallowing over with, I gathered up my strength, grabbed a spoon. Not one sound came from the house. I lined myself up by the kitchen door. From there I knew I could quick march past the pantry and right up to the table, without bumping into anything. I sprang up onto my cushion, and gulped down my cold rice pudding, not hungry, but hurting hard.

COG LEE BROIL

I knew the reason why my mammy did not take me down to the welfare clinic, like other mammies did. It was not that it was too far to walk there, or she could not be bothered to take me. My mammy was frightened that they would take me off her, and put me into t'institution. So it was our neighbour who brought the bottle of cog lee broil for me, when she went to buy concentrated orange juice for her baby.

Now seeing how we'd got this bottle of what I knew as cog lee broil, my mammy thought that I might like to give it a try, just to see if I might like it.

"You never know," she said.

So there we were on our hearth, me standing in front of Mammy, and her sitting in a chair, explaining with great eagerness, all about this oil, about the fishermen who went out to sea in their boats of a night time, how they caught these fishes in their nets for me. And she reminded me, "Now, you like the shipping forecast, don't you, now?"

That was true. The shipping forecast was my favourite programme on the wireless set, and I loved the sunshine too. It turned my black and white world into colour sometimes, besides warming me through.

Now this oil, Mammy was sure would make my body grow strong, and my bones grow straight. It was just for young people like me, the under-fives, although there were some kiddies who did not like it. If I was one of those, I could have a sweet to eat after it. Mammy showed me a red boiled sweet, wrapped up in cellophane paper. I felt the little flat bottle. I held it up to the window light. I could see through it. It was yellow, just like the bottle of fizzy pop I chose for my Sunday dinner. So now, knowing all about it, I opened my mouth wide for a teaspoonful of sunshine.

It was not warm like sunshine. In fact it was very cold. It did not fizz on my tongue like Sunday pop. It just lay there, thick and slimy. Something stopped me from swallowing it. Something about it would just not go down, although I did try. I just stood there, waiting for something to happen. So did my mammy. Her jam pot bottom glasses gazed steadily back at me, the spoon and bottle still held high in her concentrated pause, while more and more of this oil kept coming from nowhere, filling my mouth. There must be dog bones growing inside my mouth, I thought. I was frightened. There was only one thing I could do; open my mouth with a loud cry.

"Never mind!" shouted Mammy, loud enough to be heard above the screaming. "I shan't make you have any more if it's that bad."

DOWN THE STREET, PEACOCKS

I heard my mammy telling somebody, "There's some shops, as I daren't tek her into." Peacocks was one of those shops. Mammy did not like going in there herself. I think that just inside the door there may have been three or four wide wooden steps to go down, as everybody's footsteps sounded hollow there and went out of time, and I knew my mammy found steps tricky. It was her heels. They were so high.

It was not a busy shop. The wooden floor creaked and the girls followed you with their eyes as you went round, she said. Once, while I stood on the threshold, listening to different footsteps coming and going, I heard some coming out which I knew were not my mammy's, and a grey skirt came close to me, with a whiff of scent, jangling her bangles or keys. She had come out, she said, "To keep you amused, while your mother selects her purchases."

I informed her, "Me mammy's only come for light grey darning wool, to darn me daddy's sock wi', cos it's on'y place as she can gerrany."

The jingling fell silent. I did not hear the grey skirt glide away, but I did hear a baby pram being rocked. The baby started crying. Its mammy came running out. Then nobody sounded very pleased. I heard more footsteps and guessed rightly that this time it was my mammy coming out. I told her that the grey skirt was wearing a silk slip.

"Now 'ow did you know that?" she said. I had worked it out. A grey skirt would be woollen, so it could not make a brushing sound. Mammy thought that I was learning fast, and there were times when I got it right, but many more when I got it wrong.

"Why do high heels click?" I asked her. Mammy carried on about wooden shop flooring. I could not believe that to be true. Wooden floors creaked, so it must be the high heels themselves that made that clicking sound.

While I waited for Mammy outside Peacocks, I was even forbidden to rub my fingers down the windows, but that lovely squeaking sound and the tingling in my fingertips was far too good to let go by. But it was the fingermarks that bothered Mammy, because when we had gone, the grey skirt would come out to give the windows a rubbing over.

One day, I thought; if I can see, my fingermarks will show up as much as that squeaking sound and the tingling feels. So I gave the windows a good rubbing down. I was expecting the fingermarks to look like mud-brown or soot-black smudges, but I could not see anything, even with my nose pressed hard on the glass. So I thought, if that's what they are saying about fingerprints is true, then it is true what they are saying. I'm blind.

It brings a good warm feeling, just to stand where you know where you are, and to know just where you stand.

Joan Vardy

BOOTS THE CHEMIST

Mammy wanted to know how was it that I could tell her when we were outside Boots' door. I could not tell her then how I knew. I may have picked up clues without knowing. Maybe the breeze from the alleyway opposite, here the street narrowed, changing all the sounds. On the street I could see some shadows of the shop roofs. It just felt right. I knew when we were at Boots.

Inside the shop was cold and dark, lit only by a skylight in the roof. So I would go and stand in the patch of light it made on the floor, where I might be safe. All I could make out in the gloomy surroundings was the white sheets of the ghosts, gliding to and fro halfway up the walls; a deadly hush, broken only by a swish of their starched cotton, and turning of keys in locks. I would shiver in the chill. The smell tickled my nose and made me want to sneeze, but I hardly dare break the silence.

From Boots Mammy bought her starch and washing soda. Both came in strong brown paper bags, but it was a hard job for Mammy to find another use for the paper bags when the starch had gone.

When we came out into the bright busy street once more, I was glad to be among the mingled noises all around me, and I could breathe and chatter once again.

A Green Hill Far Away

WOOLWORTH'S

There was one shop which we both loved to visit. Once inside, Mammy and I would go our separate ways, arranging to meet up again somewhere, although I was never quite sure where that somewhere might be. We might meet up again quite by chance, each of us with a story to tell. Mammy told me of a time when once you could buy a saucepan for sixpence at one counter, then take it to the other side of the shop, where on another counter, for † thrupunce, you could find yourself a lid which fitted it the best, if you were quick, before they had all been picked over, that was.

From here we bought Daddy's seven o'clock razor blades. I knew there was a picture on the packet. It was of my old friend, Big Ben. In the same way that he could come from London and I could hear him on our wireless set at home, I could go to London and stand on the street, listening to him chiming, looking up at the bright blue sky above him, not just stand in Woolworth's with a packet held on the end of my nose.

For me there were no goods set out for sale to see. The counters were so high that I could not stretch up to get a grip on the edge and walk up the counter fronts to try and see. I thought the counters were fences, and I imagined all the goods for sale laid out on the floor, over the other side. I would drum on the counter fronts with my fists, listening to the rumbling sounds, like thunder rolling away.

If sunshine streamed down through the high windows, I could watch the reflected light shimmering in the polished panels as I pummelled them, and on warm days, they smelled lovely, of lavender polish. But on dull days, Woolworth's was a weird and wonderful place. The shop was full of shadows. There were green pools of light cast down to the floor by the gaslights. I would dare myself to dart from one bright pool to the next, keeping close up to the counter fronts to guide me through the blackness. I thought that the floor rose and fell, like waves with the sea going out. I loved to wander freely through this wooden-walled maze. And when I could smell carbolic, that was the place to turn about and walk out of my dream world on the cold side of the shop, where I might find my mammy, with all the other mammies. There she might be pondering over the cosmetics, still in her own dream world.

† thrupunce – three pence (single coin) thre'p'ny bit

TREASURED TIMES

After shopping, Mammy might choose a quieter but longer way to go home, where her shopping bag did not feel so heavy and I could tell she was not tired any more. Her voice and her step were light. Maybe in the shade of trees, where the leaves hid the sky, but the sun shone through, sparkling like water on the ground, which moved when I tried to tread on it. Maybe where autumn leaves fell on my face or flew off the road sweeper's barrow when he turned his back to gather up more of them. Maybe where bare branches drew pictures on the pathway, tracing for me the shape of trees I never would have seen if they had not been put at my feet for me to bend and see them. Mammy and I would laugh, just because we were both happy.

Then there were the swings on the Lammas. They belonged to the church school next door, but only their children could use them. Any of us kids seen having a go would soon be sent off. Mammy could not see properly over the crocodile tooth wall, but she could peep through the gate to see the swings. More often than not they were hanging up and padlocked, but if they were dangling loose, we might go through the grumbly gate and over the grass. Such a treat to walk over the grass and make sweeping sounds with my feet. Mammy would squeeze my hand and giggle, thinking back how she used to like a go on the swings. When we reached them, she would pop down her shopping bag and lift me on the seat. She would say, "I should think they wouldn't mind if it were you, I 'ope," and give me a push.

Treasured times, when I was just Mammy's, and she was just mine. Golden moments, to treasure.

FRIDAY PENNY

Those big old pennies were special to Mammy. Each time she got back from shopping, she would look through her purse to see if she had been given a penny bun in her change. If she found one, and she could see Vicky's bun, that had not been completely worn smooth, she would put more value on that one than twelve for one shilling. That copper would be carefully saved with some others, but they could turn from brown to green if you did not look after them properly, Mammy said.

On Fridays, after our little dinner, us kids were each given one penny to spend at the shop in the row. Mammy had been given a Friday penny when she was a child, but she said she could buy a lot more with it in those days.

The little shop would be packed tight with kids. Each in turn would place their one precious penny on the rubber money mat, and say, as well as they could, "One pennyworth of kayli, if you please."

Kayli was our name for sherbet and one penny would buy enough of the white fizzy powder in a cone-shaped paper bag to dip in a finger, suck, and belch the whole long afternoon through. I always stood at the back of the crush, clutching my big brown penny, happy to hold it just for a little longer, feeling it growing warm in my hand. If you squeezed hard enough, your penny would leave its mark on your hand, the kids said. And it was me who taught them that for a while after you got out of the little shop, you could sniff your hand to smell the penny. It was almost as though you had not left it behind you.

When there were no kids left in the shop but me, the shopkeeper would say to me, "Your turn now."

The good thing about being served last meant that I still had kayli to suck after the other kids had finished theirs.

One Friday, when I thought I was the last kid in the shop, the keeper did not speak, so thinking that this was yet another step on my way to growing up, I stepped forward, unsure of myself. I saw the black money mat on the counter, but I could not see my own hand, so I breathed a sigh of relief as I felt the rubber ridges under my fingers. Then the shopkeeper spoke before I could. "Jar's empty," she said.

I thought she might be just saying that, because I had done

something wrong, so I went through a check list in my head. I had not touched the vegetables at the back of the shop. I had not rattled the pop bottles in their crate. I had managed to place my penny on the rubber mat, and not on the scrubbed wooden counter. And I had washed my hands before going into the shop. So I could not have rubbed my grubby little hands everywhere. And I had not had time to ask politely. Any one of this list might have meant me leaving the shop empty-handed.

The shopkeeper leaned forward, arms on the countertop, dropping her head in the crook of her elbow. She was sobbing. "They i'n't any. I can't 'elp it, it's not my fault. There weren't enough for the regular 'un. I gi'd em a bit. And I think 'is mam not mind, if I gi'e her 'apenny back later."

I was staring at the kayli jar. It looked just the same as it always did, just two shiny lines reflecting the glass from the door. The window was always kept blacked out. I had forgotten all about the kayli. I was wondering how a glass jar that I could see right through to the other side, could shine silver, and how it could look the same to me, whether it was full or empty.

The shopkeeper stood up straight, blowing her nose hard. "No use, no use looking," she sniffed. I turned to go. "Take your penny," she called after me.

On my way home, I threw down my penny. The shopkeeper said it were no use.

Joan Vardy

NIGHT SOIL

Mammy did not want me to go without kayli again, so the following Friday I was sent to the shop in the morning, all on my own. On the way I heard a motor coming up the road, and it stopped, but the engine was left running, so I knew where it was. When I got near, a mester was coming out of an entry, and another mester shouted at me,

"Go away from this. This is germs."

I thought, you don't sound like you live round here. He sounded more like the man who sat behind the desk at the coal office. Daddy would have called him a gentleman. The gentleman carried on.

"This is night soil."

I thought, night soil, in the daytime? That's funny.

"This will give you fever," he went on. "You should put your handkerchief over your mouth."

The other mester said, "Kids round 'ere don't 'ave 'ankichieves."

"You have not got a handkerchief?" questioned the gentleman.

I had never heard the word 'handkerchief', so I thought I had better say "no". That way I would get the answer right.

"Then you cannot come here on Fridays," he said.

I told him, "Friday's the only day I get a penny."

"Then tell your mother to give you a Saturday penny instead," he said.

That would not do, I thought. I would never get any kayli that way. I could not tell what all the fuss was about. It smelt all right to me. That was until he sprayed the entry, and his motor with DDT. I knew what he was doing, because Mammy did it sometimes on Friday mornings. As she pumped, I could hear the liquid sounding hollow as she sprayed the window ledge, just above the net curtain. Mammy knew I would not touch it if I knew where it was.

Then the gentleman changed again. He had taken off his dark jacket. His shirt was a lovely pale blue. I thought, that must be his best one. Then he hung his jacket on his motor, and at once it blew over the side into the night soil. The gentleman cried out. He had changed again this time, inside hisself. Now he sounded like he had a horrible tummyache. He was saying that it was his only jacket, and he did not know when he might get a new one.

Back at home, I had a lot to tell Mammy, while I dipped and sucked and belched, and she got to grips with her fireplace. I learned that a handkerchief was a proper name for a hankie, like the one Mammy kept in the sideboard drawer ready for dabbing her eyes when we went to watch the funerals. And then it was put back in the drawer again when we got back in the house.

I learnt about the pan lavs. When my daddy was young, he used to take night soil up to Granddad's allotment and it never stopped folk from buying stuff off of Granddad. We were lucky, Mammy said, not to have a pan lav. That was one reason why we lived at this house.

Then I told Mammy the story about the gentleman's jacket, and she changed. Not friendly any more, she said it were a good old joke, but she did not believe me. That did not seem fair. I had never before thought that anybody would ever tell something that was not true. That was an unsettling new idea in my life.

Joan Vardy

RUNNING ERRANDS

Sometimes I would be sent on an errand to the little shop in the row. I could only guess when I reached the shop, by the metal advertising board under the window. All the houses in the row were red brick. This board was orange, which looked almost the same for me. I was frightened about what might happen if I walked in the wrong door and found myself in somebody's house. So to make quite sure that I had found the shop, I would kick or bang on the metal board, making a heavenly sound like deep-down dinner gongs or crashing cymbals. Then the shopkeeper would appear, just her top half, leaning out of her doorway, reciting above the thunderous sound, for all to hear her. Her party piece always began with,

"What in creation...?" and ending with, "You'll awaken the dead," accompanied by the dying reverberations of the metal plate.

These outbursts could not upset me because I would be so full of joy. My tummy would wobble just like the board, and I would be so pleased with myself that I had found the shop. Then the shopkeeper found out why I always banged her board. She came right outside her shop and tried to show me how her window was not the same as all the other windows in the row, but all the windows were higher than me, and I told her how I could not see any of them. Then we both agreed that we would have to be friends and wait a little while until I grew.

One day I dared myself to walk straight in through the shop door. By way of reward, I was given a bucket of soapsuds and a cloth to give the board a wipe over. The suds were nice and warm, white as snow. One customer said what a waste it was. When the shopkeeper came out to see how I was getting on, she said she could not hear me from inside the shop. I was not rubbing hard enough. Then she gave me a real treat, by telling me of all the things in her shop window. It was just like listening to the shipping forecast, but not far away places. This was poetry live, right here on our road where I lived.

Then somehow I was made to understand that it was never the shopkeeper who minded all the din I made, but her neighbour. So it would not matter one bit if I happened to make a noise. Then I put everything I had got into it, and I gave that advertising plate the very best I had, and I made a jolly good job of it.

BOTHERSOME BUSES

I wondered and worried about all the different coloured buses. There were two red buses which went past the front, but they seemed the same to me. But I knew a green bus from a blue bus. Somehow I could tell everybody what colour bus was coming, even before they could tell me. But if I did not know the colour, how could I tell them what colour the bus was? It took me a long time to learn that the buses were run by different companies, so they were made by different companies, with different engines.

But it was bothersome to me, and I asked everybody how I could tell the colours but could not see the colours. Nobody knew. Daddy told me there were two red double-decker buses that went past the front of the house on their route. It seemed to me like there was just one bus, so I asked him, how did he know which was which? He knew because one red bus had a cream stripe on the side. That was how he knew.

Then I wanted to know why they were called double-deckers. He told me that double-deckers had stairs inside them. I tried to picture our stairs inside the bus, but they would not fit. So perhaps Daddy was joking, I thought. I knew I had got about as far as I could with Daddy, when he started telling jokes and stopped answering questions.

Then the two bus companies joined up into one. Folk were not very pleased about it, I was told. The buses had both been painted red and now nobody knew where they were with them, or where they were going with them.

I showered Mammy with questions about green buses until I thought I knew about all the wonders of the world around me. How did Mammy tell which bus was which, of all the green buses which went up the road at the back of the houses? Mammy thought that there was only one bus. It was called the 101 bus. I thought it was called the 101 because it went past after one o'clock. I knew that when the bus had gone to take the workers to the factory for the afternoon shift, I could go out and play quite safely.

Mammy said, "The 101 *is* the green bus. Yes, that's the same colour as the blanket on the back kitchen table. That's there to hide the things under it. Yes, your chamber pot and the shovel. Yes, they do have shovels on the buses in the wintertime. The conductor has to get off and clear the snow away so the bus can get through. Some folks call the bus the tramway because it runs along the tramlines. No, they've gone now. They've gone to the war. They cut them up into bits. No, big bits. I know because I watched them do it at t'time. I didn't think that two men could pick up one bit and put it on t'lorry, but they did. After that I used to get my bike wheel fast in them there ruts, and it were frightening. They've filled 'em in now. Any road, that's why t'bus is so noisy. It rattles. It's ruined. Some folks call it t'factory bus because it takes workers up to t'factory. That's why it goes so fast, yes, and fast on again, so as they can get their teas on t'table. No, you'll have to wait till your daddy comes 'ome for your tea. Because it's not cooked yet!"

It was getting dark. I went out on the back to wait for Daddy coming home from work. I could see the lights on the bus as it went past. Mammy had said it went every two minutes at shift turnover time. But it still seemed to me like there were a lot of buses. But Mammy had been quite plain about that. The green bus was the 101 bus. Some folks called it the tramway bus, some folks called it the factory bus. But there was only one bus, so it must be a very, very, fast bus.

The little blue school bus went along the front of the houses after little dinner. It was to take the kids back to school. We would all go out to wait for it, for what seemed like quite a while. But at the first sign of the little blue bus, the kids would raise a cheer. They knew that if it could, it would come for them, and bring them home again. The fare was just one penny, but if you had not got a penny, a ha'penny would do. But if you had not got a ha'penny, and your dad was at the war, the school bus would take you anyway. The driver made long, loud speeches about that, saying, "It wain't be my fault if thee dad's come 'ome, see what a state t'country's in and they kids not eddicated."

I yearned to go on the school bus. Mammy guessed as much one Wednesday when I asked her for my Friday penny. So she asked the other mams to help her keep an eye on me. Our neighbour said she had more than enough to do keeping her eye on her own kids. She seemed to be telling me, not my mammy. The kids urged me, "Say your dad's at the war."

I knew that would be no use trying, but I could dream. There was no need for me to ask questions about the little blue bus. I knew that it was just like the Toytown bus in the picture on our Spadger's jigsaw puzzle. Mammy and I made and remade the jigsaw puzzle together. She would always tell me about each piece as it was put into place. There was a little white duck in the bottom left hand corner. She was wearing a scarf and carrying her basket, which had one piece missing from it. This scene came alive for me as I heard the children climbing aboard the school bus.

I pictured them with their shoes clattering, them laughing and shouting as they scrambled for seats. As the little blue bus dawdled away, I could see the kids in my mind, as on the Toytown bus, piled one upon another, hanging halfway out of the open windows, the boys wearing their brightly coloured school caps, the girls waving their white hankies, and I followed in my mind as the little blue bus purred airborne into the distance. I could see it come down to the road every now and then, making that 'chug chug' sound, with fluffy white cotton wool balls floating up from behind, just as Mammy had told me on the Toytown bus jigsaw puzzle picture. And after, just for a few seconds, a silence would fall on the road.

Then bit by bit, it would clear away. The road would fill up again with the sounds of the unhurried afternoon, making for me a true life picture, each detail being pinpointed out. Down a side street, a child wailing, its mam stating loudly: "Teacher wain't a' you wi'out shoes."

Somewhere I felt I had a friend who I may never meet. Somewhere in this picture of the real world, which I only had to hear, but need not ever see, this unlovely place. But beside me, a kind voice might say, "Come and play wi' our babby."

Everybody had got too tired of my questions about red,

green and blue buses, so Mammy and I sat down together and she talked while I listened. She set out my problem for me.

"You should know the two red buses, because you do know the green one, and you do know the blue one. Now, we don't know how you know when the buses are coming, what colour they are, so we can't help you. You must help yourself. You've already got the answer, so what you have to do now, is find it."

I was just given one clue; it was nothing to do with the colours. It felt really good inside, standing at the end of the row of houses, waiting for buses to come, just standing there, asking myself, how do I know if a bus is coming? How do I know which way it will turn at the island? It felt better now that I was doing something about the bothersome buses. They seemed to be a bother.

After that, every time I knew a bus was on its way, I would stop whatever it was I was doing, and ask myself about it. But I did not know any more questions to ask, so I did not come up with any answers.

DANDELIONS

Mammy had an idea to get the kids to play with me. She invited them all round to play on our back yard. She put out pegged rugs for us to sit on while we played. There were more than eight of us to join in with the hand games. 'One potato, two potato, three potato, four. Five potato, six potato, seven potato, more. O-U-T, you're out.'

And another game, 'Eeny meeny miny mo, sit the nigger

on the † po, when he's done, wipe his bum, eeny meeny miny mo.'

I could chant the rhymes with the other kids, so that was all right, till it was my turn to be on. Then I could not see the circle of fists held out for me to tap. So they said there was no room for me to sit on the rugs with them. I sat on the yard. I was used to not taking part. And it was not just because of my bad eyes. I was also one of the younger ones in the group. But this day I felt an outcast. I was with the kids, but not one of the kids. This day I felt downcast. I thought the war was to blame for everything. I was in the war with everybody else. It was quite normal for us kids to be hungry or cold, quite normal to be wearing grubby and wet from the inside clothes. This day I hit rock bottom.

Mammy let me take my dolly Jenny out to play with me for the first time. Then the kids taunted me and laughed at Jenny, because she had no clothes to put on. The back yard was numbing cold, so I sat on Jenny to keep myself warm. Being made of celluloid, she made loud cracking sounds. Then Mammy got mad.

This was the first time in my life that I felt utter loss of hope. While I had been fighting the world and the war, waging my own war against the world, it did not hurt me like it hurt me now. Now that I had left off fighting for one moment to take stock of what I was up against, it was as though I carried the whole weight of the world on my back. Its giant feet climbed onto my shoulders to pin me down and grind me through the cracks in the back yard.

I wandered off, and the little one followed me. We went up the roads at the backs of the houses, picking dandelions on what I thought was waste land. I saw the dandelions. They were bright yellow dots. They shone out for me against their stony grey background as stars shine in the sky, but not for me. I had never seen that star up in the blue, that Mammy sang of with me, but I could reach down for the dandelions. I did not know that there was a row of little cottages that stood back from the road just there till I heard a door slam.

A woman's voice came booming towards us shouting to us as she came up her yard.

"Be off! Be off, you'll † tiddle the bed!"

I studied her voice. The sound wrapped itself around and around me again. As the woman got nearer and nearer, the sound got more frayed. It stuck on me. Just then a thought sprang to my mind. I thought to myself. I can make a sound. I can stop a sound. I can reach out for sound, and bring them back to me, like on elastic. My elastic stretched me up until my feet almost left the ground. Filled with new-found faith in myself, I told the woman, I did not believe her tale of picking dandelions would make us both tiddle the bed.

She was lost for words. She went away. My little friend thought I was very brave. And he believed me. So we went on picking dandelions together.

He said, "I've found you a garden. I thought you'd like it."

† po – potty, chamberpot
† tiddle – urine, urinate

CLEANING UPSTAIRS DAY

At our house, Monday was the day for changing the beds and cleaning the bedrooms. There was lots of things for feeling, and lots of space for running about in upstairs. Best of all, Mammy would open the windows in both the bedrooms to let the fresh air blow straight through. Sometimes it was cold and then we wore our coats. Sometimes it would be really windy.

Mammy liked to do her work. We both liked the pillowcases with their satin stitched embroidery. There was a bolster on each bed, a long pillow that reached from one side of the bed to the other. Bolster cases were embroidered on both ends. Mammy would take a few moments to wonder at the needlework, the patience needed, and remember her kind friend. Feathered eiderdowns were soft on the underside, shiny on the top side. The one in the back bedroom was green, and the one in the front bedroom was pink.

Dirty washing lived at the bottom of the garret steps in a light green canvas bag with long handles. The brushes were kept there for cleaning the bedrooms. The one for sweeping the lino was very soft to stroke. But the hand brush for the rugs was prickly. Mammy said it had to be hard enough to shift the fluff that stuck to them. There were two half-moon rugs. Mammy said they looked good at the bottom of the beds. The one in the back bedroom was golden fur, with a leather backing to stop it from slipping on the green lino. It was a wedding present from one of Daddy's friends. Mammy had made the rug for the front bedroom. She had bought some new wool every week to work another flower or some trellis for it. In the back bedroom there was a tall set of drawers with Daddy's tool chest on top. In the recess there was a cupboard for keeping shoes in. Dirty shoes were always brushed on Mondays. Others were just dusted over. Some shoes had springy shoe trees pushed inside them to keep them in shape.

The front bedroom had two wardrobes and a dressing table. The big wardrobe was for clothes. The little one was for sheets, my green crocheted frock, liquorice allsorts. It had a high shelf for Daddy's trilby and bowler hats. Mammy would let me try them on and pretend to look at myself in the dressing table mirror. There were two mirrors at the side that could swing. Mammy said that she could see herself twelve times at once in those. She would chuckle and say, "I don't know what your daddy would say if he could see you." Then she would give the hats a brushing and put them back up on the shelf. On the dressing table, there was a tortoiseshell ring tree and a small bowl to be dusted. Under the window was a tea chest for keeping spare blankets in.

Mammy had some good stories to tell about tea. On the top of the tea chest in the sunshine, Mammy kept two green bowls full of shamrocks. She loved those shamrocks, and in the recess was a wickerwork chair. But Mammy was not so fond of that. It gathered a lot of dust.

Both bedrooms had a little metal fireplace with fancy patterns for feeling, but I did not want to feel the walls. I had an idea that walls hung from the edge of the ceilings like curtains hang down and if I touched them, they would swing. Mammy said, "God only knows why," then she blamed herself for the fingermarks she had to put up with after that day I had told her about the walls. She understood how I needed to touch the walls as I ran about from room to room.

To get from room to room we had to go down a step and up a step again at the top of the stairs, so we had a safety gate to keep me from falling down. One day I leaned over the gate by standing in the back bedroom, and reaching over. Mammy cried out and grabbed me from behind. She said she would chop the gate up for firewood herself, so that it could be never used again. She thought that if I was going to fall downstairs, she reckoned it would be better for me just to fall down them, than over the top of the gate.

The sash windows could be cleaned inside and out by lifting

them up and down. They made lovely squeaking rumbling noises. I could hear the carts going past on the road below and listen hard to try and make pictures of what I could not see.

And then there was the fun of getting out all that dirty washing and sorting it into different heaps. I could help do that job. It was great fun. And we would take one load back downstairs with us, for putting to soak in the ponch tub overnight, ready for washday in the morning.

But before we went downstairs, Mammy always got out a book to read to me. My favourite book was an alphabet book. Each page had a large letter on it and a picture that Mammy helped me draw with my finger to trace the shapes. Each picture had a rhyme to go with it, and that was how I learnt about the fishermen who fish at night. There was a doctor who came when you were ill, and a goat who tugged at trousers hanging on the washing line, and a nurse who gave you medicine.

That was a lovely time with Mammy.

THERE'S FEAR, AND THERE'S FEAR

Real fear is when I heard them say I was not old enough to know, yet I was old enough to be standing up. One time I was in the corner by the front door. I thought the fear was coming to knock me down, so I reached out my hands to find some furniture to steady myself with. But there was nothing within my reach, so I clenched hands full of air in my fists. I did not need to know all the words. The tone of the voices told it all for me. I did know what it was. I could see, flashing in the sunlight. I saw it in use every day. It was the blade of the breadknife shining in the sun.

The fear was heavy and hard inside me. As my eyes clouded over, I thought, yes, it is right what I have heard them saying about me. I have got bad eyes. But they did not know it all. It was not just my bad eyes. I never heard them say I had got bad legs, but at times like this, when I was frightened, my knees shook. But still my eyes were clever, I thought.

They made me feel inside myself what I could not see, but they could see: a rolling mass, like smoke. I listened, I waited, too stiff, too terrified to turn away my mind, even for one moment to pray. That is real fear.

Another kind of fear came when our Spadger was playing with the fire. If Mammy had to go out she would say to me, "Tell me if she plays with the fire." It was fear that told me whose side to be on. I could smell the hot paper as it got nearer the flame, and the flame got nearer to our Spadger's fingers.

There are childhood fears, when we think we know things and we do not ask any questions to get any answers. Or if we do ask, the answers we get can add to our fears, until we grow out of them.

LION

Spadger and I were moved into the front bedroom and now Mammy and Daddy were sleeping in the back bedroom in the double bed that Granddad had brought. In the back bedroom our Spadger had been frightened of a little man she said she could see climbing up the drainpipe outside the window. I told her that was very silly, but I kept quiet about the fierce lion who lay under the bed in the front bedroom.

When I was alone with Mammy one day, I told her about Lion. She said, "Try not to think about him. He wants you to take notice of him. If you don't, he will soon get tired and go away." And she added, "For the Lord's sake, don't tell our Spadger."

I drew in a sharp breath, squeezed my lips tight shut, just in case I should say one more word. I didn't want my Lord to cop it if it was found out that He had anything to do with fierce lions. So when Lion reminded me that he was there under the bed, for the sake of the Lord, I tried to take no notice of him.

Sometimes Mammy and I played at friendly lion games together. She would take me on her lap and I would feel her mouth open wide as she roared. Then we would both giggle and snuggle up together. Then it would be my turn to be Lion. We did have fun.

One day I made up my mind to find out if Lion was still under the bed. If he was, I would tell him that he could go away now. So I went upstairs on my own, closing the bedroom door. I got down on all fours by the bed and looked underneath. But it was too dark under there for me to see anything, so I told Lion how I was his friend, and reached out to stroke him. Yes, he was still there. With my fingertips, I felt his fluffy mane, but I kept on talking softly, stretching out my arm further to feel his warm body. But all I found was the dust on the cold lino. So I knew now that Lion was dead, because some people thought that when you die you go to heaven to live with Jesus. Some people thought that you just turned to dust. So that was what had happened to Lion.

Next week when Mammy cleaned the bedrooms, she was singing softly to herself as she swept under the bed. I listened as she gently scooped up Lion onto her shovel and wrapped him in a newspaper parcel. Poor Lion, I thought.

LIGHT SHADE

I could see our bedroom light, when it was switched on. Not the bulb, the shade, the flex or the ceiling rose. For me it was just a light, something that just floated in the air. Mammy said that I could not see the light because of the shade. She was wrong. There was no shade or shadow in the bedroom at all. It was when I could not see the light that I was frightened of it. Then I did not know where it might be. It might land on the bed. It might be hot, heavy or hurt me, because it was bigger than a bucket, I thought.

But at spring cleaning time, the light was taken down. While Mammy worked, she told me what she was doing. She told me about the flex hanging from the ceiling that she wiped clean. No, it would not come down. It held the shade and the light bulb up there, near the ceiling. She showed me the light bulb, and she showed me how it fitted into the light shade. Then I was allowed to hold the light shade all on my own. It was a very light shade and no bigger than our kettle. I was careful, because I knew that glass could easily be broken.

When I looked closely, I saw the delicate colours of patterns or flowers, and because I saw, just faintly, they were all the more beautiful. The light shade was so fragile, I thought, that

I hardly dare touch the patterns in case I should rub them off.

Now I knew all about the light shade, a great wave of peace swept over me.

LEEKS

I could hear a tapping sound on nasty nights. It came from behind the dressing table in the corner of the bedroom. Mammy told me it was the roof, but that could not be right, because the tapping sound came from the floor. Some men did climb on the roof and make a noise like thunder, but they did not stop that tapping sound.

One day, I saw my mammy pull out the dressing table and put a bucket behind there. When I asked about it, she said it was for the leeks, but when I looked in the bucket, there were no leeks. There was just an old rag-come-floorcloth in the bottom. I could tell those leeks bothered my mammy, but it was the tapping noise at night that bothered me.

So I asked Daddy about the leeks. It was one day when we were up at his allotment garden. He said he did not grow leeks, because him and Mammy were not bothered about them. Now I was more mixed up than before. Maybe Mammy thought that Daddy might bring some leeks home from the garden, and if he did, we might have to hide them in case somebody saw them and wanted them. So I left this muddle to sort itself out, and it did, eventually.

That was the end of my childhood fears, although there would be moments to come, when my eyes played horrible tricks on me, and moments when I would know no fear at all, when there were dangers which my eyes could not see.

THE SEWING MACHINE

Mammy's sewing machine had had an electric motor fixed to the back, which drove the belt, or for want of a belt, anything would have to do, like a piece of strong elastic. But when Mammy sewed, she needed a clear space in front of her, and not just to use the light from the window. Often the makeshift belt would snap, so it was a good idea not to sit on the settee while Mammy was sewing, even with her split-second shout of warning. Ping!

The motor was worked by a foot pedal, which had to be plugged in every time Mammy sewed. The long flex trailed over the side of the table and down on to the floor. The harder Mammy pressed her foot down, the faster the machine would sew. But she could still turn the wheel herself like she used to do, just for a few stitches when coming to a tricky part.

When Mammy had finished sewing for the afternoon, she could tidy away the foot, as it was called, by wrapping the long flex around and around it. It was a good idea not to go round by the hearth while Mammy was sewing, as it was quite easy for anybody to catch their foot in the long flex.

Next, out came the machine oil. Mammy would give the little can a squeeze at each oiling hole. Plip plop, plip plop, said the oil can. One day Mammy found an extra hole that she had been looking for. She had read about it in the manual, but that was not very clear. The sewing machine ran a lot smoother and quieter after that. The smell of the oil would hang about the house and stick to your clothes till after they were washed. It has stayed in my mind, to take me right back home in a moment.

Next, the sewing machine had to be plugged in. The socket was on the wall near the kitchen door, high above my head. But the flex would hang down in front of the doorway across the room about table-top height. So it was a better idea to go out playing while Mammy was sewing. But if I did run back in the house for anything, she would remind me to bob under the flex with her shout of warning, "Duck!"

It would be a Wednesday afternoon, when Mammy would gather together her glasses, her scissors and her cotton tin. First, she would wind herself a few shuttlefulls of cotton of different colours, as it could be a nuisance if one ran out halfway through a job. The first jobs would be the mending and patching. Then Mammy might make new things from old things. She could make new sheets by putting the sides to the middle. That would make them last a bit longer. Then when they were worn out again, she could make something new from the ends of the sheets, like a warm underskirt for me.

A piece of thick maroon cloth was just big enough to make a new pair of leggings and a new pixie hood to match for me. Two old cardigans were turned into bathing costumes for me and our Spadger. Hers was a royal blue one, and mine was bright red. They were so stretchy, so itchy, that cotton gussets had to be sewn inside to keep them in shape, and to make them more bearable to wear.

Mammy made me a grey skirt, with a white vest top sewn on to it, and a white blouse with tiny red dots all over, too tiny for me to see. There were no white buttons in the button tin for this white blouse, so Mammy sewed on tiny red ones, in twos, in a row down the front. Then she sewed press studs on the back of them for fastening. With elastic threaded through the waistband, this blouse looked as though it was tucked into my grey skirt. I can remember wearing it over my itchy bathing costume at the seaside.

After an afternoon's sewing, the machine was packed away again in the cupboard near the fireplace. Then there was the job of picking up the pins. But however hard Mammy looked for them, there was always another one to be found by Daddy when he got home from work.

THE YELLOW FROCK

Mammy liked to make clothes for herself too. She said what a game it was, juggling clothing coupons. She saw two frocks for herself in the twenty-week club book that she ran. She really liked them. I have reminded my sister about them. She laughed and said, "Cor! They really were awful. They had big bright blue flower motifs on 'em. They weren't really our mam at all. One of 'em were a bright red 'un. T'other one were a brighter yella."

I could not see the red frock, but on the first day Mammy wore her new bright yellow frock, it made her so happy. It put a new spring into her step. But it was not my mammy any more. It had made her into a new woman. For the first time ever I could see somebody moving about the house. Wherever I went, this bright yellow frock was never far from me. It frightened me. It could move quickly and quietly from place to place, when I would not have known if it had not been for that bright yellow colour.

Mammy was nipping to and fro, from the boiler to the kitchen sink. From the table to the kitchen sink. From the table to the pantry. From the table out on the back yard. And back in to the sideboard drawer. Right around the table to the window and the settee.

I had not known that my mammy tidied the house like this every morning. I could not believe that this new woman *was* my mammy. The only place she did not seem to go was in the corner by the front door. So that was where I went, and I stayed there all day.

The woman in the yellow frock spoke in a high, happy voice, but I cowered in the corner, crying for my mammy. By evening I was down on my knees with my face to the wall. I could feel the cold draught on my face, coming from under the front door, cold, yet somehow comforting. Then my cream blanket, the one with the green stripes along the edge was laid over me. I was picked up and wrapped up. I had no strength left for struggling. This woman in the yellow frock took me on her lap to nurse me, wrapping her arms around me, rocking backwards and forwards, singing lullabies.

"Do you want the stars to play with, or the moon to run away with? They'll come if you don't cry."

That was a strange, stretching feeling I felt inside myself, knowing the words, knowing the tune, but not knowing how I knew them. I joined in as the woman in the yellow frock sang, "Lula-lula-lula-lula baby."

She stopped rocking, relaxed her arms.

"Why, you remember," she said. She said she had not nursed me since I was a tiny baby. So we sang together.

"Big round moon is shining, stars begin to peep, now's the time for all piccaninnies to go to sleep."

Part of me knew that this woman in the frock must be my mammy. Yet next morning it was not much better. The sun was out, shining on the yellow frock, making it even more frightening. So again I cowered in the corner by the front door. Then this woman in the yellow frock put on my mammy's coat. She said, "It comes to summat when you've got to wear your coat in t'house. I can't get me work done in it."

Later we went down the street and Mammy bought herself some new material to make two new frocks for herself. When we got back home, she took off the coat and said, "You'll 'ave to put up wi' me for a few days while I get this stuff made up."

She showed me two neatly folded squares of material. It did smell nice. One of them I could not see.

"Mmm. Well, that one'll be alright then," she said, putting it on one side.

But she sounded a bit worried about the other one that I said I could see. But sounding very cheerful, she told me it had little flowers in an all-over pattern on it, tapping each one with her finger. I pictured them inside my head, but to me the material looked green, light, but not too bright.

After a few days, I got my old mammy back. She was wearing a new, cool cotton frock, which she hoped I liked. I said that I did, because I could only see it close up. That was the sort of silly secret that could only be shared by me and Mammy.

She said, "Oh, well, I'm glad about that, then. We'll both be 'appy now." About the yellow frock, she said, "I'll just 'ave to keep out yer way, while I'm wearing it, that's all."

She frock was washed and washed and hung out on the line to dry in the bright sunshine, till at last it came out cream.

Joan Vardy

OUR LEADER'S HOUSE

Our leader lived next door to the chip shop, and to me, each made the other all the more important for having that place in the row. Our leader's daddy was a miner, so they had a lot of money, and everybody could tell that by their house being the only one in the row to have a coat of shiny brown paint on their front door. I thought there was no need to put paint on the door, but my mammy thought it was good that folk made things look nice if they could.

I liked to go around to our leader's house early in the morning, when his mam would be sitting by the fire, cleaning the copper kettle. She could bring it up till it shone so brightly that I could see it shine, if the sun was shining, even from where I stood, at the back of the table. That was where you stood in their house, unless you were asked.

"Come and sit ye dahn on t'settee. There now," said his mam. "I can 'ave a nice cup of tea now I've finished rubbin'." She told me that she would not enjoy a cup of tea if her kettle were dirty.

Our leader had a big sister. She could make pretty bangles and if the shop had some pieces of coloured wire for you to buy, and you had enough pennies to buy it with, she would make one for you.

Our leader's dad believed that education was a good thing, but not just to be taught in school, so he spent his time in teaching his son and me, if I was there. One day we were shown a globe, and he was pointing out all the pink bits that belonged to us. He was going to tell us where the coal came from, and I was holding the globe, when it split into two halves in my hand. His dad said it was all right, I had not broken it.

"I were just gettin' round to that," he said. But I was worried. I could tell that the coal had all gone from inside of the Earth. The Earth crust itself was so very thin. I could see the world was hollow. It was like looking down into a golden syrup tin, deep and golden, somehow bigger on the inside than the outside.

Our leader had a bike. Not just a kiddie's tin tricycle. His was a big three-wheeler bike with red mudguards, a leather saddle, rubber pedals and handle grips, and on the handlebars there was a bell, and it had brakes. Nobody, but nobody was allowed to ride it except our leader, and me. But I could only ride it from their house down to the jeweller's shop on the corner. That was where I must use the brakes, like he had taught me, and that was as far as I could go safely, but I must be sure to get the bike back before his dad got back from the pit, because his mam didn't know what he would say about it.

The three-wheeler was kept in their back kitchen by the pick, standing on its head, not its handle. One afternoon I was just steering the bike back into its place, when I heard our leader's dad scraping his boots on the doorstep. I turned round and saw a black figure that almost filled the doorway. Bad things that might happen to me came into my head. I had learned that wishes worked, so I turned inside myself to find help. But I wondered if help came when you were in the wrong. Our leader's dad moved into the kitchen, making a low grunting sound in his throat. Then he spoke, "Huh, it's you, is it? I knew somebody'd been on it, but I didn't know who."

I heard the rustling of his work clothes as he passed by me through the kitchen, now out of my sight. But I could still hear him talking. He was saying it was all right, as long as it was only me. But how I could ride the thing, he didn't know, as it was far too big for me, and his son should not keep things from him.

Our leader was in their house. His dad went through to him but just in a few words that was dealt with and done with. My fear turned to joy. I had not called Jesus by his name, but my prayer had been answered. I felt safe enough to stay. The leader's mam said she knew that was all he would say. She was peeling potatoes in a large enamel bowl in her shallow stone sink. I told her that we had a bowl like hers. I could remember being bathed in it when I was a baby. She said everybody had one, and they bathed their babies in it. But I should not have said that, because I should not remember that far back. People might think that I was a bit strange. She knew me, so she would not think me strange, but there were other folk. So yet again I had been told that I was not the same as the other kids.

But I could remember. I was sitting in the enamel bowl on the table in our house. The table then was covered in the same yellow protective pad that we still had. Beside the bowl was a big green bar of soap and a white towel that had been unfolded. I was sitting with my knees bent. Mammy was standing on the hearth in front of me. She was saying that I was getting too big for the bowl now. She lifted me up to stand and hold on to her white terry towelling pinafore straps while she washed my legs with her slippery, soapy hands. When she sat me down again, the water was warm and grey. Then Mammy picked up the towel. She held it up in front of her for a splashing, laughing game. I could see the big white towel, and hear her saying, "Hidey bo, hidey bo,"

THE RULER

Mammy was sewing, but the cotton kept breaking in the machine, so she gave that bobbin of cotton to our Spadger, and she gave me Daddy's old folding ruler from out of her sewing tin. He said it was no good any more as some of the marks had rubbed away with continual use. It amused me how the ruler folded this way and that.

I'll get some chums now, with this, I thought, and went out to find the kids. I could hear them playing on our leader's yard. He had a fence but he would not let any of us touch it. If there was nobody about, I would trail my fingers along it for a guide, but today all the kids were there. So I was glad that the sun was out and I could see his white yard.

But I did not know the kids had strung our Spadger's cotton on the fence like a spider's web. I got caught up in it. The more I tried to get free, the more it tangled itself around me. I had never heard the kids laugh so much before. It took more than one mammy to come and sort it all out.

I let all the kids handle my new ruler, but they showed little interest in it, just handed it back to me. Then I hit on an idea. I could share my new toy with them. It would break easily into sections. I broke it and gave away three of them. Then the kids asked, "What can we do wi' 'em now?"

My heart sank. I had failed yet again. Now I had neither chums, nor a toy. The kids were more interested in our leader. He had made a bet with them that he could write his name on their kitchen wall, without using a pencil or a stick of chalk or even his wetted finger. I got to the front as we all gathered round him to watch. With his hands clasped together in front of him our leader stood and studied the brickwork under their kitchen window. I watched in wonder as the wall changed from a dull pink to a shiny red. The kids called out each letter of his name, but before our leader could be dishonoured, out came his mam with a steaming bucket.

"Get it scrubbed off. It'll smell," she said. The kids ran. But I stayed to watch the bubbles bursting in the bucket, and for the first time I noticed the white roses growing by the door. I begged, "Let me in on it. Let me in on it. I want to learn."

It was just like that day with the chalk on the gate. He spoke softly but kindly. "I can't. I just can't. I'm in disgrace," he said. And he sent me home.

Our leader's mam were quite right about that bucket. The smell of it was so strong it got right to the back of my throat.

When I got back home with my share of the ruler, three other kids' mams had returned the other sections. Now I was in disgrace. I knew just how our leader felt, and for the one and only time, Mammy said to me, "Wait till your dad gets home."

But she had her say first. I could not be given anything. I was destructive. Mammy had tried to understand me. "God knows I have," she said. That surprised me. It gave me comfort to think that, with God knowing, things might not turn out so bad in the end. But I had a long think about me. No wonder nobody else could understand me, when I could not understand me.

We all knew it was my bad eyes that stopped me from seeing, but I did not want to see. I only wanted to be able to play with the other kids. I was losing hope. I got hurt if I joined in with their rough, rowdy tumbles. In a game of † Tiggy, I could only stand there in the group while the kids darted about me like sparrows after breadcrumbs. In a game of chase, I could hear their running footsteps, but I was not fast enough to keep up with them. My heart and my soul went with them up the road. I could only listen to their glad to be aloud shouts carried on the wind. I would screw up my eyes to stop the tears from falling, so I would not know whose kind hand would take mine to lead me back to our gate.

Yes, we all understood about my eyes, but nobody understood about me. The few words I knew then could not tell. The few more words I know now; are they far too late?

† Tiggy - Tag

THE ECHO ON THE CLOTHES LINE

I wanted to climb our back wall, to be like the other kids. I knew I could not see enough to walk along it like they did, but just to stand up there; that would have to satisfy me. I have sworn on many oaths, never to tell just whose belief it was that everybody should do as much as they could do.

Before my lesson began, I was told that if I did not manage it, it would not be because I was not brave, but my legs might not be long enough just yet. I must be wearing good shoes. I must wait for the right time, and check that it would not rain in the next few minutes. It is beyond me now, how Mammy agreed that I should be playing out in my best shoes on washing day. It was beyond me then how I could tell if it might rain or not in the next few minutes.

But when Mammy was scrubbing the back kitchen floor, hopefully too busy to watch out for me, or for rain; it was then that I first got a foothold in next door's railings with my left foot. With my right foot on the dustbin handle, I found the handle on the dustbin lid and pulled myself up. Then I found the wooden clothes post to steady myself with, put one foot either side of the lid handle, standing up straight by walking my hands up the clothes post. Then I stretched up in good faith, reaching up with my right hand. Sure enough, I caught hold of a long loop of clothes line, which had been pulled down in readiness for me, as had been promised. Using every muscle and all the strength I had, somehow, by remembering my lessons, I was standing on the top of next door's railings, holding the bars on the top of the clothes post.

There I learned how the clothes line was wrapped around and tied on. Then I stretched out with my left leg, towards the wall, but I could not reach it. Perhaps I was not near enough. I thought if I move along the top of the railings, I might make it. The trouble was that nearer the wall was farther away from the clothes post.

But then my right foot got stuck in the railings and I could not get it out. I thought these new shoes are a bother to me.

Just at that moment, a bus was coming up Lammas Road. By now it was second nature for me to stop, to try and ask myself questions. How do I know?

For a while I had submitted myself to sound. Sounds had bombarded me. But this day, on the top of the railings, I faced the sound. I went out to meet it, like I did that day when picking dandelions. I boomeranged it back. I had heard the sparrows chirruping, nestling between the chimney pots to keep themselves warm. Mammy had told me. But even before this bus got to the end of the row of houses, their chirruping was covered by its roar.

Before this day, I had supposed that the whole of the bus made that roar. But now I could tell that the bus rattled all over because of the ruts in the road, and it being ruined. But that big roaring noise puthered out just from one part of the bus. I could tell it was tired out. The noise rose up, tumbled over our wall and it went right through me. It bounced on our back yard, rolling over, murmuring by the back kitchen door, before going down our grate.

Standing there on the railings that day, I found all my senses. I looked for the noise. I could not see it. Yet I could see the dirty birdlime on top of the clothes post. That felt sticky to touch.

I had found the answer! The one I had had all the time, like Mammy said. She was right. It was nothing to do with the colours of the buses. It was that that big noise had gone down my ears. I was so happy, that I let go of the clothes post. Just balancing there on the railings, I tugged on my ears for joy, and yelled for Mammy to come, to share my joy with me. She came hurrying up the yard, saying her prayers out loud. I wondered why.

Just then, I lost my balance, but Mammy's prayers were answered. I fell forward, saved by the clothes line and my foot being still stuck in the top of the railings. Mammy quickly calmed down. She said, "While you're up there, you can take t'pegs out of your dad's socks for me. You're nearer than I am. It'll save me stretchin' up for 'em."

We made a game of it. I felt along the line for the pegs and tugged. But I thought I had been cheated. Our pegs that us kids made into dollies and aeroplanes, my mammy had used for pegging socks out with. I had wondered how they stopped up there.

I stood by our back gate to wait for the bus coming back from the factory. When it came, the noise was not the same. I had been teaching myself. There were lots of reasons. Now the bus was full, now the bus was going down the hill, and now the engine was on the other side of the bus.

THROUGH THE RAILINGS

We were brought up to call everybody either Mister or Missus. That was because they were married. But our Spadger could not get her tongue round the name of those who lived next door through the railings. 'Andy' was all she could say. So that is how things worked out. It made things more comfortable for everybody, said Mammy.

We did not often go round to their house, but one morning, quite early, I was sent round to Andy's with a message about the twenty-week club. Of an errand, as Andy might say. I helped her to do the dusting and tidying. Their house was neat and warm. A special thing about Andy's house was she had a china cabinet.

Among her treasures behind the glass doors, I loved the most a thatched cottage. It was for keeping biscuits in, but I never found out how to get them out through the front door. Also, there was an artificial peach covered in blue, they said, which I thought was dust that would not rub off.

When we had finished our dusting, Andy dabbed perfume behind her ears and mine.

"She would," said Mammy when I told her. Turning to our fireplace, she said, "We'll see, one day."

One night when we were very young, Spadger and I had to go round to Andy's to be looked after. She put us to bed on the settee, saying, "Mammies can't always be with their children, even if they love them." She settled us down, one each end, and covered us with a blanket. Spadger was soon lying quite still. I could hear her breathing noisily, but I lay awake with a tummy ache. It was a cold and frightened tummy ache. I cried, but Andy was firm.

"It can't be helped," she said. "When children are in bed, that's that until morning."

Their mester worked down at the gasworks, so their house was lit by gas. The light glowed green. It hissed and spluttered. The letterbox rattled and the wind blew gusts of cold air at me from behind the door curtain, and the door curtain shivered and shook. I tried going under the one blanket without pulling it off our Spadger. It was so rough and so dark under there, I cried myself to sleep. The next morning it was found that I really did have a tummy ache, and Andy realised that one blanket was not enough to keep children warm, and she was truly sorry.

After that day when I had climbed Andy's railings and found the echo on the clothes line, we became great friends. She said that she had been trying to think of a way of how she could give me trifle without my mammy seeing it, because my mammy did not want me to have leftovers. Andy had watched me climb her railings and she was glad about it. So now, every Monday morning, after my breakfast, when I went out to use the lavatory, Andy would be the other side of her railings, calling softly to me.

I had to stand on the bottom bar and hold on with one hand, and reach up with the other. Andy could reach over the railings and hand me a dish of trifle. It was from their Sunday tea, she said, but not leftovers. "I set one aside for you."

I would climb down again and she would pass the spoon through the gaps in the railings. The trifle, ready chopped up for me, slid down a treat, while Andy cooed, "Be quiet, be quick, be careful."

The first time I passed the empty dish over the railings, the spoon fell, making a clatter on the metal grate. After that, I would hand back the spoon through the gaps. Then I had to climb onto the bottom bar again for any evidence to be wiped away with a clean white table napkin.

It was Andy who was first on the scene at my birth. Mammy told me part of the story over and over again as I sat on our settee, while she cleaned our fireplace on black lead days. Mammy and Daddy knew that I was coming, so Spadger had gone to stay with Auntie. Daddy had lit the fire on that cold morning before going to work. Mammy told me how she kept herself busy, resting every quarter of an hour.

"That's the best way to do it," she said. She peeled potatoes, because men need a good dinner when they get home from work. She boiled water and gave herself a good wash all over. She made the bed with old sheets. Then she was just leaning over to put more water on the fire to boil, when I came, onto the bare hearth. She grabbed the towel, which was hanging on its hook near the fireplace, and she sat on the hearth with me on her knee. It were about ten to eight, she reckoned. Mammy had been knitting a bonnet for me and it was on the corner of the table ready for its ribbons to be sewn on. So she reached up for it and put it on me. And that was all she could do, she thought.

Later, Andy told me her part of the story. "I ain'd hear yer mammy knocking about, and it were turned nine a piece, so I went round, and I did all I could, but that weren't much. And as I came to wipe your eyes, and I seen as thee is, I wept." She told me she blamed herself for my blindness, for not wiping my eyes properly. "I'm afraid," she said, "I had to help myself and your mam to some brandy, and I wondered if I didn't ought to gie you a teaspoonful, but I didn't."

Mammy continues the story. "When t'nurse came, there was nothing she could do. Fire had gone out, there were no water boiled. So she sat down to have a smoke. I was her third baby that morning. Mothers should not do things like that all at the same time. About my eyes, she thought, seeing how I had got myself into the world, I should manage the rest quite easy. She told Mammy that medicine was for soldiers, and there were mothers losing their sons that morning, and they had been brought up, and their mothers were too old to have any more. So my mammy might consider herself well off. She was still young.

"Just wrap her up and keep her warm," she advised.

Just in case I never get the privilege again, may I say now that Andy and I grew nearer and dearer to each other, through her illness, in her blindness, until her death, which never quite separated us.

Thank you, Andy.

TRAILER TO OURSELVES

Our luggage was too heavy for Daddy to carry to the trailer, so we had borrowed a wheelbarrow from the man at the big shed. On the return journey, I begged for a ride in the empty barrow. It was not a home-made wheelbarrow like my daddy's. It was made of metal which shone so brightly in the sunlight that it made my eyes water, but I could not stop staring for the wonder of it. Anything new gave me a feeling of pleasure. But the wheel did not twitter like a little bird singing, like

Daddy's wheelbarrow did. He was so sad to think that the wheelbarrow might never carry chrysanthemums or tomato plants. No wonder the man at the big shed had been hesitant about letting us borrow it.

We were taking tomatoes to thank him, and it was not easy for me, riding in this new barrow, trying to sit upright with my legs up the slope. Daddy's was a flat barrow and I could not hold on to the sides with holding the tomatoes in my hands. But I could tell it made Daddy happy to push this grand new wheelbarrow.

The wheelbarrow man did not sound at all grateful for the tomatoes. Mammy said, "He's 'appen got two greenhouses and twice as big as yours at home."

On this holiday, our trailer was light and airy and we did not have to share it with another family. This time we had it all to ourselves. It was less cramped inside and I was free to move about. But I had to find my own way of getting up and down the steps. I crawled to the light of the doorway to find the steps, in case I should fall down them. I found the best way was getting down on my tummy and slithering down head first, with my hands to feel the way. I could see the treads of the steps. To me, they looked like one grey wool rug.

But the way up took more thinking about. I can remember sitting on the grass with my feet up on the first step for a long time. But feet first was not the way. I tried waving my arms about in the air. I sometimes found the very thing I was searching for by reaching out blindly, but still, I was not getting anywhere. On the way down I had seen the treads of the steps, but now I could see no steps at all, just the green grass in the gaps between the steps. I did not know how I could climb up something that was not there.

At last I found myself lying down on the bottom step. Now I could feel the grey wool rug with my whole body. From there

I climbed up sideways, like an intrepid rock climber, one limb at a time.

Safely in the trailer once more, it was thankfulness I felt, not achievement. Mammy and Daddy were sitting at the table, talking together. I heard Mammy saying, she had thought she would have to have found some way of stopping me falling through the doorway, so she was glad that I had found a way of my own to get up and down the steps, because it was so pleasant to sit with the door open.

Every day, at lunchtime, Mammy would put the vegetables to boil on the trailer cooker while we all took our dinner plates to join the queue outside the big shed. Inside the big shed, the wheelbarrow man cooked and carved the meat, which he served at a fixed price per person.

As we waited for the big doors to open, I heard grumblings from some folk who thought that the portions might not be equal. But when the first two in the queue were served, they sounded quite satisfied. There were more grumblings coming from behind us in the queue, from folk who thought there might not be enough meat to go round. One man who had brought two plates was only served one helping of meat. And one toddler was served no meat at all. The wheelbarrow man called out, to make it quite plain for everybody to hear him, "No meat for any child under two years old."

I was four years old by now, but quite small. I worried that I might not look more than two years old, but I felt very grown up as I handed over my plate and my silver coin to pay for my own meat. I had been wanting to see what meat might look like, and was disappointed to see just a brown patch on my white plate. I thought; that meat is the same colour as the shed doors. It had been a privilege for me to carry my plate to the shed. At home I would have been told I was too young to do that. But I was glad that I did not have to try and balance my meat all the way back to our trailer. Daddy said, "It will take you too long," and he carried it for me. And I was surprised to hear even my mammy having her little grumble. It was about everybody having to eat their meal at the same time, whether it suited them or not.

When my white plate was put on the white tablecloth, it seemed to vanish. I picked it up and put it back down again a few times, and it worked every time. So it was magic. At home good table manners must always be observed. But I heard Mammy saying quietly to Daddy, "It's 'er meat. Let 'er enjoy it." And I did enjoy it, too.

At home, Mammy was used to cooking on her coal fire, and she did not like this cooker. "What use is a cooker, if you haven't any food to cook?" she asked herself. Then she had a sudden idea. She could find a use for the oven. It would be good for me. I could learn to cook safely, and have a lot of fun, so together we made milk bottle top jam tarts. They were white cardboard pastry, with red writing jam in the middle.

Milk bottles were new. Only Daddy had seen milk bottles when he worked in London. At home our milk still came round by horse and cart, in a milk churn. Maybe one of us had had a new pair of shoes, as I cooked a shoe box cake. My games of cooking were so real to me, that even if we were eating a meal, I could smell my cake burning, and have an irresistible urge to get down from the table to test it. I could even feel the hot shelf. Once, when I jumped back with the pretend heat, Mammy came quickly to check, just in case the oven had been turned on.

She thought it was good for me to be treated the same as our Spadger, so we were both bought an exercise book, even though I could not draw. Our Spadger drew seriously, not wanting to be disturbed by me. I tried to draw in my book, but the lines I drew with a pencil were too faint and too fine for me to see. It made me feel hateful. Mammy showed me the front cover of the exercise book. It was an orange colour with a black silhouette of an old-fashioned pram on it.

That gave me an idea. If I could see that pram, I should be able to see what I drew on that page. But when I did draw, I learned that although somebody else had drawn the pram, it was a naughty thing for me to draw, because the book must be kept looking nice. I asked myself, why is it that I can see that pram? Is it because the front cover is orange? Now I would never know.

Mammy and Daddy were sharing a bottle of something. I thought it was pop, and I thought that I had a rights to a share in it. I must have helped myself to a drink from the bottle. I felt gloriously happy, bubbling over with joy. Mammy told me, "It's not pop, it's cider."

Daddy sounded cross as he held up the bottle to the light to see how much cider I had drunk. I heard it swirling around in the bottle. He told me to go to sleep, but I was not one bit tired. I took hold of my exercise book and ripped it in two pieces with one tug. I was glad to have put an end to the book, and the bother of it.

Spadger and I went out to play on the grass. The world was going around and around, and to try to keep still, I twirled round and around myself. Then without trying, I learned the thrill of roly-poly. Our Spadger joined me, and we played together, as we had never done before, giggling and squealing as we rolled over and over in the grass, and did I hear my Mammy saying she was glad I had had that cider?

On this holiday I enjoyed the long walks. The paths were broad and level, with no stones and tree roots to trip me up. They were a light sandy colour, so I could see them, and I felt safe and happy to venture on ahead alone. On this holiday, there was just a gentle, warm, buffeting breeze, as if it had hopped and skipped coming over the flat fields. There were no strong winds puffing and blowing after having to climb over the high hills. Mammy and Daddy just wanted us all to have a quiet time, when we could be together.

One afternoon, I was sitting quietly on my own at the bottom of a grassy slope. Looking around me, there were no walls to spoil my view. Close by me the grass grew fresh and green. There were no weeds at all for me to see. As I gazed slowly up the slope to the horizon, the bright green of the grass gradually faded away, until I reached the boundary of the field of my vision, where the sky comes down to the ground and turns green, and the green turns white. There were no sounds, just silence.

It felt like I had found myself. It seemed as if I was the same as what I saw, filled with calm. I could stretch my whole self out to touch eternity. I was given a knowing far beyond my years in a different dimension of reality.

Later I stood by the trailer table, watching Mammy. She was spreading the bread for tea, yet my tummy still felt full, and I had no questions to ask her now. I had nothing to tell her, because I did not have the words then. Even now, I cannot put words together as I should like to do, but I do know that I was nearer to God's kingdom then as a little child, than I am now, with my little knowledge.

I CAN CAN

I was learning to live without the kids. They were noisy and nasty. They swore, they spat when they were well out of the way of their mams' earshot. So by choice on my own, I set out to find the dandelion patch again, with a long afternoon ahead of me.

I felt for the crumbling wall and the stony ground. But there were no bright yellow dots to see, so I thought I might not have found the right place. I crouched down to feel for the dandelions, but just then the sun came out, throwing long dark shadows across the ground. To me the shadows looked something like railway sleepers I would have to clamber over.

Then it seemed that things had turned about. Now the dark lines were deep, deep trenches. I dare not move, or I would fall into one and not be able to climb out again. So I stood between two trenches. I could feel and hear my heart thumping. I was trapped until I was rescued by a little woman.

She took me into her cottage. Inside the fire burned orange. The walls were green. The table was covered with a white cloth. I fingered the edge, just gently. It was starched stiff for Sunday best. I guessed they had company.

"She were lost," announced the little woman who had rescued me. "What's your name, gal?" I was asked, and then introduced to everybody there. They were all so friendly, so I felt quite at home, even though there was a house full of them.

There was an auntie and uncle, come from such-and-such place, and another auntie and uncle, who had a gin-jar tom who had died.

"Tha would a liked him, now wouldn't ya, gal?" Auntie asked. I agreed, but made a note to ask Mammy what a gin-jar tom was.

And there were cousins, come from such a long way off, part way by carriage they came.

"Now, haren't we honoured to be hentertaining such guests?" said the little woman. I remembered to use my

Sunday best manners to match their Sunday best tablecloth, but I spoiled my manners by stumbling over the name of the last man. I could not get my tongue round his name. It seemed I called him something that was rude. He got cross about it, and I had to say just how sorry I was.

He was calmed down by the offer of a drink, and glasses were handed round, chinking. I saw the bottle's long dark green neck as my drink was poured. It was like the bottle my mammy used for rolling out the pastry with. She filled her bottle with cold water. This bottle was full of some red drink. It looked like medicine in the glass. A small glassful was put down in front of me. After a speech, the man with the rude-sounding name coaxed me. "'Ave a drink, gal."

Very carefully, I felt over the tablecloth for the glass and drank down my drink. Then the little woman shook the bottle to see if there was enough to go round for another glass for each of us. The visitors thought so, and the medicine was carefully measured, for fair shares for us all. "Drink it dahn, gal, and then we'll 'ave a sing-song," I was coaxed again. But they were not songs I had ever heard before.

"Join in, come on, join in with us," they all called.

After the sing-song, we all joined hands and danced around the table, going first this way and then that.

"Mind the fire," someone called out, and we all collapsed into armchairs in heaps, giggled, cheering and then clapping our hands. Then the little woman thought I had better be going on home, so I said my goodbyes and thank yous, and she took me by the hand, and we danced up their garden path. She taught me how to hop, skip, hop and skip, and how to hold up the hem of my dress with my finger and thumb, and we danced down the road showing our white petticoats, singing, "I can can, if you can can," all the way down our back yard to our kitchen door. We were so happy, we could not stop laughing.

My mammy was not laughing. "Don't go there again," she warned me.

I tried to make things better for myself. "I was lost," I lied. I thought how lucky I had been to have met such carefree, kind and happy folks. I asked Mammy later,

"What is a gin-jar tom?"

UP THE ROAD

Once a week, Mammy and I went up the road to fetch the meat, and some money for her to keep me, but it was more than just an errand for me. It was a signpost between washing day and black lead day.

But first, there was the getting ready to go. There might be a parcel to send back to the twenty-week club. Wrapping parcels was a crackling task. Mammy would fold the brown paper into neat V-shapes on the ends of the parcels and loop string around to make a cross. Then I could help by pressing hard with my finger on the first knot, while she tied the second. Then she would say, "Leave go," and I would move my finger quickly as she tugged hard on the string.

Sealing wax must always be used on parcels, to make sure that they were not tampered with in the post. Mammy would hold the little red stick above the knot, warming the wax with a lighted match, being careful not to let any of the melting wax drip onto the brown paper. It smelt nice, but I could not touch the knot until the sealing wax had hardened. If I looked closely, I could see a shapeless red spot, but when the wax had cooled, I could feel the bumpy, lumpy knot underneath the wax.

Then I must be given a wash, but Mammy would not only wash my face, she would wash Jean's face too. Jean was our Spadger's big doll. Mammy thought that folk would think I were well cared for if I carried a dolly, and they would know that she was trying. But my dolly Jenny had no clothes to put on, so I could not take her. Jean wore a blue frock and a green corduroy coat, and matching beret. She made my arms ache, but I was so pleased to have a go with her, that I never moaned.

At last we were ready. It was just a few minutes' walk along the road, but it seemed such a long way for me, placing one foot forward, then the other, with the grey road stretching as far and wide as I could see. It was like being on a treadmill. It might go on and on forever. There was one thing to listen out for on the way. It was a friendly sound, like the air raid sirens, but softer than the sirens, like the blast of the fire engine's bell, but when it was far away. 'Wood yard,' Mammy called it. There the trees grew tall, with birds singing in the branches, drawing a picture in sound, outlining the trees' shapes, with the gaps in between.

Now that the railings had gone to the war, my mammy could see over the walls into the gardens of the big houses.

"I don't suppose they like it," she said.

I said, "If they took the walls to the war, then I could see the gardens."

Mammy laughed. It was one of her sad laughs.

We often walked along in a chummy silence, with just a few words now and then. Once I looked up and saw the grey sky through a bare bush in wintertime. I asked Mammy, "Who's scribbled on the sky?" The answer was a long time coming, giving me space to find the answer for myself. *How silly, I thought. Nobody has scribbled on the sky! That's not the right answer. It just looks like that to me. The sky has cracked, gone crazy, like pudding basins do when they've been in the oven. Now that is the right answer.*

Mammy once said that the sky just looked like the sand with the sea gone out. My answer was a long time coming. I had never seen the sand left in ripples when the tide had gone out. I looked up and saw rows and rows of threaded white beads, strung across the sky.

We often talked like this, clutching hands as we trudged along, building bridges over broken pathways of thought, forming a very special bond between us, of inner calm and deeper knowing, drawing closer on the inside, my mammy and me.

THE GAS MASK BIKE

One morning we saw a pushbike with a sidecar for a child. Mammy wanted me to find out about it for myself. I found the black box with the yellowing window. I peered through it. From inside I could hear a small child whimpering. At once I was back in my baby gas mask, cold and shaking, drowning in my fears, with waves swirling all around me. I tried pulling off my scarf and unbuttoning my coat, gasping for breath.

From somewhere far off, I could hear Mammy calling my name, and I came out of myself into her arms, on the quiet road. The roaring waves had gone.

Mammy said, "I did believe you, when you said you could remember things, but now you've shown me. I know where you've been." It worried her. She did not know how I could be helped.

That morning Mammy opened up her heart to me for her fears for my future, and I learned that I must let go and live.

A GOLDEN MORNING

"Sunshine is good for you!" Mammy always said that. So if we could, we always walked on the sunny side of any street. There was one house that we had to pass going up the road. It was a house like ours, with a front door opening onto the coursey. There, Mammy would take Jean from me and send me on to run ahead, just in case of something, while she followed, blowing her nose hard, or trying to clean her glasses with her hanky.

One morning, just as I reached the front door, I heard a little girl giggling, and bent down and saw her hair. It was fair and curly. The little girl was peeping out at me through a broken panel in the door. *At last!* I thought; *I have found a real chum.* And I crouched down to join in the game. We were both giggling so much that I lost my balance and tippled head over heels through the broken door. We both landed in a heap on the floor inside.

It was too dark in the house for me to see anything, but for a few moments we sat together giggling, sharing a perfect, wordless friendship. It may have been her daddy who spoke slowly and softly, maybe to hisself.

"Oh my, she's just an ordinary child, just like am. She

laughs. She's norra..." he broke off. Then to me, he sing-songed, "That's it now. Back you go, same way you came."

I climbed out through the hole in the door, stinging my hands in the grit on the coursey. We were still giggling, and he was saying, "Well, bless me, well, bless me."

When we got back home that morning, Mammy had nothing to do. She said she had, but it could wait. She just thought that I might like my hair washed and some fresh clothes to put on. So she would just pop me in the tub.

It was good in the tub by myself on the hearth in the warm sunshine coming through the window. Then afterwards Mammy thought, as the water was still warm, she might just dab out my clothes with just a spot or two of Dettol. Shaking the bottle, she reminded herself to use a little less next black lead day.

This was a golden memory, finding a real chum, the tub all to myself, the extra loving care and clean clothes in the middle of the week. A real golden morning.

TOP COAT

Another morning there was a very large parcel to take back up the road, so that day we did not take dolly Jean. We had not gone far when we walked under a ladder and a paintbrush passed my nose and fell at my feet. I jumped for joy on seeing the paintbrush, for just one moment, but not the next. It was magic to me, how it could just vanish out of sight by my feet. And more magic! How, without even touching me, the paintbrush had put bright green tiddlywinks on my brown coat. I liked them. Not Mammy. She was talking with the painter, saying there must be something to do about it. He was saying it was not superstition, but common sense to walk round a ladder.

I studied. I had jumped for joy on seeing the paintbrush, believing that at least there was one thing that I could see. It was paintbrushes. But I looked again on the ground for it, and at my tiddlywinks. And I learned that I could only see bright colours close up, like paintbrushes passing by my nose. Not even knots under sealing wax. Just bright colours, close up.

That night when Daddy got home from work, he seemed to like my tiddlywinks too. It had evened up the score with Mammy, because that coat was the same coat I had been wearing one day up at the allotment garden.

In Daddy's garden, I often helped myself to fruit or vegetables if I felt hungry. I knew the feathery fronds of the carrots, and I could feel along the rows for those ready for picking. I could rinse the soil off them in the water butt. To reach the water, I would need to climb up the water butt, so that was where I was that day when Daddy was shouting. He lifted me down and I thought that I was bad for picking carrots before they were ready. No. Daddy was surprised that the carrots were ready so early.

Was it that he had just painted the water butt and it was still wet? He had not told me, he said, thinking that I would not bother going near it if I did not know it was wet. I thought I had spoilt the water butt. No, it was not the carrots; it was not the water butt that was upsetting Daddy. It was my new brown coat. He asked me, "What will I tell your mammy? It's your new brown coat! And it'll be no good for the rug now, when you've grown out of it!" He thought he had at least to pick a boiling of carrots to take home for Mammy. The paint was dark brown, same as my coat, so I could not see it. But until it dried hard and stiff, it felt like sticky treacle.

Now Mammy sat with my coat on her lap, saying I could not wear it again. It seemed odd to me. Brown water butt paint would do, but green tiddlywinks would not do. She told Daddy, "We can't buy another top coat, but she must be kept warm. There must be something to do about it."

Daddy jumped up, laughing. "She shall have a new top coat, warm and waterproof," he said. He picked up my coat, swinging it round his head, singing and dancing into the kitchen. I was marched up the stairs to bed, assured that I would wear my coat again, and it might even have to have the hem let down for next winter.

THE BUTCHER'S SHOP

At long last, we had reached the butcher's shop. I could tell when we were nearly there, with a privet hedge with a golden wavy top. The butcher's was a bright white shop with a half-open stable door. "To stop dogs from gerrin' in," said Mammy. On the counter there was a little white gate. I could see through the gaps into the window. There, there was a large white space.

"Fisher legs, if there is any," said Mammy. All I knew of meat was; liver was black, sausages were pink and they must be pricked with a fork. But for some people, the butcher would disappear into his fridge. On coming out again, he would proudly say how nice it was this week.

One morning the butcher disappeared into his fridge. The door slammed shut behind him. None of the customers knew how to open it, but one was sent to find somebody who did. One lady said she had been in his house before, so she went through into the back and put on the kettle to make him a hot drink, and it was on the counter waiting for him by the time the butcher was let out of his fridge.

THE POST OFFICE

The post office was over the road, opposite in many ways. Their door was shut, and inside the walls were dark brown. It was so dim that on dull days, the post office was lit by a spitting, hissing green gaslight above the postmistress. Once I was picked up to see her stamp on my book. I could see she had light green hair and I was glad there was a metal grill to stop her from getting out. She stamped loudly on my book with her foot, I thought.

I knew that that postmistress gave my mammy money to keep me, but I supposed that if she did not give my mammy any money, she would keep me for herself in the post office, behind the metal grill. If I could, I would stand close to the wall at the back, clinging on to dolly Jean. There, there was a writing table with a pink blotting paper mat on it, where folk could write their postal orders, but everybody could read the blotting paper backwards, and know who had been before them, and the price of their postal orders. So my mammy would be careful to blot her name and the price in different places.

There were some pretty rubber bands hanging up in cellophane bags, at 3d a bag. I should have loved one. Mammy told me they perished with being in the post office for so long. I agreed. It was perishing cold in there. It was always nice to get out again, but Mammy tried not to laugh. The postmistress said a lot about rubber bands.

Rubber bands were not for sale. Rubber came from over the seas. Things were not right. We all knew that, but things had to look right, so that people could think right, and rubber bands were there because rubber bands should be there.

OINK OINK PIGGY PORKER

Daddy and I did not always go up to his garden on Sunday mornings. Sometimes we went to see one of his sisters. I had a lot of aunties, and have many muddled memories of them, but there was one auntie who I clearly remember visiting.

It was a good walk to see her, over the Lammas and through five fields, where Daddy would encourage me to walk without him, when the path was not too stony. Once, a bird flew out from a bush, almost touching my nose as it flew past. Daddy said, "That wun't a' 'appened if I'd been 'olding your 'and." He had been wondering how I would ever be able to enjoy nature, and now he knew, so everything would be all right, he thought.

On the corner of Auntie's street, right on the coursey, stood an old school. Its stone blocks were blackened with soot. It was near the pit. All the miners had coal to burn and smoky chimneys. The school's windows were above my head. I could not see the sky making them shine blue, with the overhanging roof which blocked out all the light. I thought the school was too quiet. Daddy told me it was Sunday. It would be better in the week. And it was better on the inside. There were books in there to learn children. He often reminded me that I would be going to school to learn one day.

The sign on the school there said 'Institute Street'. On the other side of Institute Street there was one long row of terraced houses. It stretched the whole length of the street, without any † gennals, as Daddy called them. So we used the unmade road round the backs of the houses, because Auntie's front door was blocked up. The good thing about that was, she said, it was not draughty, and besides, it stopped the kiddies from running in and out.

When we got there, I could go through to the front room to play in there with my cousins. There was plenty of space for playing, as there was not much furniture. My youngest cousin might be sitting in his carry cot on the floor, wearing what I thought might be my old brown coat. We would turn him out of the carry cot, if we had a special need of it. Our shoes might get a bit wet from the puddles, but Auntie did not mind who had made the puddles. Nor did she mind about the noise we made, not even her toddler's howling. Uncle would take us up to see his pigs on the allotments at the end of the street.

My cousin's granddad owned the house on the end, and he would show us his fowls. We would take coal for cooking the pigs' food and they would come grunting to greet us. Uncle would give them lumps of coal to chew. I might be lifted up to see over the pig pen wall. Then I could reach down to scratch their pink bristly skin, and find their curly tails. My cousin could climb on to the wall, shouting excitedly, "Oink, oink, piggy porker, oink oink, piggy porker."

When mammy pig had some babies, my cousin had already been in the sty to see them, and mammy pig had not minded, so Uncle was sure that she would not mind if I went inside to see the babies either. I felt timid. I did not want to be thought of as a baby. So I agreed to be lifted down into the pig pen. I went forward as he coaxed me, through the low opening into the pig sty. Inside it was warm, and the floor was covered with a deep bed of straw, but it was too dark in there for me to see. But I could hear the piglets softly squeaking and squiggling in their nest. It sounded like there were quite a few of them.

Then their mammy came in. She stood in the opening and by the sound she made I thought she wanted me to get into the nest. It seemed to me that she thought I was one of her own little babies. She was telling me, "Get back in that nest again." I thought if I did, I might step on a piglet and hurt one. So I dare not get into the nest.

Mammy pig got more angry with me. She came towards me, shrieking. Uncle was calling out, "Come out! Come out", and by the sound of his voice, he had changed his mind, and now he thought that mammy pig might harm me after all.

She was shrieking louder now and nearly touching me. She was taller than me, but now I could see the daylight in the opening. I pushed past her towards it. Uncle was banging a bucket on the trough. All the little piglets came running out with me, making happy sounds. We were followed by their mammy, still shrieking. I ran to the sound of the banging bucket, falling with my hands in the pigswill in the trough.

Some time after this, we all went to Auntie's for Sunday tea. They were not busy then like they were in the mornings, and they made time to show me round their house. A bright fire always glowed in their back room. They kept their coal in a big bath down the passageway off the kitchen. It was very cold in there, Uncle said. It took a lot of hot water to fill that big bath, and it soon got cold again, so that was why they had a bath like we did at home, in the tub on the hearth, in front of a nice warm fire.

Auntie was very kind to me. She showed me her two ornaments, which she dearly loved. She took them from the sideboard and put them on the table, where I could reach to feel them. I felt them all over, but I had no idea what they were until Auntie told me that they were a pair of Alsatians. This was a good chance for me to know just what an Alsatian looks like. They were both standing with their front paws on steps. I asked Auntie, "Where they going?"

She says, "They're going nowhere. They're posing." She explained how and why she thought them handsome and admirable. And she took time to explain all the long words she used.

After tea the light was switched off while we watched a film show. All I could see from my place in the corner was a flickering light on another wall. Beside me was a click click noise of the thing that made it work. This was the corner where the sheet was hanging. "Hanging up to dry," said Auntie, just in case anybody should ask.

I knew that behind the sheet was the dead mammy pig, and anybody who came would know that. Their nose would tell them so. A sheet could not hide that stinking pig. I had to breathe in that stink. I could not get it out of my nose. It made me feel not quite well.

I thought the film was all about the pig, and I thought that the pig might come back alive and come running after me, shrieking, like she did that day in the pig pen. So I was crying. Mammy was trying to comfort me. She did not like the film either. That flickering was giving her a headache, but she told everybody that I was frightened of the dark.

One of my cousins joined me in the crying, remembering that he was frightened of the dark. But Auntie did not comfort him. She told him that he was not frightened of the dark two minutes ago, so he could not be frightened of the dark now. That made sense to me, and I learnt that in the dark we all simply cannot see the things that are still there about us in the room.

But without touching the pig, somehow I could feel it. It was a death chill I knew of, without even knowing of death. After that we had a sheet hanging. "Hanging up to dry," said Mammy, just in case anybody should ask.

Our sheet hung over a line in the corner at the bottom of the stairs, even though we always had a clothes line stretching from the stairs door over to the window. That was always taken down at the weekends. Behind our sheet at the bottom of the stairs hung one quarter of the dead mammy pig. At night after the front door had been locked, Daddy took it down and carved. Mammy cooked. She fried it on the fire. She thought that folks might smell it, then they would know. She cut mine up into little pieces, handing me my little fork. She said, "Tuck in!" But I could not take one mouthful of that dead mammy pig.

I had to pass under the mammy pig to climb the stairs for bed. Night by night that stench changed and grew. Everybody who came would know about it, I thought. It was not long before Daddy thought the pig had not been cured right. Then it was grudgingly agreed that the pig reeked. Daddy talked it over with Mammy. I was not supposed to hear. They discussed ways of how they might get rid of it. They decided they needed help. They had given help in the past, and thought that that favour might be returned.

Next morning when I went downstairs, the air was cold and fresh. The stench, the sheet had gone. It was being washed, and after, it was hung over the line in the house at the weekend. Mammy thought that folk would not think it was funny, hanging a sheet up to dry. They would not say anything about it. They would just think that I had needed a clean one on my bed, even though she had proudly told them all that I had been dry since I was three. She was still quite sure they would not say anything.

It seemed I often came in handy when an explanation was needed.

† gennal – covered pathway between two terraced houses.

THE WET WALK

Mammy was worried. We all knew that our Spadger was really quite poorly. So our pram was brought down from the garret for her to ride in while I walked. The end of the pram was lowered to make it like a big pushchair for her to fit, wrapped up in her cream blanket with the pink stripes on the ends.

Our Spadger was crying all the time these days, and Mammy was always trying hard not to do. Only I liked that walk. Mammy put my hand on the side of the pram handle low down. That was much better than having to stretch up my arm to hold her hand. The handle was firm to hold. I could reach my fingers right around it.

In the rain the pram wheels made short sharp snapping noises in front of me, leading me on. The pram handle tilted one or two paces before me, letting me know to step up or down at the kerbs, and near my feet there were ripples in the puddles, making gentle trickling tunes just for me.

Just for me, that was a lovely wet walk.

THE SWEEP

It was the same every day at our house. Daddy would soon be coming home from work, and it would soon be dinnertime. Two saucepans were wedged together in the fire grate, leaning towards the bars so that if the coals settled, they would not slip the other way and put the fire out. Our Spadger said the water was trying to do that, it was lifting up the pan lids and spitting at the flames, she said.

So Mammy took the lids off. She said, "Pans is boiling over because they're not big enough for a family. It'll be better when t'cabbage 'as boiled down a bit." I thought that we had to wait for our daddy to come home before we could have our dinner. I did not know that my mammy could time it for the dinner to be cooked as he came in through the door. I was hungry. The smell was tempting.

Then all at once, it was silent. The water had stopped bubbling, the orange glow of the flames had gone. The room was filled with a strong smell, nasty, new to me. Mammy was shouting at the fire grate. I did not know why, and I was crying. Then Mammy was shouting at me, when Daddy came through the door, and Mammy was shouting at him, how it would have been all right if the saucepan lids had been kept on, and she did not know why I was crying because I hated cabbage. And wasn't I four now, and too big to be crying?

Then Daddy was saying there was no wonder I was crying. By now I had got enough sense to know there was something to be crying at. Then between them they set to work. The cabbage and the potatoes were rinsed in the colander. The fireplace was wiped down, and soon the fire glowed orange again. The cabbage and the potatoes were put to boil again. Then we sat down to dinner. It was the same every day at our house.

Daddy thought it was time that the chimney was swept. Mammy thought it would be a lot of hard work for her. Then, one night, before I went to bed, Mammy told me that the sweep would be coming in the morning while I was still asleep. But if the noise woke me up, it would be best if I stayed in bed. But she did not know what time the sweep would be leaving, so she told me, if it was late and I came downstairs, I must not be frightened, because all the furniture would be covered up with white sheets. Mammy told me again how she did not want me to be frightened.

The racket did wake me up. It sounded as though it was in our fire grate in the bedroom. Our Spadger sat up in bed and she screamed. Then I heard a mester saying, "You should have told me there were kids in bed. I could 'ave frightened 'em to death."

I believed that he was Santa Claus who had climbed down the chimney early to bring our toys. Mammy said, "There's summat not quite right in t'chimney." And she took me and our Spadger downstairs, reminding me again about the sheets covering up the furniture. I felt the strong white canvas sheets. The whole room looked white, just all over white, no furniture shapes under white sheets, just white, white and cold, like there was nothing there to touch.

Mammy told me that everything was covered in soot. I

could smell the soot. It was in my mouth, and it seemed to me like I could just put up my hands flat in the air in front of me and touch it.

When the sweep came back down the stairs, he wanted to light the fire. Mammy did not want him to. She thought that if he lit the fire, it would go out. He said that it was his job to light the fire, and where were the sticks and the coal? He got his way. Mammy fetched the sticks and the coal. The sweep lit the fire, and when he had gone, it went out. But the chimney was all ready for Santa Claus to climb down with our toys.

MY DOLLS' HOUSE

I have forgotten now what it was I wanted for Christmas when I was four years old. But whatever it was, Daddy told me that Santa could not bring it, so he would be bringing me a dolls' house. Not knowing what a dolls' house was, I could not get excited about it. But Daddy did.

On Christmas Eve, without much joy in my heart, I hung up one of Daddy's socks near the fire place. Then as I lay awake in bed, I heard some mesters talking outside in the road. One said, "No kids live round here." Another argued that there was, there was a lot of them, and they were all to shut up, or they would spoil it for them. Then it fell quiet.

I heard the sound of real sleighbells, and held my breath as I listened while they jingled gently into the distance. Up until now, I had had doubts about this Christmas, what with my dolly Jenny being bright as a penny with her flat silver nose and no clothes to put on. Then last year my wheelbarrow turning out to be a dolly pram after all, just because it only had one handle and three wheels too many. I had not raised my hopes about a dolls' house, but somehow now I knew that Santa would see me right.

On Christmas morning our toys were laid out on the table downstairs. What a pleasure it must have been to see our Spadger's face light up with joy on seeing all her toys at a glance. But I had to find my toys one by one, quietly ignoring her shrieks of delight. And I would not be led to come and see the dolls' house.

At first I was happy enough to feel that Daddy's sock was now heavy and lumpy, a sign that there might be better things to come. I pulled the lumps from the sock one by one. An apple, an orange, then some nuts. I held the nuts in my hands, feeling their different shapes with joy in my heart. Down in the foot of the sock, there was something new. It was long and felt rough. To me, it looked like it needed a good scrubbing. I put it down. I should have to think about that one later.

Later Mammy told me that it was a pear. She said, "It's all right to eat it, because it's fruit." So I bit into it. I thought it tasted like a turnip, but as turnips go, it was not that bad, so I ate it for Mammy.

Behind Daddy's sock on the table, I found a small plastic car. It was such a bright red on the white cloth that I could see it. And because I could see it, I liked it. I could not do much with it, but it taught me what a car looked like. Next I found a metal motorbike, and at first this toy was fun. When I wound it up with the key, I could hear it travelling across the table. But when it fell over, I thought about the rider getting his leg trapped. Mammy said, "It's only a toy, it can't get hurt." But I did not wind it up any more. The rider could not get off his bike, so I had to feel carefully to make my mind up where his arms ended and the motorbike handles began, and which bits were boots and which bits were bike, was only guesswork.

Next to the motorbike I found a white plastic horse. It was being ridden by a soldier, wearing a bright red jacket and knee high boots. It was by feeling the soldier's boots that gave me clues to the motorbike rider, because the soldier could get off of his horse, although he was far too stiff to stand up straight. I remember one day before Christmas being in Peacock's shop, and asking, "What's that, Mammy?" When I had seen three soldiers on horseback riding across the counter, and now I knew what a horse looked like. But I did not know that a soldier was just a man wearing a helmet. I thought his head was very big, some sort of an animal, I supposed he was.

I had two more years of growing up to do before I can tell the story of how I learned the truth about horse guards just being like my Daddy, and dressed up to look like soldiers.

At last, at the back of the table stood my promised dolls' house and I was truly thankful that it was not big enough to put my dolly Jenny inside of it, as I thought I might have to do. It was a real little house, not a house in a row like ours; this was a posh house with windows on both sides of the door, and bow windows, at that! On the outside it was painted with red brick walls and a grey slate roof. And now I knew what a house looked like, and how the roof sloped up to the chimneystack and the chimney pots on top, all ready for when the chimney sweep comes, so that his brushes can come out at the top. I knew that.

On the inside, all the walls were painted cream. The whole of the back wall opened up like a door, so that I could play with all the rooms at the same time. On either side of the hall, doorways led through to the sitting room and the kitchen, and a flight of stairs went up to a bedroom and a bathroom.

Daddy told me that the house was still so new that it still

had no kitchen sink or bath. In the sitting room, there was a wooden fireplace with a three piece suite to match it. Countless hours for years and years to come were opened up that day for me to be absorbed in play.

Through the years, as each new piece of furniture arrived, it went in through the front door, round the stairs and down the passageway to its proper room. One day I played at moving house and the fireplace got stuck in the hallway, and the front door had to be taken off its hinges. I could tell that Daddy was smiling when he said, "You don't take the fireplace with you when you flit!"

On that Christmas Day, Spadger and I had a look at each other's toys for a while. She had a box of bricks, which by turning them about, she could make six different pictures with them. One was of footballers on a field, but all the bricks looked like grass to me on every side. Spadger had got what she had asked Santa Claus to bring her; a doll's cot. It was painted pale blue. It stayed in the recess by the fireplace for years after. Mammy showed me how to put the side up and down, but I could not think why our Spadger played for hours tidying the covers for her doll Jean, and Rough her dog. Daddy told us that this boring doll's cot and my dolls' house were both made by a man who could not use his legs any more.

Then at long last I found the very best of all toys. Daddy and Mammy had forgotten all about it. Beside the dolls' house on the table, there was a set of garden furniture. This on its own became my daydream toy. It was just the right size to fit into the dolls' house, so sometimes I put it in the kitchen, but in through the big back wall. Because the toy was made of lead, the little things were heavy enough not to move at my fingertip touch. There was a round red table with a sunshade umbrella and four yellow wickerwork chairs, just the same shape as Mammy's, upstairs in the front bedroom. But I could feel that the weave was not the same pattern. The table was set for a tea party, with four tiny green cups stuck to their saucers, and plates, and four painted leaden children sat up to the table.

To get an idea what they looked like, I had to put them right up close to my face. There were two girls wearing frocks. One was yellow, the other was pink. There were two boys wearing short trousers and summer shirts. One was in dark blue and the other in bright green. They were so well made, that I could feel the shape of the children's bodies through their clothes. Each tiny doll had dark hair and wore white ankle socks with shiny black shoes.

After their tea party, the children were just as comfy sitting on their three piece suite round their fireside. Mammy had not thought of that. This toy was made so small that what I could not see, I could but feel. It was made so lovingly, that what I could not feel, I could but imagine, and with a toy such as this, a child has not so very far to go to be free.

ACROSS THE ROAD

All the mams and dads had had a chat about it. They thought that kids were sensible these days, and they weren't half as much trouble as they used to be. Now the big ones were old enough to look after the little ones, and the little ones knew not to run straight across the road, so my mammy told me, now that I was getting a bit bigger, I could go with the other little kids when they went across the road in front of the houses to play with the big kids. There were good times to come.

THE GARAGE

Straight across the road from our house stood the garage. In front of it stood a row of dark blue petrol pumps on a raised area. The edge of it was always kept beautifully white, so I never tripped up that step. When I heard motors coming, I could go and stand on there, then I knew I would be safe, and not get run over. I often stood there at the garage, waiting for motors to come along. I enjoyed talking to the drivers, and they were always kind and talked to me. Mammy said, "They might think you belong t'garage, an' they 'ave to do."

Some days the garage man would say, "When a motor comes along, say 'sorry, we have no petrol today,'" so I would, and the motors would pass on by. But now and then the garage man would come running out to 'fill 'em up wi' watter.' That is what he said when I asked him about it, but I could hear the smile in his voice, and my nose told a different tale, which I kept to myself.

THINGS ARE LOOKING UP

I was in our house and I could hear the kids running up and down outside, shouting. They were selling torches with batteries in the garage.

"Boy oh boy! Things *are* looking up!" said Mammy. She told me and our Spadger that it had not been any use to buy us a torch without batteries before, but now she counted out enough coppers that she had been saving in her purse for a day just like this, and we all went together across the road to join the queue outside the garage.

All the kids who had bought torches were playing outside with them. It was a very dull day and I could not see my torch light up when it was switched on. Mammy told me that I would when it was dark. So after dinner when it was dark in our lavatory, I switched on my torch, but still I could not see it shining. I thought, *I am shining it at the door, and the door's dark. If I shine it at the wall, I should be able to see a bright spot on the whitewash.* Because in Granddad's lavatory, I could see a bright spot from his torch, and his wall was green. But it was still black in our lavatory. Then I looked straight at the bulb. The kids said that you should not do that, but there was no light at all.

Later it was found out that our Spadger had used up the batteries in her torch and mine as well. Because the torches were both green, Mammy had not noticed her taking mine outside to play with. Spadger had taken my torch to play with a kiddie who had no money to buy a torch with.

But as our neighbour over the wall said to me, the torches were only toys, not made to last, and her little one didn't have a torch either.

FIRE FIRE

Once, when a lorry came to the garage, my little friend, who was standing there with me, calmly told me that there were flames coming out from underneath it at the back. He told the driver, who sounded very grumpy. He thought my little friend was playing a trick on him.

But my little friend's voice was not tricking me. I shouted, "Fire! Fire! Fire! Fire!" till the garage man came running out. But I thought there would be trouble for us both if my little friend had been tricking.

The lorry driver was shouting at the garage man. The garage man was shouting back at the lorry driver to go away, and for more of his own men to come and help him. The lorry was shooed off down the side street, followed by the men running after it. When the fire had been put out, we were both highly praised by the garage man. His voice was so upset, that I thought we were going to get a telling-off. He told us how a fire can be a very bad thing, how we had both done the right thing, and if we ever saw another fire, we were to do the same again.

He made us feel very good on the inside.

THE GIFT

Sometimes from inside the garage came a hollow ringing, like an old clock striking. It drew me to the garage doorway, but I would not go inside, because in my mind I could see the floor. It was like our garret floor, covered with tools laid out in their places. I might trip over them. There may be precious things that I might break, or dangerous things that I might hurt myself on. So I would just stand in the doorway and get soaked in the sounds. But the other kids went in, but not me.

These sounds I heard stayed inside the garage. I could not hear them from the outside. They were great metallic sounds like falling and flinging. They rose to the roof space like steam, breaking into bits, and coming tumbling down, sliding down the walls, curling themselves up in every corner.

I had no notion what made these sounds. I had no picture inside my head of mechanics and motors. It was the sounds like solid things that I saw with my ears. But not with my ears only. This grand show was put on for me alone to go and see. The sounds turned over like tablecloths, and faded on the wrong side, weaving with new sounds coming upwards, bouncing on the floor, then threading through more new sounds, mixing together, making more new sounds. And I was part of the pattern, receiving, reflecting.

I would search back in my mind for a question to this answer that I had found. The question had no words to tell of this glorious gift that only I had been granted. Steadily, the last sound would roll itself up and rest in a corner. I could not see it there, but I knew it would still be there.

And now it was the sparrows' turn to flutter their wings and chirrup in the roof space and the road outside would be quietly about its business, as before.

PENNY HEN

The paper shop was next to the garage, but you had to cross the little road to get to it, the road where the burning lorry had been shooed down. But the paper shop was not for me. It sold old comics very cheaply. The kids would keep a keen eye on the windows.

One morning I was at home with Mammy when our Spadger came running in from playing. She must get a threepenny bit out of her purse. The paper shop had had some farm animals come in, and they were selling out fast.

She was soon back with the one she had chosen. Mammy made her show it to me. It was quite a big animal, a light brown animal. I did not know what it was, but I wanted one like that. So Mammy sent our Spadger back across the road to buy one for me. She was soon back with a hen, a very little hen. Spadger was upset. "It was all they had left," she said.

The little hen's legs were hidden in its clump of grass. Its comb and its wattles were much too small for me to find. Mammy thought it was not worth the threepence we had paid for it. So she took me with her to the paper shop, and after some haggling, I was charged only one penny for my little hen.

SEWER PIPES

We were all playing across the road on the wasteland down by the Drill Hall. Some pipes had been put there, ready for laying the sewers. The big kids were on the fat pipes, but they would not let us little ones climb on them. We were sent to play on the thin pipes, but we joined in their game of walking along, trying to keep our balance. Then my little friend told me that the big kids were going through their pipes and coming out at the other end. So we thought, *we'll do that.*

He crawled in first, and I got down on my tummy and went in after him, pulling myself along with my arms. But as I squirmed further, my clothes got tighter and tighter, pulling on my shoulders and round my neck. Then my little friend got frightened of the dark. He was shouting for me to go back. So I tried, but I could not go back. I was stuck. But he came back, crying and kicking my head, and he had made the pipe wet on the inside.

My ears were ringing. The big kids were shouting up both ends of the pipe at the same time. It sounded so loud and horrible. Now we were both frightened. I felt myself rolling over, but we were still stuck in the pipe.

Then I could hear mesters talking about why they could not break the pipe with a hammer. Then we were turned about, tipped upside down, shook and jerked about all ways. I felt myself spinning into space.

When I opened my eyes, I was lying on the ground, so close to my little friend; I could see his white face. *Is he dead?* I thought, and fell back to sleep. I woke up again with the little one shouting me. He said he had woke up before, and thought I were dead.

I could hear the mesters talking. They were saying they had put us close together so that we might not be frightened when we came to. They sounded very worried about us, not knowing what to do for the best. Then they were saying there must be a patrol kept over the sewer pipes. The mesters must take turns to keep a guard over them, because you could not keep kids in. But the kids could all go in for tonight and tomorrow the mesters would see the council.

Joan Vardy

THE STEAMROLLER

On the morning the steamroller came to spread tar for the new road, my little friend and I stood at the garage to watch. The steamroller went forwards and back again, over and over on the same piece, before moving on to the next piece.

My little friend showed me some plasticine he had been given, with a promise of a big ball of plasticine for throwing this little bit in front of the steamroller, just at the right time, when he could not be seen by the steamroller mester. The steamroller rumbled towards us, crackling on the road. It stopped with a crunch in front of us, before rolling back again. And then I saw the plasticine. It was stuck on the roller, looking like a giant golden dandelion, bigger than me.

We both gasped. Then my little friend, knowing how naughty he had been, shouted to tell the driver. The driver sounded very pleased about it, saying how glad he was that the little boy had told him, because if he had rolled forward again, the plasticine would have been stuck on the road. Then the whole lot would have needed doing again.

It took a long time to scrape off the dandelion, and as the morning rolled on, folk did not sound so pleased. My little friend said he would have shared a big ball of plasticine with me, but he had been tricked. The big kids now said that they had not had any plasticine. They said they had never had any plasticine at all.

Somebody was sent to the paper shop, to see who had bought plasticine, and he was not pleased. He said that he had never had any plasticine to sell either. My little friend wished he had been glad with the little bit of plasticine he had been given.

The garage owner got grumpy. What with that steamroller stuck there, and state o't'road, he had not had one customer all morning. My little friend's mammy had been keen to get t'little beggar out of t'road for a bit. Now she was telling the steamroller driver, she knew it were her kid what 'ad done it, but it weren't 'is plasticine. Where did folk think that she could get money from for plasticine, wi' all her kids to feed?

Then the steamroller boiler went out, and it was her who had to find sticks to relight it. Then the steamroller needed water. "It had better be boiling," said the driver. Boiling kettles came from everywhere abouts.

After the last dandelion petal had been scraped away, the stony road was covered with smooth tar. Cartwheels stopped spitting, buses stopped bumping, motors moved faster, and there were more and more of them.

On rainy days, kids could watch rainbows of petrol on the new road, and young men on motorbikes would take the corner too quickly and skid on this new road. And with our house being the first aid post, it was not long before a young rider was helped in.

He had had his ear ripped off and a big bundle of old sheets was held tightly to his head while he waited to be taken to the hospital.

WHITSUNTIDE WALK ROUND

There was something coming up, I could tell that, but I did

not know what it was they were all talking about. Folks were too busy these days, and there was no time to do the things that had never not been done before. Footsteps were quicker, and folks had no time to talk, just to ask one or two questions, and they were on their way.

With all this buzz in the air, I wondered why Mammy should try and find time to make new frocks for me and our Spadger. She told me, excitedly, "They're for the walk round."

The material was light green satin, but it was not easy to make up, Mammy said, as every pin she put in and every tacking stitch she made, left its mark. Our Spadger's frock was not too much trouble, though, because she was more grown up now.

I was not old enough to wear a frock with a waist, so mine had smocking on my chest. Mammy gathered up the material and hand embroidered rows of pretty patterns. As each row was worked, she let me feel the different stitches with different diamonds and different satin tucks she had made, and she told me about the different colours she had put into it. It took her hours, but she enjoyed doing it.

Then there was the standing still for the fitting. The satin was shiny and thin. It felt cold and sounded crispy. Then Mammy showed me the buttons she had chosen. They were not a perfect match, she said, but she wondered if I liked them, and if I did, it would be all right. The buttons were very fancy, like inside-out shamrock leaves.

On the morning of the big day, the kids went round in their new clothes knocking on doors for a few coppers. At first we all went round together, but then we split up. Our Spadger went miles with a friend, and when they got back, they shared up their money. She had the little silver pennies, and her friend had the big brown ones.

I went around on my own, and kept going back to Mammy

in our kitchen with my few coppers, and she put them up on the mantelpiece. When a little lad came to our house, he was invited in. I saw him standing up straight with his arms down by his side, and his feet together. He was given a few coppers. I heard Mammy telling Daddy how he had not got any new clothes, but somebody had put a bit of polish on his shoes and he was so proud. She had just had to give him a copper or two.

I was proud wearing my new frock and Mammy could understand how I did not want to spoil it by eating dinner. So she gave me a little something which she thought would not make a mess.

The Sunday school teachers had said that any child who wanted to walk round could do, whether or not they attended Sunday school. They wanted to see lots of children walking round. I thought I had already walked round, but I was wrong.

There was so much going off, and everybody seemed very happy, so I calmed my wobbles and went along with Mammy and the other kids to the start of the walk. Mammy lifted me over a rope, and stood me in the road. That surprised me. Then she put my hand on the rope, near a rose that had been tied on with ribbon bows. She told me I must keep holding on and follow the kiddie in front. But I was not the only kid who was not too happy about this walk. We did not keep the rope tight, and we all bunched up together. With the sun shining so brightly, I could not see the kiddie in front of me.

Then they put some bigger, Sunday school scholars in amongst the little kids to keep the rope tight, and we set off again. We all soon got the hang of it. The Sunday school scholars were singing hymns and the folks on the courseys were clapping.

When we got up to the Co-op stores, my mammy was standing there with the other mammies and daddies. She picked me up, and lifted me over the rope, and stood me on the coursey. I was not happy about it. She told the woman next to her that she was not going to let her kid get the shoes ruined in the melted tar. It should have been the adults who stood in the road. They could look out for the tar, and the kiddies should have walked on the coursey.

But my mammy need not have worried. Because of the tar, the walk was broken up. It was agreed that we had walked quite a long way, and the smaller ones must be getting tired by now.

WVS

Mammy gave me some Smarties. She had told me she would when she could, but for so long and so many times, I did not raise my hopes about it. She sent me out of the front door, saying, "Give a few to each of the kids, then they might let you play."

I had never had Smarties before. They were in a white bag, a proper bag with two corners. I picked up a few, and dropped them in ones and twos. They felt smooth and round, sounding like little pebbles. Each kid took a few of my tuffees, and I went with them up the road.

We were being taken to be shown a house. It seemed a long way to go, but we were kept going by being told stories about it. When we stopped, I could not see the house, just the steps going up between two walls, with black hedges growing over them. It was said that if anybody was to go up into the garden, no matter how quiet they were, the woman would hear the slightest sound, and come out and catch them.

The stories had been about what had happened to some kids, so who would dare to go. The other kids fled in fright. *Just fairy tales,* I told myself. I climbed the steps up to the top and sat for a while with my back against the door, dipping into my bag of pebbles. I had forgotten what Mammy called them, and kept trying to say the name, but it did not sound quite right. So what? Nothing had happened yet.

On both sides the garden was level with the top step behind the hedge. I could sit there and feel the ground. It was weedy, stony and dry. And behind that black hedge in the garden, the sounds of the world outside were softened. The wind was calmed to an unhurried breeze for the unworried weeds to wave in. This was a garden of another kind, where time and troubles made space for thoughts to grow and fears to fade.

Slowly and gently I felt the door ease itself away from my back. There stood the woman, with 'a lot of barge', as Daddy might say, on the boil, then boiling over, airing her thoughts to the morning, not me, steaming about always having to send the kids off. Her voice sounded so high above me, even higher than where I had imagined the top of the doorway should be. As she simmered down, she drew in her breath, so I had my say.

I told her that it should make her happy to have a garden all of her own. She ought to spend more time in it, and take more care of it.

The woman soon changed her tune, as Daddy might say. Then she sounded much lower down, as she explained to me how things were, not speaking to me as most adults did, in too babyish or too grown-up a way, too sweet or too sour a tone. It was what with the Master being away, some of the weeds were flowers once when he was at home. She wondered what he would say when he saw them. Everybody was doing their best, she told me, and when he came home, the Master would have to learn that.

Then there was her boys. She gulped and swallowed. The war had been so very bad and children had not been told. It had been kept from them and that was right, but children should learn that everybody was doing their best, but you could not always tell that they were.

It was her WVS work that took all her time, and tired her. The woman knew that my mammy was doing her best for me, because she did not have to keep me. I could be put away. She said, "I can tell she does love you and cares for you, or she would not give you sweets. So stay and eat them."

The door closed with no more sound than a puff of air, scented with lavender and metal polish. Now that I had been told to finish my tuffees, I would not have to give any more to the kids. So I sat there on the step, dipping into my bag of pebbles, till they bounced about in my tummy.

Alone in the road, a long way from home, it seemed I was locked out of the world. The wind blew cold. I turned my back on it, just hoping that that would be the right way to go. A woman passing by told me to keep going, but it would take me a long long time. "But you will know when you're getting towards home," she told me. A long long time was what I needed to store away in my mind the truths I had learned that morning.

By the time I had got home, I had things all sorted, but for one thing I needed to ask Mammy. She said, "I don't know where you get them from," coaxing the fire with the poker. "A W vest is for a woman to wear. Your daddy has large vests. You can tell it's a large one because of the ticket in the back. It says so." Because of the war time, my vests were utility.

I had seen the big utility mark on my mammy's mattress,

so I knew what the one in the back of my vest looked like. It was just two little eyes staring at the back of my neck. This was going to be a long story. I went round to the settee to sit down and listen, till Mammy got round to answering my question.

She knew a lot, my mammy did. She knew more about vests than I thought there could be to know about them, and that was not half what she knew about utility marks. Whenever I asked a question of Mammy, even when it was not the question I thought I had asked, I had to listen to the end for an answer. I caught odd words that Mammy said, odd phrases, and even Winnie and the Cabinet got a mention, but not the woman with the unloved garden.

Mammy put the kettle on to boil. It seemed there would be no end to what she knew about vests. So fancy her saying, "I don't know where you get them from."

THE JEWELLER'S SHOP

There were two lockup shops at the end of our row. One was the barber's shop, and the other was the jeweller's shop. Before the war, when my mammy's sister had bought her wedding ring from the jeweller's shop, she was given a carving knife for a present, so my mammy went there for her wedding rings too. She wore two wedding rings. Then the jeweller gave her six egg spoons from out of the window, but they soon turned blue. Mammy supposed he could not sell them, "And that was something to do with the war, I should think," she said.

Now every day my mammy made tea for the jeweller, and

our neighbour from over the wall complained. "What were you givin' 'im all that tea? I 'ave to keep cleaning my lavvy out. No norrafter 'im, after them there kids o' mine before he can use it." Their lav was the two-holer.

The jeweller would bring his teapot round to our house, and Mammy would put it to warm while the kettle boiled, and they would talk, not just about the weather. They would discuss and debate, and I was thought too small to grasp their meaning, but I listened and learned about the war, about how people were kept awake in rooms where the lights were never switched off. And more - of kings and ministers, countries and cultures.

My mammy had always been clever at school, and ever since, she had learned new words in the dictionary at breakfast every morning, and she would use them during the day. I have never heard her talk to anybody as she would talk with the jeweller then. The kettle would impatiently rattle its lid, and spit at the fire, but it would have to wait till the talking was over. Yet Mammy said she did not want anybody to talk when there was nothing to talk about.

So it became my job to go to the jeweller's shop to fetch the teapot. The shop door was not on the end, like the barber's. It was on our side of the road, just after our neighbour over the wall. Inside, the shop was almost dark, but for one small patch of light I could see by the window, where the jeweller worked. From there I would hear a low grunt of welcome.

All my memories now are mingled into one memory. I stood there, happy to wait while the jeweller finished his job. I had my reason for being early. There were clocks to listen to on the shelves all around me. I could see each one with my ears, and see them all at the same time, because you do not need to turn your head to see with your ears. I was wrapped up in their ticking and carried away to seventh heaven.

I homed in on the clocks one by one. I noticed how each one was on his way to recovery. There were wheezing, climbing up the hill clocks, lame clocks with one stride longer than another, cross-patch clocks stamping their feet, and marching on the spot clocks. They seemed to be getting nowhere. There were whispering clocks, telling secrets as they ran on, out of step, lady clocks with all the time in the world to chitchat and tittle-tattle.

Then a jangling alarm of clocks shattered the peace to remind all the clocks that if they could, it was now time to sound the hour, each clock waiting its turn, so as to be heard without being interrupted, to shout or sing in agreement. Then, for a second or two, after the last chime had died away, their ticking tocking shushed while they all got their breath back, and the other clocks waited for them to catch up; except for the tiny watches, having no time to waste at all, with just a slight pitter-patter, pitter-patter, they went running along.

I knew I should jump when the jeweller scraped his chair on the wooden floor. His job always lasted long enough for me to share his love with him. He came over and put his teapot on the counter. Its lid fidgeted. Then, holding a warm pocket watch to my ear, the jeweller said, "Now, you listen to this." The watch tiptoed softly, just wearing its socks.

The jeweller said, "People think that this watch is beautiful on the outside, but you and I, we know where the real beauty lies." I asked about some of the poorly clocks. As they were mending, they were moved along the shelves. Then they sounded stronger, so I had to listen hard to those I knew, but even in the darkened shop, I could find them and point them out, as ears need no light to see.

"Oh," he said. "There's not much wrong with that one now, but if you could have known the gent that owns it, you'd be proud."

Another clock seemed to fall in step with it, so I asked, "Is that one a gentleman's clock, too?"

"No, now that one belongs to a lady," he said. It sounded just like the gent's clock. I did wish that I could get things right for people who gave up their time for me.

"Yes," said the jeweller. "I thought it was a strange clock for a lady, but she has a care for it and that one next to her. That one's missing a part, and I can't get one while... and that one there. There's nothing wrong with that one at all now. Its house has been locked up. It's come to stay, just for a while."

I pointed to another, sounding old and tired clock. The jeweller sighed.

"He was brought in to be mended before the war, and his master won't be coming back for him." He sighed again. "Do with him? Why, I'll wind the little feller up of a Tuesday night. Why? Well, his master always went out of a Tuesday night, and I'm sure he wouldn't think of going without giving the little feller a wind first, so as he could keep going till he got back home to his fireside."

It was time for me to stop asking questions. I could just pick out the shine of his little teapot to reach up for it. I would carry the teapot home by its handle and spout, so as not to spoil its roses that Mammy had told me about. She thought that maybe the teapot had been the jeweller's grandmother's, and had a place in his heart, what with all that fancy work and roses on it, she told me. All the more beautiful the little teapot was for me, for having, now I was not sure, was that invisible, or silent roses?

My mammy would put the little teapot to warm, while our kettle came to boil. Soon the jeweller would come to collect it, to take it back to his shop. They would be talking, I would be listening. The tea would be made and stewed, and gone cold, and still they would be talking, till Mammy might offer, "Shall

I make you a fresh pot?"

AROUND THE STREETS

The kids were always playing out on the streets. On the first street up from us, my great-aunt kept the shop on the corner. It had a lovely tinkly bell. This street was a through street, from the main road at the front of the houses, to the main road at the back of the houses. There were some streets that led off of this street, but they were much of a muddle to me.

There was one game played on this street that I was always allowed to join in. It was not the same as any other game the kids played. A group of them would be playing at each end of the street, while some other kids with notes from their dads, went to one of the houses. But when one of the kids playing at the end of the street caught sight of a bobby coming up or down either of the roads, a hooting call was sounded, which was taken up by all the kids to sound like just part of the game.

I would be playing with the little one, halfway up the street, and on hearing a hooting call, those kids with the little slips of paper, now tucked away safely in their pockets – you had to have pockets if you were one of the ones that needed the slips of paper – they would come running towards us and play with us in the game that we liked to play the best; a ring a ring of roses.

The cobbler's shop was somewhere in the muddle of the streets. He sometimes had leather for sale in his window. My mammy would ponder for a long time, making her mind up whether or not it might be the right thickness for Daddy to mend shoes with.

Once when me and our Spadger had some new shoes out of our twenty-week club, Mammy took out the laces, because they were black and the shoes were red. She sent me and our Spadger up to the cobbler's, wearing the new shoes. It was hard to keep them on without any laces in them. But Mammy thought it might be worth it to try. "You never know, he might have some red laces, and he might sell them me," she hoped.

The cobbler said, "What's so special about you two? You can't use string like everybody else?" So we had to use string, like everybody else to hide the big fib that had been told, that the shoes had been sold to Mammy without laces. The black laces were put in for Sunday best.

One sunny morning, I was standing by myself, gazing over at the sandy island. It was near the jeweller's shop window. Just there was a big black pram. So shiny it was, just like a funeral car. I knew my mammy loved a good funeral, so surely, I thought, she would not like to miss seeing a pram as grand as this one. So I ran back home to fetch her, but she was too busy to come.

But she was worried about the baby, left by a young mother, she expected. The pram would be on a slope there, and could roll down onto the road. So I was sent back to mind it. I was glad to stand and stare, supposing that much black lead and elbow grease had been used to make it shine brighter than our fireplace.

When the lady came out of the jeweller's shop, I politely told her what my mammy had said. She sounded quite upset, and asked me to thank my mother. She had not realised the danger, and said she would not leave her pram there again, and she searched through her purse and found a penny for me.

Another morning, all of us kids were sent out to play, and

some of us had not been given any breakfast and were hungry. This was a good chance for me to get in favour with the kids, I thought. So I did not let it pass by, and I was so pleased with myself when they let me lead them all the way up to my daddy's allotment garden. I did not knowingly look out for landmarks on the way, picking up clues of sounds or senses. I used another sense. If it felt right inside me, my feet followed my heart.

We went through the garden gate and I shut it properly behind me, like Daddy always did. I stood all the kids in a line along the path. Then I brought fruit and vegetables to them. I picked ripe tomatoes and runner beans, without breaking any plants down. I felt along the rows of carrots, finding those big enough to eat, and washing them in the water butt. None of the kids' dads dug an allotment garden. They did not know anything. I even had to show them how to pop a pod of peas. I gathered gooseberries by stroking under the branches towards me, letting only the ripe fruits fall into my hands, filling the kids' pockets for the journey home.

On the way home, there was one feeling lost and wanting mam, but it was not me. My mammy was happy to see me. She said she never would have believed that I could find my way to the garden like that, or that I could have learnt so much about gardening. She joked, "I should send you to pick the peas for our dinner, but you're not old enough yet, so I can't."

That night, Daddy got hot and bothered, and he went straight away to check things, but he would not take me with him. When he came back, he could not believe it. All those kids on his garden, yet nothing had been broken down! And he knew the gate catch was awkward, and even that was closed properly.

On Sunday mornings and Wednesday evenings, the cadets would march along our road and around the sandy island.

Their beating drums and squeaky bugle calls would call me to the kerbside, to sit there with my little friend. We would watch and listen as they passed by. For me their khaki uniforms merged into the background and were lost. So their flashing white gaiters was all that I could see. Their drum rolls were more than enough to satisfy me. I felt my heart beat hard, and even tears filled my eyes as I followed them with my ears into the distance. How I wished that I had been born a boy, and that the war had lasted long enough for me to join the Boys' Brigade.

Mammy did not like to hear me saying that. She told me that if I was a cadet, I would have to scrub my gaiters. I told Mammy I would scrub them. I would scrub them really hard. She said that I was a good girl. All of us kids marched around the streets.

That was the day the rod man came to our house. It was when our lavatory got blocked up. To pull our lavatory chain, I had to stand on the rim, hold on to the pipe with one hand to balance myself, while I pulled the chain with the other. For a while, the water had been coming up to the top of the bowl and going down again. But one morning it came up and up and over, just like a fountain. Mammy did laugh to find me at the top of the pipe, clinging on to the cistern.

That morning the rod man came, all the kids were on our yard. He lifted up the cover of the grate and pushed his rods down into it. He said that only when folk had pan lavs we used newspaper. Now the sewers had been put in, and we should all be using tissues. So he gave Mammy a packet of stiff strong-smelling squares.

"I wouldn't use that on my skin!" she said.

All the kids went home to fetch a comb. We wrapped the paper squares around the combs and we marched around the streets in our comb and paper band, blowing till the paper was soggy, and our mouths tingling and sore.

"There, I knew it!" said Mammy.

THE FORM AND THE FEAST

For just 6d, the chip shop's form could be borrowed for dos, so my mammy asked for it for the summer feast, when aunties and uncles and cousins to me unknown, unnamed, unnumbered, would come and fill our house, overflowing onto the windowsill and the back yard.

The form had been borrowed for a kiddies' birthday party the week before, and had been taken back to the chip shop stuck up with jam. So Mammy had to promise to scrub it before taking it back. She did, and she scrubbed it before our do on our back yard, because when it came it was covered in chip grease.

When families had a get-together, it was the custom for adults to eat their tea before the children, but my mammy said she did not want kids hanging round her while she ate her tea. So she gave us our tea first, so then we could be sent out to play, while the adults could sit down to their tea in peace and not be hurried. One auntie thought there would be nothing left for them, but Mammy told her that there was plenty of food left in the pantry.

So as to keep the form clean, the home-made jam tarts were on the back kitchen table. The huge meat plate had been brought down from the garret to hold them all, and it was full to the brim. We each took one jam tart on our way out to play, but we kept popping back in to sneak another and another, until the plate was clean, but for crumbs. Mammy did not mind, but one auntie did.

That evening we all went to the † wakes on the Lammas. That was something new for me. The kids got excited about going on the helter-skelter, but Mammy thought I would not manage it, so Daddy took me to put pennies in a box and pull a handle, and he got excited about that too. Mammy did think that I would manage to go on what she called, 'the big 'osses.' I was lifted on, and showed how to hold on to a pole. I had no idea that I sat astride a wooden horse, or that it would go round and round and up and down.

That evening the sun was setting a gorgeous golden red, but I did not know it was the sun. I had never seen a sunset like that before. I thought it was a light, flashing on and off. I did not know that it was me going round and round. I called out for Mammy, "Put it out, put it out," and there was a great noise that kept coming up to me, and just when I thought it would grab hold of me, if kept going away again.

Everybody was especially kind to me that evening, but I could sense their despair, what with that setting sun stinging my eyes, and the uneven field under my feet upsetting my balance, and the relentless din of the fairground all around me. People were shouting, but I could not know what they were telling me. So I was even frightened by the candy floss that stuck to my face and got in my hair.

I fear I dampened that feast for the whole family.

† wakes – the fair

BUS RIDING

There was a big change in my life. It was because of the peace. Now anybody could ride on a bus at any time. In fact there were new changes every day, and I was getting more and more mixed up. Some things which I had been so strictly taught, now I could just forget about; yet other things stayed the same.

The weekly routine of washing day and black lead day, with clean clothes for kids on Sundays, was the same, but nobody had time to listen what the kids had to say any more. Yet anybody could send a kid to run an errand for them, to anywhere, at any time, for anything. Kids would run errands just for a few coppers, but I was rarely sent, so I did not have the extra coppers to spend on the new things coming in the shops. Mammy had always sent me on little errands for her, but she never gave any coppers away. Nowadays, it seems that errands were made up, just to get the kids out of the house for a while.

There were things that we had managed quite well without before, but now it seemed we must have them. The blackout had been ditched, Mammy said, but my gas mask, which I would not part with, now lived in the wickerwork chair in the corner of our bedroom, and was not allowed on my bedpost.

The S for shelter sign still stayed up. Tuffee papers, fag packets still filled the gutters. I was told, "Men have better work to do these days."

If folks were lost in the street, now we could tell them where they were and the best way to get to where they were going to. We could tell folk when the bus was coming, and where it could take them. What's more, we could even have a ride on the bus ourselves, and that was the biggest change in my life so far.

So sometimes on Thursday afternoons, while Daddy was at work and our Spadger still at school, Mammy and I could go for a bus ride to see Mamam and Granddad.

On the first day at the bus stop, my tummy churned around and around. I could feel the fear growing inside me as I waited. When the bus came, I was still so small, I had to be lifted up on to the platform, and again up the step to get inside the bus, but before we had found a seat, the conductor had rung his bell and the bus started up. It did not stay still under my feet like the coursey had. It swayed and bounced down the hill, making my legs wobbly. I had to hold tightly to Mammy. I could not see anything else to hold on to.

At the front of the bus they had a heater, like a big riddle hanging up on the wall. We had one hanging up in our coalhouse. Daddy used it for riddling the coal with, when it was more slag than lumps. On a cold day, Mammy would find us a seat as near to the front of the bus as she could, and on the kerbside. That was out of the draught of the open platform at the back.

Some journeys, before the bus could start, the driver would jump down from his cab and climb up onto the bus engine. If we sat on the front seat, I could see him as a dark shape. I did not need to ask why he did this. I thought I knew why, and the reason was that the bus was a clockwork bus, and it had to be wound up. I could hear the key being turned and it sounded just like my toy clockwork motorbike that I had but would not play with.

The bus was usually quite full, and I would have to sit on Mammy's knee. If she sat near the window, I could see the daylight, but if she sat next to the aisle, all I could see then was coats of the passengers standing up beside me.

But there was plenty for me to listen out for. The conductor calling: "Any more fares?" as he squeezed past the passengers standing in the bus. There was the ding ding of his ticket machine. Everybody had to have their pennies ready to buy their tickets, and they had to hold their tickets out to be seen by the conductor.

I should have loved a ticket. They were all different colours for different prices. Folk threw them down. I should not have thrown mine down. I was told that I could not have a ticket, because I was not five years old. But when I was five years old, it seemed there was a shortage, and I would have to be quiet, or the conductor might not let me ride on the bus.

The biggest change of this new peace was on the inside of the grown-ups. The bus bell was helpful. It told me when the bus was about to stop or start. Then I knew to hold on tightly to something or other.

Along the route, the conductor would call out the names of the stops, and I learned that the bus would turn at the cross, slowly chug up the hill, and, at Station Street, it would jolt us over the railway lines. The level crossing gates would often be closed. Then we would have to wait a very long time, so the driver would switch off his engine, and the bus would be still. Then the passengers would talk quieter, or everybody on the bus would hear what they were saying. They always sounded pleased when they could hear the train coming. But it might be a trucker. Those trains could not have gone any slower without stopping, Mammy said. She could lose count of the coal trucks, there were so many of them. The trains were so long, the trucks would grumble, clink clonk, clink clonk, and there would always be one truck out of step. He sounded like loose or unoiled chains clanking. I could hear a train long after it had gone past. We might be held up at the crossing for another train after that one, a train that stopped at the station, with slamming doors and a shrill whistle. Then a quiet pause; with sighs of relief from the passengers as the level crossing gates were being opened again by a man. Then the bus would shake itself, ready to go.

At the next stop, the Nag's Head, I would be lifted down onto the coursey, sometimes by the conductor, with my legs still wobbly. On that first day, Mammy told Daddy about it when we got back home. He said I must have been on edge all the time I was on the bus, and perhaps it was not good for me. It had tired me out, but he said I would have to get used to it.

One afternoon, when we were going to Mamam's and Granddad's on the bus, there was room for me to sit beside Mammy on the seat. The seat was made of wooden slats and it struck cold to me as I sat down, and I knew why. Before coming out, I had had a little mishap, which had been forgotten about. So I told Mammy, but she was not listening. So I told her again in a loud clear voice, "I 'ent got no britches on."

But Mammy still did not hear me. She gazed out of the window, muttering to herself, "Kids. Who'd 'ave 'em?"

Now, on Sunday evenings, we could go home on the bus from Mamam's and Granddad's. If it was dark, the windows would just look black to me and all I could see inside the bus was the lights. So I could not help but look up at them, even when I had been told not to do it. There was nothing else to do but sit on Mammy's knee while she chatted. She seemed to know every passenger on the bus. I noticed that if there were mesters who were drunk, Mammy would always be very nice to them. She said, "It's best to keep them sweet."

One night trouble broke out, and the conductor rang his bell four times. I think the conductor would ring his bell one to stop, two to start, three when the bus was full up, and four to go straight to the police station. So this night the bus went straight there, at great speed, and Mammy said that any passengers who were not too pleased about being taken past their stop kept quiet about it. She said that anybody who was not quiet would be helped off the bus by the policeman, and straight into the police station.

THE STOWAWAYS

On Saturday evenings we might all go a ride on the bus to see Auntie. Then my daddy would let me travel under the stairs in the luggage space. As soon as he lifted me up onto the platform, I would dash under the stairs with other kids, while the conductor was too busy counting passengers going up the stairs and inside the bus. He did not notice stowaways. That way, we might all get on the bus before the conductor called, "Move down the bus, please! Room for one inside. One more on top."

I had some good bus rides under the stairs. The fun of hearing noisy shoes climbing up and down, just above my head and being in the dark made me and the kids the same, just for a while.

The jumping, jerking bus was all part of our games. On one journey to Auntie's we were held captive, bound hand and foot on a let's pretend voyage to be sold as slaves. At one bus stop a gentleman with a huge suitcase got on. The bus moved off and he bought his ticket, but he had to stand on the platform to stop the big case from falling off the bus. But at the next stop there was no space for a passenger to get by it to get off the bus. So the conductor wanted to put the case as far under the stairs as he could.

He called to us, "Come out." There were more than five of us. We clambered over the suitcase. The conductor had not realised just how many children could fit under the stairs, and now there were too many passengers on the bus, and somebody would have to get off, he said.

He rang his bell. The bus stopped at once.

"I've paid my fare!" said the gentleman.

"I can't put the children off the bus," said the conductor.

There was quite a to-do. It seemed that nobody on the bus had a child, or if they did, they could not recall bringing it on the bus with them. Nobody could be persuaded to come and collect a child, and get off the bus with it. So each one of us was lifted down and stood in a row near a steep grass verge in the muddy gutter with rain pouring down.

The conductor got the suitcase partway under the stairs, then he got each one of us back onto the platform.

"You'll all have to go back under," he said, and each one of us was helped to climb over the suitcase into the gap behind it. I saw the little lad before me, lifted by his coat collar and the seat of his trousers, to be scuttled over the case. I tried to pull myself up over it, and my legs were lifted up behind me like wheelbarrow handles. Turning head over heels, I landed on a wriggling, giggling double-decker heap.

The gentleman was worried about the health of his suitcase, but not about the health of the children piled one upon another. Now and then, when the bus stopped, a parent would come and sheepishly recall that he may have a child after all, and may even have brought it on the bus with him.

If a child could not be instantly recognised by an overhanging limb, the conductor would pull us out, one by one, standing us on the platform, till he found one resembling the child required. I was hauled out. The conductor said,

"How about this one? It's got pigtails."

"Mine's a little lad, I think," recalled the parent. Next a little lad was hung up by his coat shoulders. "That one's muddy, "whined the parent.

"They're all muddy," said the conductor. "Won't it do for you?"

At last, a child was claimed. The conductor said it would help if we all knew where we were going. Then he would know which one of us to put back under the first. Most of us were going to aunties, but one, who was going to visit grandpa was upset that he might be on the wrong bus. One little lad began crying when he was not claimed, thinking that his daddy had got off the bus without him.

"Can't say I blame him," said the conductor. Picking the little one up collar and seat fashion, to scuttle him over the suitcase, he said, "You can go in first then, laddie. Don't worry; we'll sort you out at the depot.

We continued the voyage, compelled to row for land to the beat of the big drum on the suitcase.

A CHERUB

Some evenings, we might arrange to meet up with Auntie. She might be waiting at the bus stop for us when we got off. Then my cousins could run through the green fields, and we could talk to horses over gates. I could feel their warm breath from their nostrils. Any one of us might get stones in our shoes, or stung by nettles, and what with all the stopping and starting, we never seemed to get anywhere.

But one evening we were all going down a street. It had long rows of terraced houses on both sides. Auntie had spoken, so we were behaving ourselves, just for once. We were going to visit somebody. We were not going to see the bomb site. Mammy thought that would not be fair. It might hurt somebody's feelings to see everybody going to stare. They might be watching from a house nearby, where they had been taken in by a kind neighbour. But we could slow down a bit. I did not find that very easy, so I had to walk a few steps, then wait for Mammy to catch up. We met a family coming the other way, and they stopped to have a few quiet words.

At the bomb site we did stop. The gap between the two houses in the long terrace made a space for the sad grey sky to come through. I could feel its breath, hear its sighs. My cousins were called off the mound of rubble, and told to put things down. I could hear the broken bits falling as they scrambled back down the heap.

Mammy was looking up. She said, "Ohh! Look at that bedroom wallpaper! I bet she loved that. It dun't look like it 'ad been up long. Roses on it. I bet she paid a bit for it on coupons. Look at the fireplace still hanging there."

I could almost feel the fireplace as she spoke, because we had a little iron fireplace in our bedroom.

"Well, who'd believe it? There's a little ornament on the shelf. It's a cherub," she said.

My other aunties and uncles stood in silence, so it was just guesswork on my part to know how the bomb site had struck them, but by the sound of Mammy's voice, even without knowing all her words, I could pick up every feeling as she switched from one to another.

We all turned and walked slowly back up the street. I felt sickened that I had been made to play a part in all this. They thought it was all right to say nobody had been hurt. My cousin said, "Well, we gorrem back for it!"

Uncle said, "Builder can purrit right, nobody'd know."

One auntie said, "Perhaps, just perhaps we didn't ought to have gone."

I judged the rest of them and found them all guilty. I had learned the realities of war. It was not just gas masks and ration books, the blackout and the roar of the aeroplanes at night. I had seen the house in a crumpled heap, seen it with the gap for the sky to come through, after the bombing and before the birds had learned to sing again. To hear them all talking non-stop, you would think they'd just seen a field full of golden buttercups.

FISHING

The kids were in a huddle outside the leader's house.

"Can we play?" the little one and I asked. They all got in a ring and held a powwow about us, where it was settled that we could play, but only if we dug up worms.

We changed our minds then. We were not going to the chip shop garden again. Then they wanted us to play with them.

"Oh, they won't be any trouble this time," they told us. "The garden behind the air raid shelter belongs to everybody."

Behind the air raid shelter, half-buried in the rough grass, lay a marble slab, which we were told was a grave. Between us all, with much effort, we managed to heave away the slab, and much to my relief, there were no bones under there, just very dark, flat soil.

We were given small tins to put the worms in to save. Seeing no worms, I thought this may be a let's pretend game. That was the best sort of game for me. I could not always tell if games were let's pretend or for real, but at least I was out there, playing with the kids. So I found a stick and poked about happily.

The big kids were talking about going fishing in the afternoon.

"Can we come?" the little one and I begged.

They said to me, "You can't come. You 'aven't dug up any worms. The little one might. But 'e'll 'ave to ask his mam first."

The little one's mam would not let him go fishing. It was too far to the Lawn Park. Then the big kids got busy. There were fishing nets to make and lengths of string were tied around under jam pot lids to make loops for handles for carrying the fish back home.

We were not wanted. The little one put his hand in mine to take me for a walk with him. He had hatched a plan, a big plan, and he wanted me to hear it. So I listened while he spoke.

"This afternoon, we'll follow t'big kids. We'll keep a long way back. If we keep quiet, they won't turn round and see us. When we've gone too far to be brought back 'ome, then we'll shout up, an' they'll 'ave to tek us with 'em. I know it's too far. I'm too little. But you're big, so if I hold your hand and tek you, you can look after me."

What a long speech. What a good plan! I thought, my little friend is growing up and getting clever.

At dinnertime my tummy had bubbles in it. Keeping the secret was hard. So we followed the big kids across the road to go and play at the garage, we told them, but just for a short while. Then we followed on, past the paper shop and the air raid shelter, past the Co-op stores and a row of houses with the little shop, on and on until we reached the Staff of Life public house on the corner of the main road. We stood on the edge of the kerb, and the little one was shaking. He asked me, "Is this far enough not to be took back 'ome again?"

I did not think so. And the big kids did not seem so very far in front of us. I thought we should wait a bit, for them to go further on. I listened to their voices fading as they went down the hill. The little one said, "If we wait any longer, I shan't see them. We'll 'ave to cross the road now. I can't see any motors. Can you hear any?"

I listened hard. "No," I told him.

"Well, then," he judged. "It'll be safe for us. Let's run."

We ran across the road and all the way down the hill to try and catch up with the kids. After we'd gone past the public swimming baths, he yelled to the kids, and they yelled back, "Oh, come on, then!"

We followed them over the market square, down the shopping street, around the corner and over the main road. Then we turned right and went up the hill to where the public library stood. I knew, because I could see the steps.

Once, Mammy had took me up those library steps. There was a lot of them, but at the top she dare not go through the door. She said, "They might not have any books for you, anyway, and you might make a noise, like you do."

Now I thought, if I can come this far, I shall go into the public library one day, all by myself.

We went on, past a church and a school, over roads and by old stone walls, till we came to a narrow gap and through it into the Lawn Park. It did not feel like going in. It felt like coming out. On the park the green grass grew as far as I could see. We walked over it and down the slope.

At last we reached the boating lake. We lay on our bellies, with our hands open under the water, ready to close our fingers on a passing fish. We waited and waited for a tiddler to swim through our fingers. But the big kids were catching fish with their nets and their worms. They saved their tiddlers in the jam pots.

Some older lads were sitting on the banking nearby, and they asked me if I could swim. I did not know that word, 'swim'. They told me to come away from the water or I would be drowned. Then they all went away, except for one who stayed with me, even when his chums called for him to follow them. He would not leave me till I came away from the water's edge.

I'm walking along, and beside me is an old gentleman, using his walking stick. As the hill gets steeper, we turn another way, not the way I had come with the kids earlier. The gentleman leans on his stick. He puts it out in front of him, standing it upright, digging it into the grass to pull himself up a pace or two. He is breathing with great effort. It is not time to ask any questions. I must wait a while. Then I ask him, "Is this a green hill."

The gentleman is smiling in his voice. He says, "It's not much of a hill for a young'un like you, but it is for an old'un like me."

"Will it be all right for us to climb it?" I ask him.

"Oh, yes," he says, "but it is hard going for me, and maybe it is a hill for a very young one."

I ask him if this is *the* green hill that Mammy tells me about. He is pleased, but surprised that I should know about that green hill.

He says, "Aren't you much too young to be asking me all these questions? You'll not be a scholar yet awhile."

At the top of the hill I met a lady. She asked me, "Are you out on your own?"

I tell her, "My chums are fishing for tiddlers, and I've been sent away from the water's edge."

She said, "You'll be safe here, if you stay under the shade of the trees, but if you get lost, just ask for the Red Cross hut. Somebody will show you. Can you see that red cross?" she asked. But I could not even see the Red Cross hut. The lady spoke kindly and told me all about it, and I told her how I was a little first aider. Then she was telling me all about institutions and how one day I would be going there, and how she knew that there I would be well cared for.

I did not know, but all this time we had been waiting in the ice cream queue, and the red cross lady bought me a cornet. She said, "Now when you have finished that one, you go and play for a while. Then you can come back and I will buy you a second ice cream."

I sat in the shade where I knew I would be safe to eat my very first ice cream. There was nobody there to tell me, "Hold it up straight. Lick the cold wet bit at the top. You'll like it, so try it. It's nice." But I could hear my mammy saying, inside my head. Sometimes she said, when I got myself in a bit of a pickle, "You'll have to learn yourself."

All around me I could hear sounds, but I did not listen to them. I had a lot to go over in my mind, sitting on top of the green hill, which the old gentleman had said was not much of a hill really, and it was not *the* green hill, the one I wanted to find, the one with God on the top.

My auntie lived in a long street, with an old dark school on the corner, and on the wall there was a sign that said 'Institute Street'. My granddad went to the institute and he liked it. So would my institute be like the school with the overhanging roof and the soot-blackened stones? Or would I like it, like Granddad did? The Red Cross lady had said that I would be well cared for there.

Later she came to take me to buy a second ice cream. My

tummy was really saying no to a second ice cream. It was not used to such treats, but I was told, "With this heat, you need more ice cream." Two cornets in one afternoon. Now fancy that!

As the sun began to set, the trees did not make any shade for me, so I was hot and unhappy by the time the kids came to go home. They had no money for ice cream cornets, but they hung around hopefully for a while. I asked if I could carry a jam pot, but they snapped, "No, you can't."

I thought: *that's just because I've had ice creams and you haven't.* I wanted to ask if I should really have eaten ice cream cones, or should I just have thrown them down, but I kept quiet. The kids were showing off with their fish, so they did let me have a look at them. But all I could see through the side of the jam pot was murky green. But the little one said that he could see the fish, and I could tell by the excitement in his voice, that he was not pretending. There were some fish and he saw them.

So we held hands and lagged behind the big kids back through the town. The shops were in deep shade now and shuttered up for the night. I studied. The little one did see the fish, so it was not that I was littler than the big ones. Seeing was not part of growing up, like things you get better at as you get bigger, like tying your shoelaces or spreading yourself a crust of bread and lard. Now the truth came clearly, I did not see things like other kids did. It was just this, I could not see.

We dragged our feet and lagged further and further behind the big kids. They kept shouting, "Come on! Catch up." But every time we caught them up, they let each other take turns of carrying the jam pots. It was the string that was the bother. It cut into their hands and none of them wanted to carry the fish for very long.

When the kids were almost out of earshot, I felt none too happy. But then they shouted, "Catch up! And you can carry the fish." I forgot about my tummy. The little one could not have a jam pot to carry, only me. So now I was one of the big kids, and not a baby any more.

I tried once again to see the tiddlers. Holding the jam pot with both hands, I peered down into the murky green water, and I prayed hard from the place where it hurts most, when what you want is the very least of little things. Without me knowing what was happening, my prayer was answered. The water began rising and turning milky white, and I did see the little fish. They were circling round and round as the jam pot filled, and as it overflowed, I saw the tiddlers, like grey-green slithers, cut runner beans. They rolled and dived, rose again and swam over the brim.

The leader said nothing. He gently took the jam pot from me, and set it down in the gutter. He plunged his hands deep into his pockets, and hung his head. Then taking his place at the front of the line, he slowly and silently led us on the long trek home.

DOWN THE FIELDS

Now the kids' games took them down the fields. They could be gone all morning, so I spent more and more time at home with Mammy, waiting in the house, listening for their shouts and running footsteps.

Once when they came knocking on our door, it made my heart leap with gladness, I was so excited, and they were too. They were telling my mammy how we had all to go to a shop, as the shopkeeper had something for us, but she would not say any more until she had got every child who lived round about. So off I went with the kids, knocking on doors and calling for all the kids around. There were little ones who had never been allowed out to play before, and others who I had never seen before. And after a long debate, we even called for the lads whose mam and dad had the paper shop.

When the kids were running, it made my legs ache to keep up with them, but I had to keep up or I might get lost. Even the little one ran with the big kids. He did not seem to be tired. He was very happy, but he kept running back for me. He did not need to hold my hand now. He was not a baby any more. Still little, but one of the kids. He tried to tell me how he wanted to be my friend and he wanted to be one of the kids. And now he had to go and be one, and he cried and ran off, calling, “Bye bye.”

I knew I had lost the little friend I once had.

When we got to the shop, we were asked to go round to the back, where a roll call was taken, but still some kids were missing and had to be rounded up. Then the shopkeeper, with a piece of paper in her hand, counted up, and told her mester that there’s enough for each child to have half, and the halves were handed out.

The mester put a thick stick into my hand. “Eat it,” he said. It was like rhubarb when I sank my teeth into it. It was even worse than rhubarb.

“You have to take the skin off first,” said the mester, and he showed me how to pull back the skin in ribbons. I took just a tiny bite. It was like soft sour turnip. I had been taught good manners, so I did not spit it out. I just swallowed the little lump without chewing it.

“Don’t you like it?” asked the mester. “It’s fruit,” he told me.

I told him that it was not like the apple or the orange that Santa Claus had brought me. I held up the thick stick, hoping it would be taken from me, and it was.

He said, "She hasn't messed it. She's only taken one small bite. One of the others might as well finish it."

Back at home I told Mammy everything. She always listened to me. She thought it must have been something like that, and she felt sorry that the shopkeeper had not managed to keep her secret for a few days longer. But she might have waited a week or more already and could not wait to treat the children. And it was good of her, Mammy said. But I wondered about that.

Through the wall from next door came the howls of my little friend, with such a belly ache for eating two halves of the fruit. And Mammy was sad. She had thought that I might at least have had one friend to last me for a lifetime.

THE SAINT MARY'S REST GARDENS

Once again the kids had gone off to play without me, so Mammy showed me safely over to the desert island to play by myself. I gathered driftwood to make myself a pretend fire. I followed footprints, which I pretended to see in the sand, bent double in my game to see them more clearly. They led me to the far shore, where I straightened my back as I stood on the sand, looking out to spy the ship. I stared in wonder to see a green haze. Was it real, or was it just a mirage over the narrow sea of road? Could there really be another island? Not a desert island like ours, but a green land? It made my heart bump inside my chest, just to think that I might have discovered another island beyond ours, no less an explorer than the best of them.

Mammy came for me for little dinner and told me, "That's the rest gardens."

I had done it again. I had asked Mammy a question, and there was no end to what she knew about the St Mary's Rest Gardens. She said, "Some folk call it t'park." And she promised to take me in there next time we were coming back from doing the shopping down the street. She told me before the war St Mary's Rest Gardens had been given to the people by the church. "On the day of t'opening, the Sunday school scholars marched round it, and they had a picnic there. Before then your auntie lived there, in a little old cottage. Been pulled down now."

The park was even better than I had pictured it. There were a lot of bushes. Each bush had its different shaped leaves and its different shade of green. There were old trees that Mammy thought Auntie would have seen through her little cottage window. There were neat lawns with paths around them and seats where folk could rest.

All around the park were high railings. They had not gone to the war. At each end of the park, there was a gate. That was so folk could walk right through, instead of along the road, Mammy said. When the gates squeaked, they let me know that somebody might be coming. From the sound of the squeak, I learned when somebody was coming in or going out, or maybe that was just the wind. The gates were locked up at night to keep everybody out.

On our way back from the shopping, I got very friendly with the Rest Gardens, and I learned a lot. I knew a little less, but Mammy did not know why she had not taken me through the park before, and after a pause, she said, "Well, I've more time these days." Now that I was her helpmate. Now I could do little jobs for myself, like fetching my shoes and putting on my coat.

On our walks through the park, I would gaze about me at the shadowed lawns, not knowing if the shadow made the grass darker or the grass grew deeper in parts, if the shadow moved or if the grass moved. I just gazed, while Mammy quietly said her prayers out loud.

Sometimes we went to the park on sunny afternoons. Mammy would take her mending. But some ladies would take along their knitting, and some mams would sit by their babies' prams, and I had to play quietly so that I would not wake the babies, and not go near them, as they were out getting fresh air, not the Germans from me.

IN THE PARK

On long summer evenings, we kids played in the park and nobody minded. When the gardener pruned the bushes to about half their size, we kids could not hide in them any more. So he said he would not cut them back again. But when they had grown, he would just keep them tidy and trim any branches that we had accidentally damaged.

The old folk, resting on the seats, thought it made the evening more pleasant to watch a few children playing happily, and they had time to talk to us. One kind lady helped our Spadger to make daisy chains.

One evening I heard the lawnmower coming and I ran to pick the daisies before they were gobbled up. But I tripped headlong onto the grass. The gardener came to help me up. He was truly sorry. I was cross and felt around for what had tripped me up. It was the raised edge of the path. The gardener said it had not been made like that to trip me up; it had been made like that to make the path look nice for the old folk. He said, "If this had been a playground, it wun't a'been there." But he was so sorry that the kids had not got a park of their own to play in. He told me that if I picked the daisies, I was not to leave them on the grass, or they would make more daisies, which would kill the grass.

When holding a daisy close to my face, I could see the white petals tinged with pink, and if I kissed a flower, I could feel each feathery petal tickling my lips. The magic of daisies was how they could close their yellow eyes to go to sleep, and that was just the time when Daddy would come to take us home for bed. But I could go to the park any time I wanted to do. All I had to do was think about it.

There were daisies on my little thre'p'ny bit-shaped plates, the ones that Mamam bought me from the auction. I used them for sandwiches at little dinner time. I could lift a plate up to my nose closely and look. That showed me that the white plate had green grass growing round the rim, with a daisy chain laid around the raised edges in a circle. I could just see, or could I just see, the tinged pink petals?

It would seem like bringing the park to me, or was that taking me to the park? I could live out my daydreams. It was so real and wonderful. I could feel the fresh breeze on my cheeks and touch the wet grass under my fingers, and smell the shower of rain. Or I could just be still and listen to the silence there, coming back home with a start to find myself sitting up to the table now refreshed to go steadfast on my way.

In the park I could not join in with the kids' games of hide and seek, so I just pretended, hoping that the old folk would not think me a silly girl. First I would hide in the bushes, counting, then I would jump up to seek for myself, hiding in another bush.

Once I found one of the kids and I was so happy. That night they let me play, just for that once, so I hid, but nobody came to find me. But at least it felt like I was playing with the kids.

Sometimes I might just be still for a long while, just watching the shadows on the grass. I could not see the branches of the trees above me, so the sunshine put the pictures for me where I could see them, and I could get as near as I needed to, lying on my belly. It made me giggle to watch the leaves jump and dance about and there were straight shadows which crept slowly across the grass. I had no idea what they could be. I just watched them.

At these times, I did not hear the kids playing, or the old folk chatting, or even the cadets marching round our desert island, beating their drums and blowing their bugles. But I did hear the church bells. That's what Mammy said it was when I asked her the question, "What is it that shines all over the sky?"

She said it was because of the peace. I could understand that. Those church bells blotted out all the nasty noises, till there was nothing left but the shining peace.

Joan Vardy

A BOMB IN THE PARK

One evening I had not noticed that all the kids had gone. There was no chattering, no footsteps, just me alone in the park. I went to the gate. It was locked up, and I was getting chilly. I waited for somebody to come past, but nobody came, so after a while, I went to play.

Now we kids kept a secret to ourselves. Deep in the bushes, there was a box. It was like a tea chest and sometimes, it ticked, so we kids called it 'the clock'. So I went to sit beside it, to recite my nursery rhymes in time to the steady ticking. I often did that when I could not play in the kids' games.

But then I heard footsteps and ran to the gate. A mester was there, but he could not reach over to pull me up. The bars on the gate were too cold and slippery for me to hold on and climb up. The mester asked, "Whose kid are you? Who do you belong to?"

I did not know.

"You've got to belong to somebody," he said.

This really hurt me inside. I had thought that I could belong to myself. I didn't know or think that I had to belong to somebody else. I knew that Daddy, Mammy, our Spadger and me all lived together in one house. I thought we could all live together and love one another, but still belong to ourselves. Till now I had felt sure of myself, but if I had to belong to somebody, I would have to let them take over. I had thought that I was free.

This truth was going to take some more thinking about, but not just now. I had other things to think about.

I asked the mester, "What is it that makes that ticking

sound in the bushes?"

At that he threw his arms in the air, and skipped around in a circle, shouting at the top of his voice, "There's a bomb in the park and a kid's locked in."

Footsteps came running and a voice yelled for him to stop shouting or it might go off. There were folk appearing out of the blue, and by this time, the sky was quite a dark blue. Even the paths in the park were turning blue. Everybody looked like black cut-out shapes.

One of them took charge. He said, "Where does t'keeper live? Fetch a ladder. Go for t'garage owner. Whose kid is it?"

Another shush-shushed him, and quietly asked me, "Can you still hear the ticking?"

"Oh yes, it's still ticking," I said.

"That's all right," he sighed. "It's still ticking. Then there were sighs of relief as a ladder came at the same time as the park keeper, jangling his keys. He soon had the gate unlocked and came through, but nobody else came through.

"Now, then, where's this 'ere bomb?" he asked me.

I showed him the way among the bushes. He would not let me lead, but then he could not go any further hisself, and had to back out again. "I've been looking for that there thing all o'er," he said. "No wonder I couldn't find it. Only a kid could get in there. Why didn't you tell me about it afore now?"

The first mester shouted, "You knew about it?"

"Oh yes, I knew about it," I said. "I only wanted to know what makes the ticking sound?"

"Well, it's an electric box, so now you do know," said the park keeper.

Then my daddy came rushing, catching his breath. He said, "I've been up to t'allotment, looking for you." Gasping, he swept me up into his arms, hugging me to him with beads of sweat and tears rolling down his face onto my cheeks.

Daddy had not asked if he could pick me up or even say that he was going to do, so it was true; I belonged to Daddy. He sobbed on my shoulder, but I had no say in it. I was his. I did not belong to myself.

With a sinking feeling inside of me, I thought, now I will have to do, now I will have to come, now I will have to be, now I'll have to belong.

THE BELL RINGERS

Everybody, young and old, loved to hear the church bells ringing, even though they filled the peace and quiet of a Sunday morning. The bell ringers practised on Wednesday evenings. So did the fire brigade and the cadets. But the bells drowned out the sirens and the drums and bugles. Things were changing and it was all to do with the peace, Mammy told me.

But it was not the peace and quiet that I had known and loved. We now had a new kind of peace, and it was a very noisy kind of peace. The bells were like a magnet to us kids. We knew we should not be, but one evening we were all in the churchyard, sitting on the grass by the church. The stonework looked yellow in the evening sunshine.

While the kids watched the bell ringers through the open doorway, the leader answered all my questions. The bells, he said, were high up on the roof, but he could not see them properly.

"Has your mam got an egg whisk at home?" he asked me. "Has she let you have a look at it?"

"Yes," I said. I told him how she let me whisk the starch up with it, on washing days, in the bread pancheon.

He told me, "That's what the bells look like to me, but upside down."

So now I could picture the bells, spinning in the bright blue bowl of the sky, and underneath a big wheel turning with its sharp teeth. But instead of a handle, like my mammy's whisk, the bells had ropes to pull to make them work.

Then all the kids scattered like sparrows when one of the bell ringers came out. I could not dart away with them. I was frightened enough to, but I could not see where to run. So I stayed put, sitting on the grass. There was nothing I could do but pray.

The bell ringer came over to me, took my hand and led me into the little house with the other ringers. Then he closed one of the double doors. He let me stand in the circle with the other mesters, and showed me his rope.

The golden light of the evening sun shone in through the half-open doorway. I could see the mesters on the other side of the circle, their white shirt sleeves rolled up to their elbows, bobbing up and down, first one, then another, making waves of warm air brush over my cheeks. I heard their heavy breathing and smelled the hot sweat of the mesters near me on the darkened side of the circle.

In the bedroom upstairs, there was a great big noise. It was like a lot of folk getting up from their dinner, scraping their old wooden chairs on the bare wooden floorboards. From somewhere far away came the sound of the muffled bells. I could feel them ringing inside my chest. Joy overflowed through me. It rippled down me from head to toe.

How long I stood there, I cannot say. Time stood still, till I found myself in the churchyard again, with the sun gone down and the shadows gone to bed.

The bell ringer wished me a good night, shutting the door behind me. I walked a few paces forward, found the grass with my feet and sat down. From somewhere I heard a soft cooing. I made my way towards the sound on hands and feet, clambering over the graves, till I found our leader crouching behind a tall headstone.

He said, "I'm proud of you. You stayed. We all ran. You were frightened, but you were brave. So you can be my second."

"What's a second?" I asked.

He said, "That's when all the kids have gone to school, you can come out with me, but they all want to be second, and they're all bigger than you are, so don't tell them, will you?"

That night, I was proud of my leader. He had waited to take me home. We went through a gap from the churchyard into the cemetery to take a short cut, but when we reached the main gates, we found they had been locked up for the night. My leader could climb over the gates. He said it was easy. It was just the first bit that was hard, but he thought that if he could climb, then I could climb. And I thought, *if I am going to be second one day, I will have to try. If only he could help me up that first bit.*

So he got up the gate so far and reached down for my hand. But the bars were just straight. I could not pull myself up to reach his hand.

"We'll have to go round a long way," he said. "There's another way. It's shorter, but I don't know that, so you'll just have to trust me to take you home."

I just had to tell my little friend next time I saw him, about me being second. He was so pleased for me. He had already been told that he could be second one day, but he did not know if the leader had meant it or not.

But now he knew he would be second one day.

THE BUG HUT

Our Spadger whined. "They'll spray us with DDT."

Mammy thought that was a bargain, to get the kids out of the house for a while, and to have them deloused, just for a few coppers. So we both set off to the bug hut, passing Daddy's allotment, picking up other kids on the way. It was on the bobby's route to where Daddy used to live.

Outside the bug hut, there was a huge crowd of noisy kids. One kid shouted, "Come and 'elp me with 'im." Her little brother was trying to get away. Two bigger kids came to help the reluctant one up on to his feet, and with one either side of him, he was marched through the doors. There, a kind lady said that a row of chairs had been put out, just for the little ones like me, and she took a group of us right down to the front.

I found an empty chair and sat on it. A girl told me that that one was wet and now my frock would be wet. She helped me find a dry chair, and told me to lift my frock up and not to sit on it because I might be asked to stand up, and if my chair was wet, I would have to go out. I was also warned not to put my feet on the floor, or a mouse might run up my leg.

The kind lady came to settle us nicely to see the horses on the screen. The kids did see the screen. They were laughing and getting excited, so I joined in. Mammy had told me I must learn to join in with the other kids. So I joined in the game as well. The aim of the game was to make a kid sit on a wet chair. It was a bit like tug o' war at first. You pulled the kid next to you by anything you could grab hold of, or you pushed the kid to try and make it move along the chairs, all the time keeping your feet off the floor, or a mouse might run up your leg.

By half time, one of my pigtails had come undone. A bigger girl in the seats behind, untied my other pigtail for me to let my hair hang down in waves, she said. "That's nice, and you won't need your ribbons now, will you?"

The kind lady came to say she hoped we little ones were enjoying ourselves. Our mammies had paid for us to come because they wanted us to enjoy ourselves. We were settled nicely on our chairs again and sprayed with DDT. I heard the pump hiss as the drops fell.

To begin the second half, I sat in 'pull you' position, with a wet chair beside me. I was coached how to grab hold of the kid sitting the other side of it. I tried to get the kid onto the wet chair, while other kids were pushing and pulling, till this kid and I were both lying on the wet chair together. I clung on to his rather stretched woolly, but the kid escaped, leaving his own chair empty for me to sit on, as there was already a kid sitting on my chair. I was coached, "Next time, hold on to something tight, because we nearly won that time."

Mammy was right about having to learn to join in with the other kids. I was getting on better now without pigtails to be pulled, and knowing that smart trick of slipping out of your cardigan if you needed to.

By this time, there was more than one wet chair, so we were having much more fun, enjoying ourselves like our mammies wanted us to do. The game ended when a big girl came to help us all get dressed. She asked me if I had come in a coat, because there was one girl who came every week in a woolly and went home in a coat if she could. Her mam would sell it for more than the pennies it had cost her to come. A woolly was pulled over my head.

"There now," said the big girl. "If your mammy doesn't like it, you can wear it when you come next week."

Our Spadger left me at the gate and ran off to play. It seemed that Mammy had missed me, that she was going to throw her arms around me to give me a kiss and a cuddle. But she backed off for a few seconds' silence. Then she made a noise of disgust, and it sounded like she had caught a cold. She said, "Ugh! I think you've brought more home than you went with."

After a few more seconds of silence, I heard the tub being took down from its hook on the wall. I told Mammy that I had joined in with the other kids, like she had said. I had enjoyed myself, like she had wanted me to. Mammy's voice had changed. She said, "Get 'em all off right where you stand." Then she went to and fro, fetching warm water from the boiler near the house fire to fill the tub in the kitchen. Each time she came with a ladleful she had more to say.

"It's a good job it's Sat'day. I was just gettin' water warmed for you. You needn't think you can go back next week for your own cardigan. I don't know what to do wi' that one. It were better than yours. Some mother might ask for it. She might not want it back. I've learned a lesson, it cost me a bit more than I thought, but it were worth a try."

SUNDAY SCHOOL

"You must go to Sunday school, now that you're old enough," said Mammy. "All children have to go."

So after dinner, me and our Spadger went off with all the other kids. Not many of the kids wanted to go, but neither had some of them wanted to go to the bug hut, and I liked the bug hut. It was about the best place I had ever been to, and Mammy seemed to think that I might like Sunday school. And it was not far to go, just down the hill.

Once inside the hall, I thought I knew why the kids did not want to come here. It was chilly, dim and brown. The walls were brown, the floor was brown and I could not see where they met. It made it look like I was in a bubble. Invisible chairs were scraped over floorboards into rows. I had not been told anything about Sunday school.

I had no idea why I was there in this brown bubble, but there we all were, sitting in rows of wooden chairs, with the little ones at the front, and the bigger ones at the back, all chattering away. I was surprised when all the kids started singing. It was the hymn I liked best of all hymns, the one that Mammy and I sang together on black lead days, about the green hill without a wall. It felt like a light had been switched on inside of me. Knowing every word, I sang out.

Our Spadger tried to quieten me. "The kids are staring at you," she said. When we had finished the hymn, the teacher said how nice it would be if all the boys and girls sang out like that.

Later we all had to go in other rooms. On the way to our room, I heard a lovely sound coming from one of the other doors. I wanted to go in there and find out what made that lovely music, but I was told, no, that room is for the babies, and I was to stay with my sister for my first day. But oh, how I should have loved to have joined in with the babies.

Our room was light, and from the sounds about me, it was filled with tables and chairs, and I was somewhere in the middle. I could not see the walls, just the daylight coming in from the windows. Another girl had brought along her little sister for the first time that day; that made me feel good, not being the only new one. And that Sunday afternoon, a few of the older scholars were away, so us newcomers were collared to call out their numbers in the register.

The other new little girl was very shy. The girl said that her little sister could only count little numbers. Our Spadger was very pleased to say that she was teaching me how to count up to one hundred.

I will never forget that night when I got the strap for counting. Spadger and I slept in a bed together and we talked till we were tired each night. Over a time, she had taught me to recite the rhyme that goes,

'One, two, buckle my shoe, three, four, knock at the door, five, six, pick up sticks, seven, eight, lay them straight, nine, ten, a big fat hen, eleven, twelve, dig and delve, thirteen, fourteen, maids a-courting, fifteen, sixteen, maids in the kitchen, seventeen, eighteen, maids a-waiting, nineteen, twenty, my plate's empty.'

The rest, she said would be easy. Now that I could count up to twenty, I could count up to one hundred. All I needed was to practice every night.

One night Mammy and Daddy had both shouted up the stairs more than once for us to get to sleep. I had counted up to about thirty-four or so when I heard Daddy coming up the stairs. He stood at my side of the bed and took off his belt, and I was strapped four times, as I was four years old. It stung and made loud cracks. Our Spadger was strapped six times. She was shaking and sobbing. But there was not one sound from me. I held my breath. I would not be beaten. But I had learned the lesson. It is wrong to count.

On my first day at Sunday school, I was not counting, just calling out one number, and I was given the number forty-one. It was explained to me how it would come after number forty, and number forty was sitting in the row of tables behind me. So I had a little chat with number forty, and I learned the sound of her gentle voice.

Some of the scholars swapped their numbers round, till a number was found that the little sister knew, and some old hands had more than one number to call out. But we had it just about sorted before the teacher came into the room. Things went well till after forty-one, when two scholars called out the same number at the same time, because one was a latecomer who had crept in without being noticed. The teacher said she had thought there were not quite that many children in the class that day.

Then we were split into smaller groups. At our table, we were each given a card, with a picture on it to colour in. We were all excited to be given wax crayons. Our mammies would not let us have them at home. Wax crayons melted in your hands, they said, and wax crayons made a mess on your clothes which did not come out in the wash, they said.

I was given three crayons; a blue, a green, and a brown one. I could not see the picture on the card, so I lifted it up to my nose. There, I could make out the black lines, but not the whole picture at the same time, with it being too close. The teacher laid the card on the table again, and traced the picture with her finger, while telling me the story. She thought I might like to start by colouring a blue sky along the top.

This was the first time I had ever coloured. I did a bright blue band all the way along the top. Then I drew a steep green hill from halfway down the card on the left to the bottom right hand corner. Near the top of my hill, dressed in his long brown robes, I coloured Jesus preaching a parable. He was standing very tall, and down in the valley, I coloured the multitude, like a flat brown field. While I coloured, it felt as though I was listening to the story all over again.

The kids were scornful. One cried. The teacher said she

liked my picture. She could tell I had a better grasp of its meaning than the other boys and girls. They did not want to learn.

But she could not have them upset, so my sister must take me home. The teacher did not think that my mammy and daddy would mind. And she told me I might soon be going away to school, and not be able to come to Sunday school each week and have my star card marked. She said that some of the children only wanted stars for the Christmas party. But she promised me, "You can come to our Christmas party without stars."

So I had learned a little more about going away to school. I would not come home until Christmas times. I did not mind having to stop at home with Mammy on Sunday afternoons while our Spadger went along with all the other kids. We made jam tarts together, or a cake for tea, and I learned how to roll backwards and forwards with the green bottle, and how to twist the cutters to make the tarts without using the pastry. And Mammy told me how she used her little finger to get the jam from the spoon, because little fingers are the cleanest fingers, because we do not use them. Then it was my job to clean out the mixing bowl.

THE CEMETERY

I did go out to play with my leader as his second when all the other kids had gone to school. His education was an all-round thing that could not be learned in school. We made the cemetery our playground, as we could not be seen in there, but because the railings had gone to the war, there was a clear view of the whole cemetery through our back bedroom window, to keep my mammy happy.

We had many happy hours in the cemetery together. The leader told me that it belonged to everybody. That made belonging sound better than me having to belong to somebody. We made friends with the man who worked in there. He thought we were an odd couple to be together, a big lad like him and a little lass like me, not much more than half his size.

He soon set us on tidying the graves. Under his watchful eye we took the faded flowers from the pots, leaving those that were not quite yet dead. We gathered up the twigs and dead leaves from off the grass, and when folks came to put fresh flowers on their graves, we carried the cans of water for them, so that they did not get their clothes splashed.

Once we went to a funeral. The vicar wanted to send us away, but the mourners, dressed in their best black, said, "No, please don't send the children away. He loved little children." And we were brought nearer to stand by the deep hole. Prayers were said and we both joined in, in the parts that we knew.

I did not know about coffins. I supposed the old gentleman lay in the bottom of the hole on the bare soil, getting his Sunday suit mucky, and I wondered if anybody would be winding his clock for him. I heard the spade being thrust into the heap of red soil close beside me. Heavy lumps were tossed down the hole, landing on the poor old gentleman in dull thuds. My leader sniffed. He had known the gentleman, and he had been a good gentleman, he said.

I looked up to see him. He had changed, his head lowered, his face bright pink. His arms were limp at his side, and now his long brown coat seemed too big for him, with his buckled belt hanging loose. He took my hand, and turning, he said in a husky voice, "Best go now."

We went to sort out the flowers on the graves. Some had big bunches, but others had none, so we took one or two flowers from the good bunches, putting a few in each empty pot, but only if there was water in the pots. When the mourners in their best black came by, I heard them telling the vicar how they did not like what we were doing.

He said, "I can't stop all of the children from playing in the cemetery. There'll always be one or two who..." and he cleared his throat. He pointed out that there was no harm being done. They could see for themselves that not all the flowers were being taken. So if they brought flowers it would not be noticed, and if they did not bring flowers they would remember how their graves were being tended for them.

One gentleman was what my mammy would have called 'well-spoken'. He said to me, "But you do not give the flowers a drink."

I told him, "I can't reach t'tap to turn it on."

"Then what about the water for the flowers? They will die without a drink of water," he said.

I told him, "God waters t'flowers."

He went along the path to catch the others up, saying something about me being too clever, leaving me to ponder.

Each morning before we went to play in the cemetery, I sat beside my leader, while he learnt his lessons from his dad. I did feel sorry for him. My leader did try, but there were all those islands far away over the oceans, with names to be remembered. And those numbers in the little squares, and pi to recite. But there were story books, and something to think about for the day. My leader had to mind what he was told. His dad often warned him that if he did not do well, he would have to go to school.

Then came one morning there were no lessons. His dad said, "This is your one last day, so you had better make it a good one."

My leader helped me up to sit beside him on the cemetery wall. I thought we might have gone to play, but we sat there for a while, while he sorted things out to hisself out loud. At last, he said, "You had better know how to get out of the cemetery by yourself, when the gates are locked up."

The best way, he thought, was for me to learn how to get in. So I would have to learn how to climb over the wall. It was an old stone wall, so he found me a place where I could get a good foothold, and I had to learn where that place was. I was taken to the cemetery gate, and told to feel along till I found that very stone for my foot. Then I had to learn how to pull myself up, using the stumps of the sawn off railings. But they were still sharp from where they had been sawn off, so I had to take care not to rip my hands on them.

It was easier letting myself down into the cemetery, landing on the soft ground, squeezed between the wall and the thick hedge that grew behind it. Then my leader went round and came in through the cemetery gates, and came up to me on the other side of the hedge, to find a place where I might get through. I crawled along to the part he had chosen and between us we made a good gap, by breaking the twigs till the gap was big enough for me to be squeezed through. This was made short work of by me lying on my belly and being pulled through with my coat sleeves, with twigs snapping and crackling all about me.

I was told that when I grew, and the hedge grew, I would have to make the gap bigger by myself. "So you'd best use it now and then," said my leader.

To get out of the cemetery, I had to crawl along the hedgerow till I found my gap. That was not easy. My leader said: "Well, if you can't find the gap, don't worry. You'll be quite safe, locked up in the cemetery."

On his last day we went home early. "There might be things to be done at 'ome, before tomorrow," he said. "No good goin' over old ground, 'ere's your gate." So I had been second, and now that my leader went to school, I was my own leader.

Outside the cemetery gates there was a telephone box, where the bobby on his beat had to make calls. He did not want me to cross the road by myself, now there was too much traffic. So he would regularly take me over from our gate to the cemetery in the afternoons. He asked me what time my daddy got home from work. I did not know. He asked me, "Where does Daddy work?"

I said, "He works on t'buildings now." So the bobby thought there would be time for me to play while he went up to the village where Auntie lived and back again in good time to take me back over the road before my daddy got home for his dinner. So when my tummy said, it will soon be dinnertime, I would sit on the cemetery wall to wait for the bobby. He was just one of the kind people I met at the cemetery.

Also by the main gates there was a urinal. Mammy told me it had been built for the bus drivers and conductors, as there was nowhere for them on that route. But they did not like to use it, because the passengers who were sitting on the top deck of the bus could look down over the urinal walls and see them while they were in there. So instead they used our lavatory. But I used our lavatory nowadays, and more than once I would be in there when the bus stopped and a bus driver or conductor pushed open the door, because my legs were not long enough to hold it shut. The passengers on the bus must have seen me, but they had to wait while I finished. So now, if there was a bus due and I really must go, I used my chamber pot. It was still kept under the back kitchen table. I could normally wait while the bus had gone past. If Mammy was working at the kitchen sink, she would see it pass by through the kitchen window, and give me a call when it had gone.

Daddy told me that before the war, all building work stopped. That was why he had had to go to the pit. I thought that was why the urinal did not have a roof, but the walls had been tiled and it was quite nice in there. I used it myself while I was out playing, if I had a need to, when the bus had gone past, that is.

Once on my way out, I met a mester coming in. He asked me, "Is they a lavatory in there?"

I said, "No, but there's a drain for t'rain watter. If you like, you could use that. I do."

He was not sure.

"But bus 'as just gone past," I told him. "Nobody'll see you, and I can stand outside and no kids'll come in."

When he came out, he thanked me for being so kind, and he sounded like he really meant it.

At night when the kids got home from school, they might play at walking along the cemetery wall. They used to show off. They could just jump down if they overbalanced. I thought, *now I am on my own, I am going to learn to walk along the wall, while there's nobody watching to laugh at me. I'll do it and do it, until I'm as good as them,* I thought. *Then I'll show 'em.*

Now I had been taught how to pull myself up on the wall, I could find my own foot holes, and I made a start by first crawling along the wall, minding the railing stumps. But then I found steps on top of the wall that I had not known about. So I climbed up as I crawled, and it was easy, without any kids watching me. But what I could not see was that the road outside the cemetery was going downhill and I was going up. I did not know just how high I was until I heard a lady calling me from down below.

She told me she did not think I knew how high I was. She was waiting for a bus and did not want to miss it, but she could not leave me so high on the wall. She told me I must creep back, till I was on the lower part. She walked along underneath me as I went. I had not tried creeping backwards before. It was not as easy going down the steps as coming up. The lady said, "You must keep going," and when I was safe again, she did catch her bus.

That had taught me a lesson I would not forget. I did not even try to walk along the wall again. I knew it was dangerous. I stopped trying to be like the other kids. I had a talk to myself about it, and let go of something inside myself.

But I still wanted the kids to be friends with me. I used to squeeze myself between the wall and the hedge, and clean out the rubbish from down there, and throw it over the wall onto the coursey. The vicar was pleased. Nobody could reach down there to clean out the rubbish but me.

There were some stones there that the kids called boulders. I liked boulders because they were round and warm and smooth. But the kids liked them because they said that if you put them up to your eye and look up to the sky, you can see through them. So I would hunt for boulders to give the kids. Then they would be friends with me for that day.

Mammy told me that there were even grown up folk who would rather not be in the cemetery on their own. I told her that I did not feel I were on my own, even if there was nobody in there with me. Mammy chuckled.

But there was something that I had no words to tell, a stillness that shielded me and filled me with calm, and I could take it back home inside of me. I cannot find the words now, but I can try to tell of the way I found the world about me then.

For me, the sun did not shine up in the sky. The sun was in

the cemetery, with me. I could feel it, even through my thick brown coat, right beside me. I could see the dark shadows on the path. They were like living paintings for me. Shadows were not the shapes cast down by tree branches. Shadows were real things.

My trees had no branches. My trees were just tall, rough trunks. I would rub my hands over their patterned bark till my palms tingled. Tree trunks could do that. I soaked up the hush of the leaves way above my head. But my leaves had no twigs to hold hands with. My leaves were like birds. They could just float on the air, and whisper without a flutter. My birds could whistle so sweetly, with no trace of shape. They were just a whistle. No sharp beak, no claws, no need of feathered wings. My birds just sailed over the sky, only the sound of their song as they glided over an unseen rainbow arch.

The rain fell from a clear blue sky, as did scented rose petals from heaven. I had no friends from my past and no fears for my future. For this season I paused, to be healed and strengthened, with time to rest on the grass as I had done with my leader, to share again with myself the stories his dad had told us, to think back over the things my leader had told me before the war, when kids wore clothes that fitted them, with eggs for the egg whisk, and cheese for the cheese grater. My leader felt sorry for the little kids. We had not known about that. We thought the war was just normal.

He had liked to talk, and I had liked to listen. He had told me of the wonders of the wide world. I did not interrupt to ask where or why, so I did not learn what. Now the days of peace had come, the days that he had hoped for, and he would grow up to be a man.

As the seasons changed, from summer through autumn to winter, I changed with them, using my open eyes and ears and heart. I learned that nothing stops the same. Everything changes. It was too slow to be seen, not too quick to be noticed, but too slow to be counted. I welcomed every small change I was given in trust. But now there was nobody there to tell me the truth.

As the days grew cooler, the breeze blew fresh on my cheeks. The golden leaves I had not yet seen, floated down, fluttering about me. Folks said they were dead. Folks were wrong. The leaves were full of life and loving it. If I held out my hands to catch them, they cheated me, by stroking my face. I joined in their dance and we ran with the wind. I followed their rustling as they scurried in circles. I studied and learned that when leaves and flowers and old folk are dead, they all go brown and crumpled. So they are all dug in the ground.

I learned that Jack Frost can make ice crystals that can change into dewdrops in the morning sunshine. Sheets of ice could sound like glass if I smashed them; then change to water in my hands. I learned that a warm wind could turn itself inside out, coming back crisp and cold and talk on the tops of the tree trunks, then turn again, bitter and biting.

Daddy called that an idle wind. "It's enough to cut you in two," he would say.

One morning the sky whistled at the top of the tree trunks. The church bell tolled. I turned my back on the main gates to leave through my gap in the hedge. My hands stuck to the sawn off railing stumps as I let myself down. I knew I would fall on the slippery ice.

I picked myself up and faced the lonely, sad cemetery. The funeral cars purred and crunched on the icy road. The mean wind moaned. It came from miles away over the fields and I got my first view of a landscape. Just like my leader, I had learned those things which cannot be learned in school, and the things which cannot be found in books, and things that I cannot put into words now.

Joan Vardy

THE CHRISTMAS PARTY

Before the Sunday school Christmas party, our Spadger taught me to sing some Christmas carols in bed at night before we went to sleep. Mammy thought it was good that my older sister could teach me, and Daddy never came up to give us some strap.

'Good King Wences Last Looked Out' was one carol, and another one was, 'We Three Kings Of Ory And Tar, Bearing Gifts We Travel So Far.' I asked our Spadger, where did the other king come from?

We all had to take our own plate and a spoon for the party. Mammy tied green cotton around and around the egg spoon handles, the spoons that had turned blue, so that they would not get mixed up. She chose the thre'p'ny-bit-shaped plates with the daisy chains round the edge, thinking it would not matter if they got broken. But I thought it would.

Mammy said, "After t'tea, when pots 'as been washed up, you'll 'ave to go an' claim y'own plate." She was sure I would know my own plate. But I was shown a white plate out of the pantry, and I did have to say that I would not know it from any other white plate. I was worried how I might find the kitchen. I had to carry the plates and the spoons, while our Spadger carried the jelly that Mammy had made especially.

It was already getting dark as we joined all the other scholars and went down the hill together. But it was light inside the Sunday school. We were all sat down at long tables, and the kids said that there was mountains of red jelly, and I heard one of the ladies saying that she thought that every mammy had made a red jelly.

The little boy who sat across from me at the tea table had brought a dinner plate, and he was crying because it had got broken in half, but he cheered up when he was told that he could eat jelly just as well off half a plate.

But the lady thought that I could not eat jelly with a coffee spoon, so she gave me a nice fruit spoon. When the little boy had eaten his jelly, the lady gave him another half plateful, because he had only had half a plateful the first time round, she said.

After tea we went to play in a dark hall. It was all lit up by fairy lights, I was told, but I could not see them. Santa Claus came. He was on the stage at one end of the hall. As our names were called out, each one of us had to go up to collect our present. Getting up on the stage was quite easy for me, climbing the steps on hands and feet, but on the stage the lights were dazzling, so bright for me, I could not see Santa or anything, just one white light wherever I looked.

I found myself holding a sheet of cardboard, so I thanked the white light most politely. I knew I could not manage Sunday school, and I did not know what my card was, but I was grateful that I had been given much more than a sheet of cardboard.

The Sunday school teacher had kept her promise. I had come to the Christmas party, and I had been treated as a child who could see. But it was too hard for me, too much for me to bear. Somehow I had to get back down those steps, but my body stiffened. My feet stuck to the stage. It felt like bumping into a white wall. I had not felt like crying, yet tears were rolling down my cheeks, and I still had my mind set on getting down those steps. But I was helpless. It was like being in a dream. Voices around me were telling each other about my bad eyes.

I stayed in this moment for I do not know how long. Then I was just floating down the steps, with somebody on each side of me, just holding my elbows with the tips of their fingers, or so it seemed. I heard a lady saying how light I was, and a mester saying, "All children's light."

"Not that light," said the lady. "That one's not thin, like some of them."

I was awake again, with the hall floor under my feet. At once I was surrounded by kids, begging. "Swap it." They had jigsaw puzzles or books. I would not be parted from my cardboard, even though I thought their presents might be better. Our Spadger had warned me before we came to hold on to my present. They said I could not see it, but neither could I see their presents.

When our Spadger got down from the stage, she had some dolls' house furniture, a bed with a white rigid plastic quilt, and a pink dressing table with a real mirror.

A lady came to say that she thought we had been given each other's presents. She asked me, "You've got a dolls' house at home, haven't you?" And I told her I had. But our Spadger did not want to swap her present with mine.

Back at home, Spadger did put her furniture in my dolls' house, and now and again we would both play together. But I kept my sheet of cardboard. Spadger did not want to play with me, so Mammy showed me how to play a game on my cardboard. She hunted through her button tin till she found two which I could see on the table. But they vanished when she put them on the board. She hunted through a drawer to find a dice. She said it had spots on it. Then she reached to the back of the cupboard for an egg cup, blew into it, and dusted it with the corner of her pinafore. Laughing, she said, "I knew I'd find a use for it someday."

The egg cup was made of dark red Bakelite, the same as the ashtrays that we kept for when we had company coming.

Then Mammy showed me my board. She traced with her

finger up invisible diagonal ladders and down invisible wavy snakes, so when we played at snakes and ladders, Mammy moved her button and she moved my button when it was my turn. But she made it feel like we were both playing together, by telling me when we climbed over snakes bodies and turned the corners, watching out for paintbrushes near the ladders.

But I could shake the dice when Mammy had found it for me and put it in the egg cup. I am sure Mammy did not have to pretend to enjoy playing with me. She really did enjoy playing, and her mood was catching. After that first game, I need only ask once and she would say, "Go and get your board out, and I'll come and have a game with you," just as if she had been waiting for me to ask her. She would leave off whatever work it was she was doing and forget about the clock.

We would both make noises going up ladders and down the snakes, and I soon got to know where they might be, how short or how long they might be. I could shake and shake the dice in the egg cup, but still land in a snake's mouth. Sometimes I got home first, sometimes Mammy got home first, but the game did not end till we were both home, and all the while we laughed and laughed, till Mammy would have to lift her glasses to wipe her eyes.

MERRY CHRISTMAS

It was going to be a long day, Mammy said. She had got to go with Daddy, and I had got to go over the wall to play with their kids. At their house, little dinner time came and went. I said I would be hungry. Mammy just said that she would have to remember when they got back. It was about the brown boots I would see up at Daddy's garden. I weren't going to see them any more. I weren't to talk about them any more. And I weren't to bother my daddy.

We were all playing out on their back yard when we heard the aeroplane coming, diving, twisting and turning overhead. The noise frightened us all and they were crying. I wished I was back at home. I could tell the kids' mam was alarmed as she came running to the back door. We all gathered around her. Then I could hear the relief in her voice when she shouted over the din of the aeroplane, "Look, he's writing!" and those who could spelled out the word with her.

M-E-R-R-Y. "He's chalking on the sky!" said one of the little kids.

Their mammy laughed. "He's wishing us a merry Christmas!" she shouted as the aeroplane drew here and there. We all clapped and cheered and shouted back to him, "Merry Christmas!"

On Christmas mornings, Santa had always left our presents on the table, mine on Mammy's side, and Spadger's on Daddy's side. But this Christmas morning, our table was covered with the best white tablecloth. This year I did not find any presents. There was a board with yellow and black squares on it for our Spadger, which she should share with me. But she had set her heart on a scooter, and was hunting out the house for it, shouting, "Where's my scooter? Where's my scooter?" wherever she looked; in the coal house, in the pantry, under the kitchen table.

Then she found it, behind the settee. It was not quite big enough for her, but she went out on the front in the sunshine, where the ice was not too bad. I hunted out the house for my scooter. Mammy kept saying, "I told you, you an't got one."

So I told her I would go out to play without one. She said that no other kids would want to play with me on Christmas morning. Then I was shouting at her, just like our Spadger sometimes did. In the end, she said, "Here, go then. Take your coat." It hit me. I clung on to it quickly, or I would have dropped it.

On our back yard, I did my best to button up and buckle up without Mammy's help. When I opened our back gate, my little friend was leaning on it, trying to get out of the wind. He grumbled at me, "I've waited a long time. I thought there must be one kid like me, who an't got a toy."

I told him about the row I had had with Mammy. We wondered what to do. He knew somewhere, but I must not tell. It was somewhere to go over the road. The road was slippery, but it was quiet, because it was Christmas day. It was the urinals that my little friend had found for himself. He knew one corner in there where he said he could sit and sleep, and sometimes when he woke, the sun would be shining on him. So we sat down together, and he was soon fast asleep.

After a while, I heard some youths coming in. I could hear that they were having a merry Christmas. As they came into the urinal, I thought it best to keep my eyes closed and pretend to be asleep, just in case there might be trouble for me. One youth sounded like he was going to cry.

"Street urchins! It's Christmas day, for Christ's sake!" he shouted.

They wondered what they should do. I heard the words 'bobby' and 'hospital' mentioned. Then some more youths came in. They were asked if they knew us.

One said, "I know one, but not the other."

Then there was a great deal of shouting. My daddy came. He picked me up and laid me on his arms. I thought I had better keep stiff, because that's how I would be if I was properly asleep. I did not have to pretend to be stiff. My arms and my legs stuck out straight. I really was stiff.

Daddy kept calling my name and I would not open my eyes. He kept on calling my name. I could not open my eyes, they were iced tight shut. The youths kept on shouting after us as I was carried into our house. I was laid flat on the table. I heard my shoes bang on the wood. The best white cloth had been taken off. Mammy and Daddy thought they would leave me and wait and see. They said, "Don't move. Don't move yet."

I did have two Christmas presents. Daddy had found them in the cupboard by the fire. One was a writing slate. "It's just for you," he said. It was a sheet of metal with holes along the edges with rubber pads on one side to protect the table. Yet Daddy thought it should go up the other way.

There was a folding ruler just like Daddy's, with knobs on one side to fit in the holes on the slate, to hold it steady so that I could write on it in straight lines. One section of the folding ruler was full of holes. The other one was covered in bumps and dents. Mammy gave me a piece of cardboard and I folded the ruler over it. There was a tiny bradawl, just like Daddy's, and I pushed it through the holes in the ruler to make dots on the cardboard, just like Mammy thought I should. But I could not push hard enough. So Mammy found me some tissue paper that the Christmas oranges had come wrapped up in. That was a disaster.

Daddy would not answer any of my questions. He said he did not know, but I should. I should be able to use my slate, because it was for me. I knew what he meant. For me, because I was blind.

The other present was a wooden box with blocks inside, like matchboxes. I took one out and Daddy asked if I could see the spots. I could not. So both presents were put away in the cupboard.

Daddy said, "They'll larn you, at school."

NO COAL FOR THE FIREGRATE

I could tell that Mammy did not like this moaning wind. She had never heard the like of it before. She asked Daddy, "What does it mean?" Daddy was quiet. Mammy rugged me up and sent me out with him to fetch something from the garden for our dinners.

On the way home, I asked him why the cars were so noisy. He told me they had chains on the wheels. I asked about the sky being green. Daddy said, "Yes." But that was all he had to say about it.

Back at home I told Mammy the sky was green. She said, "Go on with you."

Daddy said, "Yes, the sky were green." We had brought home with us a whole stalk of Brussels sprouts, which Daddy hung up in the empty coal house in the kitchen. Mammy said there was plenty of room to hang them up in there, without any coal, but what use were sprouts without coal?

Daddy said something about burning the stalk to cook the Brussels, but it was not less than a miracle that he had also brought home a bunch of bronze chrysanthemums which he had grown for Mammy. Those were her favourite flowers. Daddy said they should have been frosted, it was too cold for them, and it was beyond belief.

Mammy cheered herself by arranging her chrysanths with great care in the tall celery jug. I had a close look and saw their golden petals all curled over evenly, just as though they had been combed.

Like the rest of the kids, I wanted to play out in the snow. Mammy said that I could and sighed, knowing better than I what the outcome would be, but nobody could tell me what snow was all about, she said. There would be some things in life I would have to learn about for myself. Some things would have to be learned the hard way, and snow was one of those things.

When I got out onto our back yard, it was covered in a coat of blinding white. All my landmarks had gone. The grate near the lavatory was not there to jump on, to make that lovely hollow din, as Mammy called it. And where were the dark railings? I needed them to navigate my course up to the back gate. They had gone.

On the other side of the road, the snow had hidden the pebbledashed wall. The drift looked flat to me, so I plunged into it and had to pull myself out again. I could not see our back step, so I could not believe it was still there, till I tripped up it. The kids had made a snowman. I could see him, like a white pillar box for posting your letters in, but it did not feel like a man. It froze my fingers. There was no joy of playing in the snow for me. I hated everything about it, and was soon back in the house. Lesson learned.

I felt the cold most of all in my tummy. Mammy knew I should have something warm to drink, but we sat together by the empty fire grate. She thought that sitting there made her feel warmer somehow. It was so cold that the pale winter sunshine came in through the window to get a warm, she said.

Mammy and I shared an orange cut in half, and we ate, while I listened to wondrous stories about Eskimos fishing through holes in the ice. Then we made igloos from the orange peel, carefully turning the halves inside out with the orange side on the inside and the white side on the outside.

Mammy asked me if I was warm now. I knew that telling lies was bad, and I did not want to hurt her, so I just said, "Mmmm." It seemed like not quite telling a lie, and I did say, "Thank you," but I was not sure why.

An icicle grew between our back kitchen door and the outside lavatory. It grew fatter and fatter, until it was like a tree trunk. It was useful for me to cling on to as I went to the lavatory. It stopped me from slipping on the ice, till it grew so fat, I could not stretch my arms around it. Mammy thought it was beautiful. Daddy thought it was dangerous.

The night he cut it down, we left the kitchen door open with the light switched on for him to see to work. It did not matter about keeping the house warm, with having no coal to burn. Mammy was sad to see the great icicle lying on the back yard. Me and our Spadger were happy, sitting on it, making a game of it.

Daddy picked up his chopper again. Crying like a baby, he hacked at his wooden wheelbarrow. Mammy reminded him that his father had helped him to make it, and begged him to stop. "There must be another way. There must be something we could do."

It was my daddy's dad who had helped make the greenhouse, and the wheelbarrow. He had used a hot poker to make holes in the wood, and made his own dowels, and not used one nail.

We were told that that night was a special night. We were not going to be put to bed. We were wrapped in blankets, and were soon fast asleep on the settee.

The next morning I woke in Mammy's arms, still wrapped in blankets. She was calling out to Daddy, "Lou, Lou, they're alive. We're all alive." She thought that as we had made it through that night, she was sure we would all make it through the winter.

I was told that I was going to fetch potatoes for my dinner. Mammy put me in the wheelbarrow, and tucked me in with potato sacks, telling Daddy that nobody would think anything, seeing a little kid having a ride in a wheelbarrow, wrapped up in sacks.

It was a sunny morning, but the ride was bumpy. I tried holding on to the sides of the barrow, but they were splintered where Daddy had hacked in despair. At the place where the potatoes were, Daddy had to do some talking to the mesters to make them agree with him.

I had to walk back home, holding onto the wheelbarrow handle. Daddy had not thought that I would be slipping all over the place, but I could not ride. The sacks were too heavy for the wheelbarrow as it was. The ice from the wheels was spitting up at my face.

We met up with a few folk, who all had sharp words to say to Daddy about potatoes. He had bet we would meet up with somebody, but he said they could not do anything about it now. It was too late. We were on our way home. We took the wheelbarrow straight in through the front door and put it between the table and the sideboard. When the sacks were opened, I felt cheated to see, not potatoes for my dinner, but coal.

Mammy said I was too young to know I could soon have a hot meal. She showed me the potatoes she had already peeled and cut up into pieces. They were in a saucepan covered with water. But before they were cooked, Mammy dabbed my face with a warm cloth and smeared Vaseline all over my scratches. Daddy said that hot potatoes were a good enough meal for anybody, and we did have hot potatoes for our dinner. Just hot potatoes.

OUR HOUSE

Our house had a living room and a back kitchen, with the pantry and the stairs in between them. Upstairs there was a front bedroom and a back bedroom that had the stairs leading up to the garret. From the front door, straight out on to the coursey, and at the back was a yard, with a lavatory, the dustbin and the clothes line.

We called our living room 'the house' and the heart of the house was the fireplace that Mammy dutifully and beautifully blackleaded every Friday morning. Now in the long winter evenings, two kettles could sit and sing gently to each other, either side the fire grate, one on the boiler top and one on the oven top.

Now and then the coals would settle themselves more comfortably in the grate, and when the fire was just right, Mammy would help me and our Spadger to make toast. She would show me where to hold the long-handled fork and turn the slice of bread round for me when it was light brown on one side.

Sometimes Daddy would open the oven door and put his feet up on the top to get warm. When they got too warm, he'd lean his legs up on the cupboard at the side, for a rest.

Our house was cosy in the evenings now the pale green curtains closed. Mammy said they helped to hide the electric box, which hung on the wall near the door where the settee was. All the woodwork was stained a warm brown, with a dado in the corner by the front door. That was where folks rubbed their coats when they came in and they might be wet.

On those winter evenings, me and our Spadger would join

in games and would play together. She did not want to fall out with me any more, now that Mammy had told her how they must all try and help me if they could. Now our Spadger knew that, we had some good games together.

The biggest space for playing in the house was under the table. It stood in the middle of the room. Under there, there were katy-cornered washing lines for us to hang out hats and gloves and the dusters to dry. Or we could make it into our tent.

There was some space by the stairs door, but there was a howling draught came from under the door, and there was no pegged rug in the corner. Mammy said we were lucky to have pegged rugs and an electric light bulb.

Now no customers came to our shop at night, opening the front door to let all the cold air come in, and Mammy and Daddy could sit on the hearth near the warm fire together. We had no more old clothes now for Daddy to finish the pegged rug on the hearth, so he might read his newspaper, and sometimes Mammy might do her mending. She would get out her cotton tin that she had got from the tin factory where she used to work. She often told me about the picture on the lid. It was of two ladies in a garden, she said.

Mammy had a mushroom to put socks on for darning. That was if Peacocks had had some light grey darning wool come in, that is. It made me feel really grown up to be asked to fetch something from the sideboard, with our Spadger's help.

The sideboard was at the back of the house, facing the fireplace. It had fancy work on the front and that was just the start of the wonders on the inside. It was fun just to open the doors and smell everything at once. That was just like seeing them, for me.

On the top shelf at the right, crammed with stuff for Wednesday afternoons when Mammy could make new things from old with her sewing machine, and the new material had a smell all of its own, there was a round clothes brush that tickled my nose if I tried to see light shining through the hole in the middle of it. When I got a fit of the giggles it made me really happy on the inside.

At the left on the top shelf, there were tea towels and glass cloths. They were all smooth and smelled of starch. There was Granddad's packets of Woodbines and Park Drives just there. In the middle of the top shelf, Mammy kept her iron. That was when it had gone cool. It shone silver for me, but it was great fun for our Spadger. She could see funny pictures in it, and she could make them move. Mammy said I was lucky to have a big sister like our Spadger.

The iron lay on the flannelette sheets that Mammy would put on the table for doing her ironing on. She would plug her iron in with the light bulb, and sometimes she had to iron at night when the light was switched on, and then the room would go light and dark, and that would be really upsetting for me. So she tried not to do it.

On the bottom shelf in the sideboard, it was crammed full with half-finished work. There was a red jumper which Mammy said would be too small for me now. She told me about the picture of the little Dutch girl and the little Dutch boy on the front. But she thought I was too big for motifs like that now.

And there was one navy Fair Isle glove, waiting for its mate, and all sorts of tablecloths, sideboard runners, dressing table mats, all waiting for the right colour embroidery silk to come in the shops, and Sunday afternoons at Mamam's and Granddad's.

Next to the fireplace, the built-in cupboard took up the whole of the recess in the corner near the window. The bottom drawer was our toy drawer, and next to that, in the corner, was a little cupboard for the penny slot gas meter. Now this was one of those puzzles waiting inside my head to be solved some day.

Above the toy drawer was a long drawer where we kept all our underclothes to keep them aired and warm. There were two drawers above that: the one on the right was for me and Mammy and our Spadger, for hats and gloves and the dusters; and the one on the left was for Daddy, for his cap and his scarf and his belts and handkerchiefs.

Above the drawers there was a cupboard with three shelves. On the bottom shelf we kept the first aid kit, with the brandy and the Dettol, and Mammy's sewing machine and her curling pin tin and the tin for the money for the twenty-week clubs.

On the shelf above that, there was the best china tea set, with real gold round the edges, and a set of glass fruit dishes with leaves on that I could feel, and glass tumblers for Mammy and Daddy to use, and there might be brown sugar, or raisins, or American cheese. On the top shelf, there was a lot of books.

Some evenings, Daddy would reach up high to the top shelf and get all the books down. He would grunt with the effort. He had some gardening books, and there were some books which had been given away when you bought newspapers, they said. These were fat books with thick covers, with their names stamped on the front. I could feel their names like big round pennies.

There was a reference book, with brown shiny pictures in it of the wonders of the world, they said, a doctor's book, and a dictionary, and one book called The Handyman and Home Mechanic. At the side of the other books, this one felt brand new.

If Daddy looked at that book, he would say, "Phew!" and whistle. Mammy said he was not good at that. She said it would make him sweat and scratch his brow.

But now and then the garage man would come over the road. He was very keen to look at the home mechanic bit. He would talk and talk about it and we all thought he was very clever. And he could take some of the pages out of the book; unfold them again and again, to spread them out on the table.

Books had always been a big thing in our lives, and we had always been taught to take good care of them. But I had not thought much about books before. They had just always been there. We had shown them to visitors when they came, and visitors were very interested to see them.

There was that little nursery rhyme book of mine, that one with Goosey Gander in. That was the only page I could find that I knew. It looked like a big white hole, and that was Goosey Gander. I said I could see the writing, and everybody said that I could read it when I was older. But it just looked like wavy blue and white stripes to me

But I could say all my nursery rhymes. I did not like that one; Goosey Goosey Gander, whither shall I wander? Upstairs, downstairs, in my lady's chamber. There I met an old man who would not say his prayers, so I took him by his left leg, threw him down the stairs.

I kept my chamber pot under my bed. I could drag it out and use it, if I needed to in the night. I had stopped asking Jesus to make my peepers better, so I thought about that old man. He must have had his good reasons to stop saying his prayers to Jesus, like I had. And what a nasty thing to do it was, to throw him down the stairs.

Spadger and I both had a little book. They both looked the same to me, so I was careful not to get hers. Mine was one about three pigs who lived in houses, and our Spadger liked it better than her book, and I liked hers better than mine, because I had been in the brick house with the mother pig, and I had been very glad to get out of it.

Our Spadger's book was about a mester called Noah, who kept all the animals safe on a big boat. So I liked that book the best. Mammy was pleased, but she had thought that I was not quite old enough for that book just yet.

Me and our Spadger both had a big book. Hers had a picture of Mickey Mouse on the front. That was the one that Mammy had shown me when I had first had my grown-up gas mask, and all I could see of Mickey was his big black ears. My big book was called Shorty Shambles. Shorty was a little fat mester who, like Noah, lived on a boat. He had a telescope in one hand and in the other; a big bottle of what I thought might have been medicine. I loved to listen while Mammy read the stories to me, but I could not say what they were about. But then we would look at the pictures together. I could see the yellow pages, and Mammy told me, "That's the sky." I learned about anchors and hammocks and funnels and flags, and it was all something to do with the shipping forecast, and I loved the shipping forecast.

Some evenings Mammy would find out her picture postcards that Daddy had sent her when he worked on the buildings down south. That was before the war. They said the postcards had roses on them and it felt like there was lace around the edges. Then there would be a lot of happy talking.

Some evenings, there would be real treats. It would make Mammy happy if she had to find out her nutcrackers to crack herself some brazils. She might give me and our Spadger some raisins to eat in our tent. Or Daddy might unwrap American cheese from its blue and red cellophane package. Then he would cut us a slice, and say, "Now you can tell everybody that you've had your cheese rations and they'll know."

This was wintertime with nothing growing in Daddy's allotment garden. This was a time for our family to grow, grow together, talking time, quiet time, a peace time. Not the

Wednesday evening peace, with the church bells ringing and the fire sirens sounding and the cadets marching, as my Daddy said, "Making a racket with their drums and their bugles." This was peace and quiet time. The clock would chime and not remind anybody to jump up and do something, a time for Mammy and Daddy to sit by the glowing fire together and now I could tell you every little sound that our house made. It was just as though I could see it. But it had taken me five years to learn it.

Now I knew it was the cupboard doors that bumped gently as they nudged each other to be closed, and it was the swivel catch that went round and round if it was pushed too hard. It was the drawers that opened and gently knocked, and knocked again when they were closed. The hard metal sound was the oven door and the squeaky tune was the boiler lid.

I could tell you how Mammy was using the poker in the fire. She could put it through the bars to lift the coal a little, or scrape the bottom bars of the grate before she put more coal on the fire. I knew the sound of the tea caddy spoon being dropped back onto the tea leaves and the sound of the boiling water going into the teapot, making the water froth and swirl.

But there were some sounds that had no names for me just yet; the light switch, which was high up on the wall out of my reach; on all of the inside doors, there was a little catch, to snick the doors before we went to bed. Daddy would do that so that we would all be safe in the night.

This was my home, my family, and this was our house.

Joan Vardy

LITTLE LANE SCHOOL

There was no doubt in Mammy's mind. When I was five years old, I would be going to the Little Lane School like our Spadger did. Little Lane was a narrow lane. The school was near a farm and the slaughterhouse, by the fire station and Fireman's Row.

On our way to the school, Mammy told me she would be waiting for me outside the gate at dinner time. I thought: *how shall I find the gate?* She reminded me how much I had enjoyed my visit to the school on the open day last summer. I had enjoyed my visit, and I remembered it.

On the open day, when we went to see our Spadger, Mammy and I had gone to the school in good time for me to use the lavatory before going inside. The lavatory block was across the schoolyard and very posh, I thought, with its green painted door. It was so smooth I just had to stroke it, and I could see it shining in the strong sunlight. Mammy was muttering something about how money was being spent on education. It looked pitch black inside to me, in contrast to the bright day outside, but I did not let that bother me. I had made up my mind to enjoy this visit, come what may afterwards.

If there was one thing that Mammy may have been worried about when I came to this school, it was using the lavatories. She sounded very pleased as I went inside.

But before I could find a lavatory, a whole class of girls came in after me, high voices chattering, strong shoes clattering. More and more of them kept coming in. I could hear the sound fanning out, so it was easy for me to trace the size and shape of the place, with all that clamour.

When we were all in, packed jam tight, the game began,

and I joined in, like Mammy said I must, with the cheering and the jeering, and when it was my turn to use the lavatory, I thought the bigger girls were helping me with my britches, because I was still little. But this was the game, the reason for the uproar. Nobody had even hinted to me that school could be this much fun.

The teacher could not say just how sorry she was to my mammy. It did feel good, just going into the school, and I got mixed up with all the other kids. But what a long way it was to the back of the classroom, to reach our Spadger's desk. It was too dull there for me to see much at all. She let me hold the book she was reading, and the kids around us said it was no good, because I could not see. Our Spadger said, "She can see it, then. It's just that she's not big enough to read it yet. That's all. She will be able to read it when she's learned how to read."

I hurt for our Spadger's sake. The kids knew me and I knew them now. Just a few minutes ago we had been playing together as equals. But now they had made it quite plain for me, as plain as the pages in the book were for me, that I could not manage at this school.

Mammy and I went round the classroom. The kids were in little groups doing different things. One group were modelling with plasticine. As we got near, one girl's work was being highly praised by the teacher. I spoke up, saying that I could not see it.

The teacher said that those people who could see had no need to touch, but if I felt the model gently, I would not break it. It was just as though I had jumped in time, or many miles in one moment. Yet it was only from the back of the room, where I had been struggling to be like a child with eyesight, to the front of the room, where I was grateful to be given the gift of blindness, with a new way of seeing with my hands.

The girl was to tell me about her work. This was the first

time I had ever thought of using my hands to see with. As I felt over her work, very gently, the wooden board was a field, and in the middle of the field stood a tiny dog. Around the field was a hedge. It was to stop the dog from getting out, I was told. Feeling a field with a hedge around it was something new for me. By stretching out my hands and feeling the whole of the field with the whole of my hands, I could see the space. A space was something new for me to think about, and I thought, what a lucky girl, to know about the field, and not just streets and walls, as in my world.

I wondered if the dog could get out of the field. The girl said, "No, he can't, because the hedge is prickly." The hedge had no prickles to feel, just fingerprints in the plasticine. Then the girl said the plasticine was blue, and I thought so that must be why her work was being so highly praised. How clever to think of using blue plasticine to make a dog and a hedge, something else for me to think about, and afterwards I thought long and hard about blue dogs, until I felt my mind stretching into a whole new land of let's pretend.

While I felt the other plasticine models, I heard the teacher talking with my mammy, saying that she could not teach me, no, not even if I was a sensible child. I knew I could not come and learn at this school like our Spadger. It had not taken me long to have my big questions answered for me.

Next we all went out on the school yard to watch what the kids could do. After a while the younger brothers and sisters were invited to join in the games. But my mammy would not let me go. The teacher came for me, saying that all children can play games. Besides it would be nice for me to come and join in. She took me to hold hands in a ring.

But Mammy was saying that if I could join in playing, I could join in working. I could not see how to play the game, but just to be with the kids for this one afternoon, was how

Daddy might have said, "Make the best of what you've got. You'll have to be happy at that."

A puddle appeared on the yard, and a little lad was taken out of the ring crying. There were giggles about the puddle looking like a worm squirming along. One kid thought it was blood running from the slaughterhouse next door. The teacher tried to quieten that one, saying, "Not today, dear." Then once again, all the kids were sent to use the lavatories. Now that was my idea of a good game, and one that I could play, and give as good as I got.

Mammy had often wondered why our Spadger came home wearing the wrong breeches, and now I knew why.

On the day when I was five years old, we reached the school. The teacher was standing near the gate, letting the kids through into the yard, leaving the mammies in the lane. When my turn came, the big iron gate was slammed to. It shuddered in its catch. Behind the bars I could see the school bell flashing in front of my eyes as it was swung up and down, hurting my ears. A shadow of a head leaned over the gate, shouting, "I have told you, I cannot teach your child."

But still Mammy did not give in, quietly pointing out one or two kiddies who might not be able to learn much at all. The teacher shouted that, "I can teach them something. Your child I can teach nothing," putting her words to the slam of the clanging school bell. She said, "She cannot come to this school."

I thought the teacher sounded like the postmistress, who gave my mammy some money every week to keep me. She stamped on my allowance book from behind a metal grill. Now I felt safer with the teacher behind those bars.

As we turned to go, the bell was still ringing gently, as it was carried loosely over the school yard. I wondered, did that bell belong to the school, or was it from off a fire engine next door? Mammy was quiet. I knew what would make her happy, so I asked to see the fire engines.

Sometimes, when we were on our way home from shopping, Mammy would put down her shopping bag to pick me up to see through the windows in the big red doors. I did so much love to be picked up. If the sun was out, I could see something shining. Mammy always sounded happy when I said I could see the fire engines. So this day I stiffened myself. I pretended to get excited, and when Mammy asked, "Can you see the engines?" I answered as quickly and as brightly as I could. There was dread in my tummy that the engines might not be inside the fire station. They could have gone to a fire.

"Yes, I can see! I can see the engines!" I lied. It did hurt me to tell that lie. It hurt like a knife cutting through my tummy.

By the time we got home, Mammy was back to her old self, saying that she would show that teacher who could not teach me. She would teach me herself.

Mammy made a good start that very afternoon, and each afternoon afterwards, she gave her time to me. She began by teaching me to find and name each part of my body, a few more each day in greater and greater detail. And for the first time I became aware of myself, and how I used my body. Mammy touched each part of my body and named it; my arms and legs, hands and feet, fingers and thumbs, heels and toes. I learned I had balls on my feet. I found the lines on my palms, and learned I had moons on my nails. That was a lovely thought.

Mammy tickled my armpits and wobbled my kneecaps. I found my eyelids and eyelashes, eyebrows, and we talked about everybody's eyes being a different colour, and we talked all about my eyes.

Then I learned about the clothes that different people wore; the bobby and the collier, the old folk and the babies.

I practiced at getting myself undressed and dressed again, feeling for armholes and elastic, mastering hooks and eyes, press studs fasteners, besides the buttons.

I learned to put words to my actions, jumping and clapping. As Mammy and I played and talked together, I learned more and more. If I shouted, she said, "That's shouting." When I smiled, she said, "And now you're smiling."

I needed to be taught every little thing. I never could have picked things up along the way like our Spadger had done.

Our Spadger had a little blackboard, and Mammy got it out.

She said, "Now, we know you can write."

So she could remember my first day out to play! That was the reason the blackboard had been put away, so that I might have time to forget. So Mammy had known about it all this time. And now I could begin again, and learn to read and write the words mam and dad. M-A-M D-A-D.

The next word Mammy thought nearest to mam was pram. P-R-A-M. But writing four letters on the blackboard were close together. They seemed to join up. And I mixed up the capital letters of P and R.

When I was in bed one night, Mammy and Daddy cut out cardboard letters from cereal boxes so I could pick those up. I could feel them, but Mammy did not notice. That was how I learned to name a few more letters, but when I laid them back down on the table, to me it looked like all the sticks and curves got tangled together. Mammy gathered them all up, saying cheerfully, "There must be a way, and I'll find it."

But just for now, I could learn about money. "Everybody must learn about money," she said. So on the white tablecloth, one shilling's worth, that's twelve of those big old pennies, were spaced out in a line. I could see them. Mammy thought that sixpenny bits could wait. But one day she put out a line of old brass thre'p'ny bits underneath the pennies. I could not see the thre'p'ny bits, but I did know where Mammy had put them, so all went well at playing shops.

Then one day, Mammy put out a line of ha'pennies – halfpennies. I could not see that the ha'pennies were smaller than the pennies, so when Mammy asked me for fourpence ha'penny in change, although I knew which three coins she needed, I picked up the wrong ones to feel them. Mammy did not know that I had to feel the money, to close my hand over it to measure it. She picked up all the money herself. Putting it into her purse, she said she thought she could make better use of it herself.

Then she hurried into the back kitchen, sobbing, saying, "It's true what they say. I can't teach you either. You'll have to go away, where they know how."

NOT MY TURN FOR THE WELLINGTONS

My sister has told me how she came to lose one of her wellingtons. It was in the 1947-48 winter. It was when she was coming home from school, while playing in a five-foot snowdrift. But she dare not tell our mam at the time.

Every time me and Mammy went out, we looked for that wellington in the melting snow. Mammy thought there was little hope of finding it, and there were none in the shops to be bought, so Spadger and I both had to share my wellingtons, and we had to take turns to go out and play. But because they were my wellingtons, I had the choice of when to go out and play in them.

This afternoon, I had let our Spadger have her turn of the wellingtons, and I was playing with the cushions on the settee. Mammy was in the back kitchen, washing out socks by hand. She used to wash the socks by pulling them onto her hands like mittens and rubbing them together with a tablet of soap. While she worked, she was singing softly.

Then I heard her crying for help. I ran into the kitchen, to find her leaning over the sink, holding her arms out over the white frothy soapsuds. I could see her hands. They were bright red. At first I thought *she must be washing out red socks.* Then I thought, *none of us have got red socks.* And Mammy had not got socks on her hands. It was blood I could see.

She was so frightened, and she had told me that blood was nothing to be frightened of. Our house was a first aid post and I lived in it, so I was a little first aider. Yet Mammy was still crying for help. So I found a towel and wrapped it around her hands together in a bundle like I had seen a soldier come in our house once before. And I held the bundle tightly. Together we walked through into the house for her to sit down by the fire, just like I had been taught.

Then next thing I had been taught, after Mammy had refused my offer of the blanket on the settee and the brandy, was to find my mammy if she was not there. But my mammy was here, and she was still crying. I rested her hands on the table, still holding them together wrapped in the bundle, and in my heart, I asked for an answer.

Straight away a mester walked into the house, without even knocking. He said he would never do that, but he had heard the screams for help. He sat beside Mammy and I was asked to fetch damp cloths and dry towels.

When Mammy's hands were wiped clean and dry, not one

cut or scratch could be found. Then the mester said it was the hot water that made her hands bleed so much. Next he fetched her a tumbler of water.

Now that was new. That was not in my first aid list. I did not know this mester, and at first I thought he might be a club customer. But as he chatted with Mammy, I was not sure that I should be listening. I caught a few odd words about school and me, and I would have gone out to play, but Spadger was wearing my wellingtons.

She had shown me how to pile the cushions up on the settee, and climb up to sit on the back. So there I perched, nursing her old dog, Rough. This afternoon, I was looking after him for her. The mester was saying that I must go to school. I knew that my mammy did not want me taken out of her hands. She cried softly now, so the mester turned to talk to me, for Mammy to hear him.

He said, "You would like to go to school, wouldn't you?"

Wouldn't I just! I would need to get my shoes on. They were at the bottom of the stairs. My heart sprang and I sprang from the back of the settee into the air. I had forgotten just how high up I was. The mester cried out, and caught me before I fell. Then I took a running jump at the stairs door, putting my hands up to find the door knob, like our Spadger had been showing me, and this time, for the very first ever, I found the knob at my very first try. I hung on with both hands, turning it one way then the other, but I could not get the door to open. Our Spadger had said that when I was bigger, I must push the bottom stair with my toes.

I asked for Mammy's help. She sat in silence. I did not want to hurt her, but I was happy that the mester had come to take me to school. So it was not really me who had to say, "Sorry, Mammy."

The mester told me that he could not take me right now.

Somehow I could not hear him. He said he would call for me another day. He was saying nice things about the school to Mammy, and about me playing with other children like myself. Then he wondered why I was not out playing with the children this afternoon.

I said, "It's not my turn for the wellitons."

He told me that at school every child had a pair of shoes of their own, so they would be able to play together in the garden. *Now what a funny thing to say,* I thought. How could kids play in a garden? My Daddy's garden was full up with chrysanths, glass cloches, the greenhouse, and rows and rows of veggies, and it could be muddy. There was no space for playing games there.

The mester was still talking, and I was wondering what sort of games could kids like myself play together, because I could not join in any of the games with the kids round here. They played hide and seek in the park, and around the streets they played tiggy on, and follow my leader.

Then the mester was saying, "Green hills," and he was still talking, but I did not hear one more word. Green hills? I must go to school to find a green hill. The one with God on the top!

Once again I tried my hardest to get that stairs door to open, and this time I found I could push the bottom stair with my toes, just like our Spadger had said I would when I was bigger. This time the door sprang wide open. It seemed a long way to drop down, but I let go of the doorknob and found my shoes. I sat down to put them on.

"I've told you, I can't take you now," said the mester. "But whatever your mother says, I will come back, I promise you. You *will* go to school."

Every morning after that my mammy got cross when I asked her if I would be going to school that day. So I kept it to myself and hung on to the hope that one day I *would* be going away to school, to be myself.

Joan Vardy

THE WELFARE CLINIC

My mammy had never dared take me down to the clinic to buy orange juice or cod liver oil. She feared that one day they would take me away from her. But now she accepted that I must go away to school, and the clinic was one place we had to visit. At the door I held back. From inside, I could hear babies crying.

Mammy said, "Come on. We're going in, now we've got this far," and I was half-pushed, half-carried through the doorway.

Inside I shivered with fright, thinking that here and now I would be taken to the institution, never again to be seeing my family and friends, my chums, my playground, which I knew and loved. The fear of unknown people and unknown places came over me like a dark storm cloud. I believed that all the crying babies were waiting to be taken away with me. I could tell that they knew that this clinic was not a nice place.

We followed the nurse to a warm, quiet room. This room was so high and huge, that even the walls and the ceiling shied away from the doctor there. Mammy got me undressed. I knew I would be having new clothes for the institution, so I thought I was being changed ready to go. I asked Mammy about it.

She said, "Oh yes, you will have new clothes." She had not thought that I was to be undressed, and made a fuss about my underslip, telling the nurse it was one she had made for me herself. She had cut it out from the sides of an old worn out flannelette sheet, a green sheet, it was.

"We don't mind that at all. It shows you care for her," said the nurse. "It doesn't matter what you made it from, as long as she's kept warm."

I could tell that made my mammy feel much better. I stood with nothing on to be checked all over, and stood on steps to be weighed and measured. Then I was led over to a table near a tall window. The window was so tall that I could not see the top of it. I gazed up in wonder. At first I could not take it in, then I reckoned that this window must go up through the ceiling.

The lady doctor who was sitting beside the table there, gave me two wires with knobs on the end. They were for me to put in my ears and I was asked if I could hear the clock ticking when the doctor put the other end of the wire on my tummy. The other end of the wire was very cold and I did hear the clock ticking.

Doctor asked if I knew any nursery rhymes to recite for her. So I rattled off, as quick as I could, "Hickory dickory dock, the mouse ran up the clock, the clock struck one, the mouse ran down, hickory dickory dock."

Mammy cried out, "Ohhh!"

"Don't worry," said doctor. "She is very nervous, but you aren't helping, mum."

Then I got the hang of the game. The idea was to say the rhyme together with the clock, like I did deep in the bushes over at the St. Mary's rest gardens.

"There now, you can get dressed again," said the doctor. "And then you can go home."

Thoughts rushed around after each other inside my head. Go home? See my daddy? Have my dinner? Could it be that I did not have to go to the institution after all? Then I realised how I really did want to go to the institution, where I would be taken good care of, where I would like it, like Granddad did, where I could join in the games with the other kids, where they would learn me. They would learn me with my hands, with my new way of seeing, I thought.

While I had been deep in thought, Mammy had got me dressed in the same clothes I had worn to come to the clinic. Doctor asked Mammy if I dressed myself at home. I did dress myself at home, now that Mammy had taught me to look for armholes, find elastic, and how to fiddle with fasteners, so I felt quite ashamed.

We were told that I must be brought back to the clinic again, to be vaccinated. So it seemed that I would be going away the next time I came to the clinic.

Mammy said sorry to me about that first day at the welfare clinic. She had had to take me for my eyes, and there was no reason for me to be undressed that she knew of. If she had have known that, she would have told me before going, so that I would have been expecting it.

HALF AN ICE CREAM

These days, Mammy always made sure that I had something to eat in a morning before going out to play. But today she had gone back on her word, and it was such a long walk to the dentist for me, without having had any breakfast, down into town and up the hill on the other side. I thought about the day we kids had come fishing for tiddlers on the lawn, that day when my prayer had been answered, when I had seen the little fish swirling around in the milky water.

The big house stood in its own grounds. We went through the open gateway, winding our way up a chilly drive, rustling leaves spitting at us from both sides, then up the steps to the front door in the sunlight. I could tell my mammy was nervous while we waited such a long time for the doorbell to be answered. Then a lady with a friendly voice welcomed us inside.

It was dark inside the hallway for me. That is why I could see through the stained glass panels that I found. They were low enough for me to brush the cold glass with my cheeks and trace the leaded ribbons with my hands. With my face to the glass, it was light enough for me to see, and I gazed at the patterns of blue and green. The sight was so beautiful, I held my breath, a gift granted to me, to treasure for a lifetime. I was lost in my own timeless world when, from somewhere far away, somebody was calling my name. I had forgotten all about my empty tummy and the dentist.

Mammy put the lady right, saying, "It's no good you just calling her name. You will have to lead her by her hand. She's blind."

At last Mammy had said the word out loud. She had admitted it to herself, and given in her hopeless private war. My public war had just begun.

The lady led me in to a bright sunny room, with a window that seemed to take up the whole of one wall. I was helped up into a chair, a bit like Granddad's rocking chair, but much higher. After the dentist had looked at my teeth, he said he would take out two of them for me. They did hurt me a bit sometimes, so I was glad to hear that. But then he said he was going to give me gas.

Gas was what the Germans might give me. I had left my gas mask at home. The calming effect of the stained glass window vanished. I tried to get out of the chair, but I dare not jump down. I could not see the floor. I was told that if I was a good girl, I could have some chocolate. Chocolate? What was that? It sounded as bad as gas. I struggled while the dentist and the lady both tried to get a mask over my face. The gas blew cold. It hissed just like Daddy's garden syringe. I coughed, spluttered and struggled, and held my breath, and stared into the black gas mask.

Then the mask was taken away. The dentist and the lady both stepped back a pace to catch their breath. The dentist spoke sharply to me, saying that I could not be given any more gas. He said to the lady, "Show her the chocolate. She can't see it from there. Let her hold it." I was handed the chocolate. It was flat, wrapped up in paper. "There now," said the dentist. "That is what you could have had if you were a good girl."

This chocolate was like a piece of wood, I thought, and I might have been able to drill a hole in it using Daddy's brace and bit in our garret. But the chocolate felt like it might have been joined together, so maybe it was a jigsaw puzzle, like the one our Spadger had of a Toytown bus. Then, in my nightmare, the room was swinging. There were bright blue lights flashing, and cracks, just like a blazing wood fire, and there seemed people all around me talking at once, in that German, like our wireless could, but faster and faster.

I am on my way home, crying in a contest with a little lad about my size. His mammy is saying that nurse said: give him half an ice cream. For my treat we bought oranges from the market. When we got home, Mammy cut one in half for me. But my mouth was too sore for oranges, so it was put cut side down on a saucer to keep fresh. I said that I wanted to share half an ice cream with the little lad. Mammy laughed. She said, "Nurse didn't say half an ice cream! She said half aspirin!"

But I still thought I should have what the little lad had had. So Mammy fetched me a drink of water. She went to the cupboard and gave me a little white pill. I swallowed down the bitter pill, surprised, but without protest, and I tried to work it out. It seemed that even though I had won, I had lost. But even though I had lost, I had won. And I did need to win, to gain strength for another day.

THE EYE INFIRMARY

It was a long bus ride to the eye infirmary for Mamam, Mammy and me. We had all had to get up very early, as everybody must be there by nine o' clock, then sit and wait their turn, and with my name beginning with the letter V, it would be a long wait.

Mammy had been before, and told me all about it. We sat and we waited in long rows of chairs. I had thought it was just me who had to be quiet, but everybody had to be quiet. Now and then, a lady shouted out people's names. I could hear a bit of grumbling and shuffling. Then the quietness would settle again. As there were more and more empty chairs, the air in the room got fresher and cooler.

Mammy had brought her glasses cases with her and she fidgeted with them in her lap. I did not hear my name shouted out, but Mammy took me into another room. It was dark in there. They had the blackout up. Thinking about the bombers coming over, I was frightened, but a kind lady in there had a torch, so she switched it on and let me play with it. I could see the light, and I enjoyed listening to the click of the switch. Switching on made a ting sound, but switching off made just a dull click.

Then the kind lady played a game with me. She held the torch, and moved about the room, switching it on and off. I was to point to it if I saw the light. I thought she was just playing with me to pass the time on while I waited to see the doctor. I had no idea this was an eye test, so I did not think it was cheating when I could point to the torch and say whether it was on or off. I was playing the game using my ears, the best way I could, the way I always did. Joining in games was not easy for me and I often had to make do with let's pretend.

Then the kind lady thought the game would be better if she bandaged one of my eyes. I was quite happy to let her bandage one of my eyes. It would not make any difference in the dark. Being blindfold was often part of a game when playing with the kids. I thought about the blackout again, so the kind lady switched on the lights, while Mamam and Mammy had a chat with the doctor.

My mammy had been in the eye infirmary in the war. At night times, the wards were lit with blue light bulbs, and they had put a smokescreen around the hospital to hide it when the Germans were trying to bomb the railway station nearby. They hit the church, but everybody was pleased, because the trains could keep running.

I was still listening for the bombers coming when Mammy took me into another dark room with the blackouts up. A doctor in there said that my mother should have taught me that there was no need to be afraid any more. He told me that he had a light, and that it was through a hole, and I could come and see it. There was a chair there, by the table for me to sit on. But the chair's seat was missing, so I just perched on the bar at the front. I was not high enough to see the light. The doctor asked me if my mother would let me sit on her lap.

So Mammy perched on the bar at the front of the chair, and I perched on her lap. I was still not high enough to see the light. The doctor sounded angry and came round to our side of the table, but on finding that the chair was broken, his voice sweetened. He was another man.

He said, "You should have told me."

Mammy said, "I thought you were having to make do."

He said, "I think we can do a little better, not much, but a little better."

At last another chair was found for me, and although it did have a seat, Mammy thought it was about like her, worn out. When I did see the light down the hole, there was spittle on the place where I could rest my chin, so I would not look again.

Somebody had to be found to clean things up, and somebody else had to be found to take me to have my face washed. It was warm water, scented soap on a flannel.

EVACUATED

I knew all about evacuation. During the war, Mamam had had an eleven-year-old boy come to stay with her. He had been evacuated. The doctor at the clinic said something like: I must come back three times to be evacuated.

It was a man I had to see, and on the first day, he said he immunised me. It did not work, because Mammy had washed me and got all the bumps wet. They all had to be done over again, and I must wear a wide plaster which nearly reached right round my arm, and I had to keep it on for such a long time that Mammy thought it would stunt my growth.

"Ridiculous!" said the doctor. We must keep coming back to the clinic for me to be inoculated.

Each time we went, there were Dolly Mixtures for me. A

huge tin would be lifted down from a high shelf. I could see the sweets in the tin. They looked pink, and I almost looked forward to going to the clinic each week, to help myself to a handful, because sweet rations only lasted me for two minutes, Mammy would say.

On the last day at the clinic, there were only three dolly mixtures in the bottom of the tin. But the doctor would not let me take them, but just have a look at them. He told me I was a big girl now. Those sweets were for a little baby. But I heard the nurse say, "Oh, doctor," and this tin was from a low shelf, not from a high shelf.

Now on my arm I had four white pennies in a square. I was so proud of them. They were like badges which must be worn by every child at the institution.

Our Spadger was feeling left out, because she could not be evacuated. I was feeling impatient. The doctor had said I had been immunised, I had been inoculated, but I was still waiting to be evacuated.

MOVING ON

Now that we only had one pair of wellingtons between us, I could only go out to play half the time, so I grew away from the kids and it seemed that all of them except me were getting cleverer. Then the five kids from over the wall flitted into a council house without even time for a goodbye, because their mam said that goodbyes were bad things.

But when they came back to clean out their house, I went

in their lav with my little friend, the two-holer where we used to sit side by side in the dark on their back yard. He told me that he would not sit on their new lav. It was inside the house. His mam was telling my mammy, "He'll have to get used to it."

He was so sad, because only big kids lived round them now. He was crying as I listened after them as they walked away for the very last time; my little friend, the one who was to have been leader one day. It did not seem fair that he was so sad, yet I was so happy. But we had said our goodbyes.

I missed the kids badly. I would stand outside their gate and listen inside my head to the little sounds that used to be; the water trickling down their grate because their tap was always left on for the kids to either wash their hands or get themselves a drink whenever they needed; their fire being settled for the kettle to be put on to boil. I heard again in my head friendly sounds that I could not put a name to, which will stay as strangers forever. Then there'd be the kids, all in a muddle, and their mam come to sort them out. It hurt to sense the silence.

Yet my life was easier now, not having to keep up with all those clever kids and being left out of their games. It was time for me to move on.

THE ROCKING HORSE

Again, Mammy and I went on the long bus ride to the eye infirmary, but this time I went without having breakfast, even though Mammy had said that I would not go without breakfast again. I knew she was doing her best for me, so I did not say anything about it. *War rationing,* I thought. She might only get upset and say, "Going without is something we all have to put up with. It cannot be helped, so there's no good in grumbling."

On this second visit, we did not have to go into the waiting room. We went in a room like the one at the clinic, lovely and warm, high windows. Like at the clinic, I was undressed and checked all over. Then the nurse helped me on with a dressing gown. She told me it was a deep red colour, with a lovely cord to tie round my waist. Mammy had a long green dressing gown, so I did feel grown up, looking just like her. But because I could not see, I did not know that I was wearing this dressing gown back to front.

The nurse bandaged my eyes, and sat us down by a radiator, for me to keep warm. I heard a baby crying. Mammy told me it had been there all the time, fast asleep in its tiny cot. The nurse thought there was nothing anybody could do to comfort a blind baby. Mammy was sad that it was left to cry, so when the nurse left the room, she picked me up and carried me over to the tiny cot. Then she pulled my bandages up for me to have just a peep, she said.

I could see a bandage wrapped around the baby's head. It was just like mine. So it made me try to be a big girl. Mammy held the baby's hand, cooing softly while it went to sleep again. She told me there was a rocking horse at the far end of the room, and how she would love it for me to ride it, as I may never have a chance like that again. But I must promise to keep my bandage on.

Mammy helped me find out all about the horse, with my new way of seeing with my hands. He was like the horse I had ridden on the roundabout at feast time. Mammy helped me onto his back. The horse did not go up and down like the horses at the Wakes. He rode backwards and forwards. I soon got into my stride, and away I galloped in time with Mammy's sing-song, "Ride a cock horse to Banbury Cross, to see a fair lady ride on a white horse, rings on her fingers and bells on her toes, she shall have music wherever she goes." I could tell that Mammy did love it, which made me love it all the more. We both laughed as I rode higher.

The nurse was summoned back into the room by our happy sound. She had come to see if I was still wrapped up, sure that the bandage had been taken off, or how could I be playing? Mammy spoke up, telling her that a blind child could play as well as any other child. But the nurse did not think so. So Mammy made her stand there to watch me playing. I rocked backwards and forwards, Mammy sing-songed. Seeing was believing. Even the nurse joined in, laughing with us.

Later the nurse held my hand to take me into another room, where I could hear other kids. They were going to have their dinner. The nurse asked my mammy if I would be upset when I could not have any.

"Not if it's cabbage," she said.

My bandage was taken off, and I was shown my cot. I was sitting up in it quite happily, when a lady brought me a dinner. But I would not eat it. I could smell it was cabbage. It made me heave. My nurse rushed over to take it from me. She thought I might be sick.

The little lad in the cot next to mine cried because he could not have his dinner taken away from him. My mammy was assured that the nurse knew best, how every child would not like every food, but every child must eat some food, and something was usually found that a child would eat just a little of.

I lay in a white space, in a dream, with a white light at my feet, a pink sheet of lint half-covering my face. We kept lint in our first aid cupboard at home. I liked the clean smell of it. This lint was bad, awful bad.

A man's voice at my right said, "She's looking at me."

A voice at my left said, "Don't be silly. She's asleep."

This man was dressed in white. Behind him there were shiny things. They might have been saucepans on a cooker. I thought I lay on a table in a posh kitchen. The man on my right was still sure I could see him. He was very tall.

Going home on the bus, I could see bright colours that were not there that morning on the journey going to the eye infirmary. When we got home, Mammy lit the fire to boil the kettle to make us a cup of tea. I stood on the hearth to watch and wait, where Mammy said I might get a tiny bit warm. As the fire burned up brightly, I saw it for the first time as orange, yellow and red, and even bits of purple in it. There were flames dancing, and beautiful blue smoke, rising gracefully up the chimney. So fire was not just the one bright orange blur that I knew.

While waiting for Daddy to come home, sitting on the back of the settee, I saw that the net curtains had fancy work on them, and flowers with frilly petals, with holes in the middle where the yellow bit should be. We had brought home a tube of eye ointment, which I must keep having in till bedtime. But when I asked why I could not always have eye ointment in to make me see, Mammy just murmured. She put the tube on the table and I stood there, looking and thinking about it, with my legs feeling like they were made of India rubber.

I saw that the tablecloth was not just plain white. It had shadowed patterns on it, which made me feel restful. It summed up the home I knew, but had never seen before, but just felt inside myself. But this was the home where the others lived.

I was happier the next morning when everything looked

normal again, spotlessly clean, perfectly straight and tidy. That was my home, the same way it had always been.

POP'S PINK TIDDLE

We loved, knew, trusted our doctor. We called him Pop. Mamam, that was my mammy's mam, paid a few coppers a week for herself, Mammy, Spadger and me to go and see Pop if we were poorly. Daddy still paid a few coppers a week to see his doctor, up in his own home town, if he was poorly.

He often told me about when he was a lad. If one of them in their house were badly, the doctor's orders were always the same; four jugs of water, from the brook where the herbs grow, and it would be my daddy's job to fetch it.

But for all our ills, Mammy could usually find a remedy. The doctor's was still the last resort. There was once, when I was small, I had a really bad tummy ache, and Daddy went to fetch Mamam to come and see me. She advised putting soap up my bottom. The thought of anybody doing anything like that to me hurt me in a horrible way, so much so that I put on a very brave face. I tried hard to smile, and suffered in silence. Then Mammy thought I had been shamming, but at least the soap was not used.

Mammy told me about how we once had a lovely full first aid cabinet. I could remember that night when the Germans rattled our house and it fell off the top shelf in the kitchen, and Mammy cried. A lot of money had been spent on medicines for us all, and when the cabinet was sorted out, all that could be saved was some yellow sulphur powder and some Fiery Jack.

When my mammy was a young girl, her dad found work at the pit and it was a house belonging to Pop that Mamam had found to rent. It was Pop who had come to see my mammy at Mamam's house while she was resting on the sofa. That was when our Spadger was born. It was Pop who had come to see me when I was really poorly with the measles that the Germans had given me.

Now we could all go to a doctor without paying any pennies, but still home remedies were always tried first. Mammy would take me on the bus to see Pop. We would go up the side street to his surgery. Once we went on a dark evening.

In the waiting room, the gaslight whispered softly. The air was thick with smoke, which made us all cough, not just the smokers. In the middle of the floor there was a big bowl, a bright blue enamel one, just the same as the big kettle we kept topped up on the oven top by the fire. That was the one we had brought down from the garret and weren't to say nowt about, if anybody were to ask.

In the waiting room, I mentioned it to Mammy. She grabbed for her hankie and choked in the chorus with the smokers. They were flicking their fag ends into the bowl and spitting on them to put them out, making them stink.

Most of the times we went to see Pop, it was in the morning. Mammy liked to go in with or after somebody else, so that she would know when it was our turn to go through into the surgery. If not, she would have to count the patients in the waiting room. Sometimes two would go in the surgery together, and sometimes one would leave without going in because they were waiting for another patient, or got tired of waiting.

Mammy said, "They might come back another day."

Sometimes the waiting room would be too full for Mammy to be counting everybody properly. Then you might have to jump up quick if you thought it was your turn. The walls of the waiting room were nicotine brown, and around the edges of the room, there were dining chairs of all kinds. Mammy said they were for sitting on.

Sometimes we would hear great arguments coming from Pop's kitchen next door. If Pop heard the row, he would come through his waiting room to settle things down. If time was getting on, he would lock the street door so no more patients could come in. But if you were too late, you could hang about outside, and the next patient out would let you in.

In the surgery, Pop would be sitting at his table calling out, "Next," and inviting folk to, "Come in. Sit yourself down, won't you?"

Just above where Pop sat, there was a hole in the ceiling, *to let out the smoke,* I thought. Mammy called it a skylight. I could see that the sky was light, but I still thought that it was just a hole. The window which looked out over the street glowed a yellow colour, but Mammy did not know much about it when I asked her if it had a net curtain which had been washed with a dolly cream bag to make it look so yellow, or was it so yellow because it was dirty?

There was a sink in the corner where Pop made up his medicines, and along one wall there were shelves behind green curtains. Pop would rummage through his medicine bottles to find the right one. He always felt sure he had just the very thing for me somewhere. As he shuffled the bottles, he would greet each one with its long name, and they would chink chink on one another in reply.

Just lately, life did not seem so good any more. All home remedies had failed, and I had got Pop puzzled too. I was taken back to see him for a second time. He talked in a gentle way with Mammy for a long while, now and then brushing ash off his papers, blowing them, shaking them. But he was still at a loss for what medicine he might mix up for me. I knew I would be able to tell which medicine I was given the first time, so I jumped down from my chair and pulled back a green curtain. Mammy tried to stop me, but Pop stopped her, saying, "She may know better than we her cure. Sometimes children do, you know."

He told Mammy that just the day before he had put his shelves in order, so I would not know where to find my medicine that he had given me the first time. Now I was not quite so sure I would know, but I felt along the row of tidy bottles, putting my hands on each one for a second or two. With my left hand, I found a bottle.

Pops gently said, "No, not that one."

Then I do not know why, but I took a bottle down from the shelf. It made me feel so very sad. I held it tightly with both hands close to my body. I felt the pains in my tummy, and I knew the one who took this medicine was very ill.

I looked at Pop, trying to ask a question, with tears falling from my eyes, but I could not. I did not have words to ask.

He said to me, "Don't worry. The gentleman is old. I feared so. I would have known so, but he did not tell me what you have told me, and we must take strong doses when we need them."

Pop told Mammy I had touched the bottles I could reach easily, and he told me that I might find my bottle of medicine if I reached up to a higher shelf. I found the higher shelf and felt along the bottles again, thinking about each one, till I found my bottle. This bottle made me feel happy and strong on the inside.

Pop said, "I hadn't thought of that one, but that one is not for you. I will mix some, suited to your age."

I told him how I had liked the first bottle of medicine. It had tasted of treacle. He chuckled from his sink in the corner.

On the way home, the bottle slid around in the bottom of Mammy's empty shopping bag. She kept reminding me what Pop had said.

"It's your medicine. You must take it all, and it won't taste nice this time." That night Mammy told Daddy how disgusting it was that her child was allowed to choose its own medicine.

Daddy said, "It's all t'same stuff, just pink tiddle. He puts a bit o' colour in. If folks thought it did 'em good, it did."

Pop's medicine was always pink, but you could tell how bad or how big you were by how much cocoa powder sunk to the bottom of the bottle and had to be shaken up. But I did wonder if this was the right bottle I had chosen.

The medicine lived on the sideboard by the Westminster clock, to remind Mammy not to forget about it. After grinning and bearing my bitter spoonfuls for three days, I did begin to feel well, in the same way I had done when I first touched the bottle. Mammy was so chuffed. She said she had known all along that I knew better than Pop. I had got my life back!

UP SMOKE

Up Smoke. Daddy told me that's where we were, but that was not smoke I could smell. That was new, a sweet scented air wafting in from the street. We were in a hollow building, sitting on a bench facing double doors. The door on the right stood open inwards, back onto the wall letting in the draught, a new warm draught.

Outside, all the motor cars were in a hurry, all their horns pap-papping, each one playing its part, joining in a never-ending tuneless tune. I thought, *the people here must be very poor.* They had no pegged rugs on their floor, just bare tiles.

To our left was a wide flight of stone steps going up to a light where a row of big windows let in a new bright light. The walls were pale cream. They gave back that new light, filling the empty echoey space with silence. Nobody spoke. We were all there, Mammy and Daddy, Spadger and me. And our Spadger chose to stay there when I went up those wide stone steps, holding hands between both Mammy and Daddy.

Just at the top, we went in a room on the left. This room did not seem to have a window of its own, so it had to borrow light from the stairs windows, and keep its door wide open. The doctor sat just inside the door. His chair had its back to the wall. His table was beside him. The nurse there found chairs for Mammy and Daddy to sit down, and kept me busy while the serious talking went on.

She showed me her nurse's uniform. She was wearing a hat. A hat in the house! My mammy sometimes kept her hat on and her scarf on in the house, but only while she got warmed through after we had been shopping on a cold day. The nurse told me she was wearing a blue dress with a white apron. My mammy's pinafores had frilly straps to go over her shoulders, but the nurse had to pin her apron bib in place.

This doctor even wanted to examine the soles of my feet. Mammy could see they were dirty.

"I did wash them," she said, "but she'll have been running round since then."

"I'm pleased," he said. "If they were not a bit dirty, I should think there was something wrong."

Nurse said, "Find the dolly."

I was tired. I had had enough already. All I could see was cream. Cream walls, cream floor, cream door.

"Where is it?" I asked her.

"On the sink," she said. No sink in sight.

Somebody else here who does not know about me, I thought, *and there's no use me getting choked up like this every time.* I told myself I would have to learn to deal with this kind of problem and this kind of person, even when I felt like crying out, "You can see that I am blind."

Like magic, the nurse turned into a friend. She led me over to the sink.

"Where is it?" I asked again.

"She's on the tap," said nurse.

I had learned that a tap would be on a wall above a sink, so I stretched up as high as I could, rubbing my hand along the wall. Nurse put my hand on a tap. That was new! A tap, fixed to a sink? She handed me the doll.

"It's got no britches on," I said. "She'll catch a cold, sitting on the sink." I showed it to the doctor.

"Can you see her hair?" he asked me. "What colour is it?"

I did not know the word for ginger, so I could not say.

"Can you see her hair slides?" he said. I could. They were pink.

"It's got no britches on," I said again. There was an uncomfortable hush.

I swapped the doll for a game. It was a wooden board with pegs sticking out of it. When I tipped the board sideways, all the pegs jumped out of the holes and onto the floor. Mammy had warned nurse that would happen, and she knew what would come next, when nobody came to help me find the pegs. I cried the tears I had held back so far.

Mammy was saying she did not doubt how many children the doctor had examined, but she knew me best. I was her child. I noticed a bright red blob slowly coming towards me. Nurse was bringing me another toy. I could not tell her what it was. I could not say what it was even when I held it. But the doctor would not believe me.

In the end, nurse told me, "It's a bus." It was beyond me to picture a whole bus. All I knew of a bus was the slatted seats and the space under the stairs. This toy was just a wooden box with holes in it. I felt around the floor to find the pegs that had rolled away. *They'll be safer in the box than on the board,* I thought. So I posted any pegs I found through the holes. Then nurse was tired. I could tell she had had enough.

"I shall never be able to get them out again," she said.

I ran through the open doorway, calling to our Spadger. The doctor panicked, coming out after me.

"She'll fall, she'll fall," he said.

"Oh no, she won't," said my mammy. "She knows the steps are there."

I was glad of her reminder, but I would have remembered as soon as I heard our Spadger call back from down the bottom. The doctor told me about the handrail on the wall for the steps. I had not been shown that on the way up, but I did use it on the way back down.

Very soon our Spadger and I were playing a game on the steps without holding on the rail. Up one, turn around, down one, up two, turnaround, down two, up three, turn around, down three, up four, turnaround....

The doctor stood at the top of the stairs, stammering. He was lost for words.

Outside on the street, in that sweet scent and the warm wind, and the noisy motor cars again, then I had the joy of finding out for myself why babies called motor cars papaps.

Mammy told Daddy, "Huh! Doctors! They know everything about nothing. He's had his eyes opened for him today."

Daddy agreed and soothed her, saying, "No use in 'arpin' on. Some folk'll never learn. They'll never learn."

MY NEW FRIEND

A visitor came quite often now, and Mammy was pleased to see that he was always dressed smartly in a brown suit, but he did look around him for dust, and once he spotted a little heap of dirt under the table. Mammy had swept it together, but it had been in the dark, so she could not see it, and she had missed it, and forgotten to sweep it up with a dustpan and brush when she had cleaned up that morning at six o' clock before it had got light.

The visitor smoked cigarettes, so Mammy would get him one of the Bakelite ashtrays down from the shelf. He taught me how to put the papers in the little tin to roll his cigarettes, but when he held the lighted match for me to blow out, I did not know why I had to blow. Mammy decided I must be frightened of fire. Grown-ups said and did such odd things, sometimes. I could just not make them out.

The visitor made friends with me. He brought a cardboard clock with him for us to play together. It was about the same size as a dinner plate, with a cream face and bright green fingers. I did feel proud to move him round to show him some of the times I already knew, but both he and Mammy tried to show me that there was something more about the clock face, but I could not grasp what they meant. Mammy said that was one of the reasons that I was going away to school.

It was Daddy who had taught me to tell the time. He would chalk up his figures for the twenty-week club on the inside of the cupboard door. He would stand me on a chair to watch while he drew a clock for me, with little feet on the bottom and bells on the top to wake you up in the morning. And he always drew fancy patterns round the edge. He showed me how to hold the chalk, and he would guide my hand as we drew the fingers together. Then he would rub out the fingers and next day, while he was at work, I would draw some more for him, for when he got home. I learned a new time each time; the o'clock, the half past, the quarter past and the quarter to the hour, then the five and twenty past, and the five and twenty to the hour.

The next night Daddy had not taught me a new time, so the day after, I thought, *I'll please him.* I dragged a chair over to the cupboard, climbed up, found a piece of chalk, and I did a little fat finger, and a big thin finger. That night, when Daddy opened the cupboard door, he was not pleased. He was upset. I had drawn over some figures he had been working out. He was cross because I had not told him I could not see the clocks he had drawn. At the same time he was sad I could not see.

"I know now. You've shown me," he said. But he would not teach me any more. Up until then, I really did think I could see the clocks on the door. I *could* see the clocks, but I could not say where it was I could see them.

Mammy thought she may as well show me the rest, now I had got this far, so with a teaspoon and a knife, and a shilling's worth of those big old brown pennies on our white tablecloth, I learned about a five past and a ten to, and then there were too many times to fit in. But that was all there was to it, and I had a rough idea about it, so we just forgot.

My new friend told me about trains and how one day very soon now, he would take me on a journey, on one train to

London, and one train to school. I was looking forward to going to London because before the war Daddy had worked there on the buildings. In the garret he had told me about it, and I learned about it from him while he shaved in the back kitchen in the evenings. I would sit on the pegged rug, even though it was cold in there. I'd listen to him singing, and my Daddy could sing. He sang a lot of lovely songs which are mixed up in my head now.

But one song about London, I knew a lot of words of, and I believed them all, even if Daddy did change some of them. It went something like, 'Oh Mary this London's a wonderful sight, where the people go working by day and by night, they don't grow no taters, no barley, no wheat, but there's gangs of them digging for gold in the street. At least when I asked them that's what I were told, so I just took a 'and in this digging for gold. But for all that I found there I might as well be, where the slag heaps of Briley slope down to our street.'

There were more words about beautiful shapes nature never designed, about roses that came away on your lips and peaches and cream.

On one of his visits, my new friend asked Mammy to put my coat on for me, so that I could be taken for a walk. Mammy was quiet.

He said, "You've got to trust me. You can stand by the door and watch."

I was used to walking, for going shopping, and to the allotment, and to Mamam's and Granddad's. But this was new, to be taken out, just to walk, like it was new to have a grown-up friend. We went out, past the desert island and the park, and over the lane to the bus stop. There, we had a real good feel at the stone wall. It was the same rough wall as the one round the cemetery, but this one was much too high for me to climb over.

My new friend wanted me to remember all about this bus stop. We walked up and down the hill a bit for me to notice how we were on a hill. He told me that if I remembered, I would know where we were while we waited here to catch the bus. The bus would take us to the city to catch the train to go to school.

I was very happy about it, and happy about the new shoes I would be bought, which I could keep for my very own and never have to share. And my new friend told me that he would bring me a raincoat to wear on the day. I was happy about that too.

Then he showed me how to say goodbye, how to wave my arm and wave my hand, and say, in a cheerful voice, "Goodbye, goodbye!"

SAYING GOODBYE

I was not so cheerful to be taken round to visit all the family to say goodbye, even though they all gave me money. It was the way they said their goodbyes, with wet tears on their faces, and sloppy kisses. You would think they were never going to see me again. Some of them I was sure I had never seen before.

Mammy had just the one sister, but Daddy said, "There were fourteen of us, and wi' me being one o' t'nippers, I were born an uncle." He said he should not wonder that I got them all mixed up. There were two of his sisters I clearly remember visiting; Auntie and Uncle who lived in Institute Street: they kept The Peaks. And an auntie and uncle who were often talked about, but not often visited. They lived up in Daddy's own home town that was out of our back gate, and up the road past Daddy's allotment garden, and past a row of terraced houses. Each house had steps going up to the front door. It made me think of my first day out to play, and the truth I shared only with Mammy about the swear words on the steps.

Each of the houses had two or three milk bottles on their steps, but our milk still came in a can, brought round with a horse and cart. Every morning our back door would be left open wide for the milkman to bring his can down into the kitchen. He would swirl it around for fair shares for all and measure one ladle of milk into our clean jug.

Auntie's was on past the football ground, where Daddy would let me look through the knotholes in the fence. It had been put up, he said, to stop folk from watching the games without paying. Daddy thought how wrong that was, not to let folk look at green grass. He said, "There were blokes working down t'pit, lasses in t'factory, it might be only green field they ever see."

Then we would come to hills, up and down, where Daddy would chuckle to hisself. It was about the times when the trams used to run and how they would slip back down the hill in the wintertime, when he would stand up halfway up the hill and put his arm out to stop one.

"Well, I were just a lad, and there were no 'arm done," he said.

My sister has told me how she well remembered that day when we went up to Auntie's for me to say goodbye, and how I was told and bribed, and threatened not to touch anything in the house. She had been brought along to help, and told to keep her eyes peeled and not to take them off of me for one minute.

I knew my manners in other folks's houses, so we stood behind the table at the back of the house. I was resisting the temptation to feel the white tablecloth, to rub the hem between my finger and thumb, so that I could tell Mammy whether or not it had been starched Sunday stiff.

Auntie asked if we would like a drink. Our Spadger's refusal was met by a silence, so when it was my turn to be asked, I thought, maybe it had been wrong of our Spadger to refuse, so I said, "Yes please, Auntie."

I heard a tumbler being put down on the table in front of me. I thought I would be having it filled with pop. I waited to hear the glug glug glug glug glug and the fizz. Auntie said, "I expect you can get one for yourself. Surely you are not waited on hand and foot at home?"

I found the tumbler and went through into the back kitchen. Auntie must have meant that I was supposed to get myself a drink of cold water. I found the sink by the door. At our house we had a brown, shallow slopstone, but Auntie's sink was deep and white and smooth, so high for me to reach the tap. I looked under the sink for a beer crate to stand on. That was where ours lived, handy for Mammy to take it out to stand on to reach up to tie the washing line to the line post. I could not find their beer crate, so I went to ask Auntie, "Do you keep your beer crate in t'pantry?"

Auntie drew in her breath. There was another silence. Uncle cleared his throat. Our Spadger told him that I was still little. Auntie sighed. She said, "If you cannot use the tap, you may use the footstool. You will find it in the corner. Your cousin used to use it when he was younger." I felt good inside to be like my cousin, who I did not know I had.

The footstool had wobbly legs. The top was cushioned, so I took great care climbing up, holding tightly to the top of the sink with my left hand, with the tumbler in my right. My mammy would not let me be doing this at home. In the sink there was a rubber thing. It was for putting in the hole to stop the water from going down. Not just an old rag for stuffing down the hole.

Then I learnt the real reason why this auntie and uncle were spoken of as being posh. On the wall above the sink, there was not just one tap, there were two taps. I asked myself, why would anybody need two taps? What could be done with two taps that could not, just as easily, be done with one tap?

It was because I had come to say my goodbye that I was invited to 'come round the table and stand on the hearth'. I watched Auntie putting coal on the fire using tongs, not just a shovel. Three lumps were carefully chosen from the scuttle, and placed in the fire grate, not just tipped on. Then Auntie stood back and asked Uncle if it was just about right. He was sitting at the table, in the same place where my daddy sat at our house. Speaking slowly, he said, "Let it not be thought that we are mean. After all, is it not Sunday? Put on another lump."

The tongs hovered in the air. "Do you really think so?" asked Auntie. "This lump? Like that?"

"Mmm... yes," said Uncle.

I had heard it said that he wore his jacket to eat his dinner. I thought I should not wonder at it. Three small lumps of coal would hardly throw out enough heat to keep him warm, even if he did sit at the front of the table near the fire.

Auntie supposed other aunties had given me money. "And how much did they give you?" she asked. Some aunties had been too kind. One had given me half a crown. I thought it best to pretend not to know anything about money. A coin was placed on the table for me to pick up. Using my best Sunday manners, I thanked her, picked up the coin and gently lowered it into my pocket, hoping it would not chink too much on all the other coins.

When we were out of earshot of the house, Daddy asked, "'ow much did she gi' ye, then?" When I told him, he could not stop laughing.

NO END OF A DAY

My suitcase had been packed ready. Mammy and Daddy had not known what to put in it. They just put in some things that they thought I might need. Then I was put in the tub and got ready for bed. Daddy and I said our goodbyes. He wanted me to go to school, to learn, get clever, and be good. We clung to each other, just for a few seconds. Then we called to each other as I climbed up the stairs behind our Spadger with a smiling feeling inside my tummy.

When Mammy came to wake me, early, I was still tired. It was still dark outside. We crept down the stairs together, leaving our Spadger asleep by herself in the big double bed that we both shared. Daddy had made a good fire before he went to work. It was big enough for me to see the orange glow, even with the house light switched on. Mammy and I had our favourite breakfast; bread and marmalade and cups of tea. Then I had a quick wipe over with a cloth, and Mammy helped me to get dressed in my new clothes.

I had a blue jumper that Daddy liked. It was out of his twenty-week club book, and a blue skirt that Mammy had made for me herself. She had bought some new cloth and used a paper pattern. The skirt straps had been a tricky job. Two squares of cloth were folded over to make triangles, then one was put on top of the other to make a V shape, with the narrow pieces to go over my shoulders. Mammy thought if she had not bothered to follow that paper pattern, she was sure she could have saved a quarter of a yard of stuff. The waistband was too thick.

She told me, “Machine wun’t tek it. I’ve done t’best I can, and we’ll have to be satisfied at that.” It was good to take to school with me, that homely scent of machine oil.

My new shoes fastened up twice. First the laces were tied in bows, real laces, not just string. Then the long wide tongues, with fringes on the ends, folded down to hide the laces, and they were kept in place with straps that buckled up at the sides. The shoes were light brown, but too far off for me to see them when I stood up. I was walking round and round the house in them, when there was a quiet knock on the front door. My friend came in.

Mammy wanted me to use the lavatory. I wanted to be off. My friend told her that he would see to it that I would be taken good care of, all day. He handed her the raincoat he had brought for me to borrow. Mammy did not say anything, but she helped me to put it on and we got in more muddle than a little with it. The raincoat was a bit too big for me. Mammy pulled the shoulders back and the sides down, trying to make me look tidy inside it. Then she fiddled with the buckled belt and found somewhere to tuck away the long spare end.

My friend was talking softly. He said, “Don’t say anything. Just cut her a slice of bread and marmalade.”

Mammy did find a voice, then, but it was not her voice. It was hard.

“She’s already had one,” she said.

He spoke again softly, and slowly he said, “I know. Just make her another one.”

The loaf was still in its place at the corner of the table,

cut side down on the folded newspaper. I heard the saw knife cutting unsteadily as she turned and turned the loaf around. The butter knife caught the edge of the pot as she scraped the hard butter, and it rattled in the bottom of the marmalade pot. I thought, that sounds about empty. Then Mammy put the big sandwich into my hand.

The front door had already opened, and my friend, with my suitcase, was already out on the coursey. I went outside and Mammy came to stand on the doorstep. With a big wave of my hand, and with happy voices, we both called, "Goodbye! Goodbye!"

Mammy could not say that word, or use the name she lovingly called me. She shouted, too loud, "Toodle-oo."

My friend took my hand in his, and said, "For her sake, wait until we're out of earshot."

We went past my little friend's empty house and the barber's at the end of the row, over the sandy island and on to the park. That was where I started to cry. My friend said, "I'm sorry. It's the dark, isn't it?" And, "You can't see, but it's not really dark, and I can see, and we both know where we are, don't we?"

We crossed the lane to the bus stop, and I was asked again to feel for the rough stones that I'd found before, so that I would know where I was. The stones were damp and cold without the warm afternoon sunshine, but I was happy again.

My friend thought I might like to sit on my suitcase. It would be fun for me. But the lock was not fastened securely. The suitcase should have had a strap round it, but Daddy thought it would have been a lot of trouble when it came to the time to take out my sandwiches, so he had put the strap inside the suitcase. I told my friend about it, so we opened up the lid, got the strap, fastened it round the suitcase, through the handle. Then I was lifted up on top with my back to the wall.

I sat there drumming away with my grand new shoes, eating my bread and marmalade. It was the best sandwich Mammy had ever made for me. It had bread as thick as Daddy liked it, and butter like you'd never heard of rationing, and the good marmalade from the bottom of the pot to suck out from between the crusts. It was hard to catch all the marmalade before it dripped down on the raincoat.

Then I heard the sound I sometimes heard when I was still in bed, early in the morning. It was the pit men in their boots. They came from everywhere about to the bus stop. My friend was sorry again. He thought I might be frightened. The pit men stood on the kerb edge, scraping their boots to keep themselves warm, laughing and joking with each other.

When the bus came, I could see it had lights on the outside. I thought: why would you have lights on the outside? That's useless!! I was lifted up so high to be put on the bus that it felt like I was going for a ride at the feast. It was so exciting, to be with the pit men, still eating bread and marmalade.

It was daylight when we got to the city. In the cafe, my friend sat me up to the table, while he went to buy coffee. When I saw the coffee, I cried with alarm. All I could see was coffee. How could coffee stand up on its own? I did not see that it was in a glass cup. My friend wiped away my tears with a big white hanky. He said that I would have to learn to feel. That was why I was going away to school, to learn. And he said, "We've both already learned a lot today, haven't we?" He folded my fingers around the cup handle.

At home, once, when we had run out of tea rations, Mammy had made us a cup of coffee, but it was much too strong for me. The cafe coffee was not too bad and I drank it down. My friend asked me if I would like some chocolate. Chocolate? I was going to find out what chocolate was!

He gave me some money and told me I could go to the

counter and buy my own. Every Friday I went to the little shop in our row with my Friday penny to spend. But this felt a bit scary; all part of going to school and learning.

On the counter there was a glass case that I did not see, and the woman did not help me, and I got upset about it. My friend took off the wrapper for me and said I would have to learn not to be upset. The chocolate was very hard, so we shared it.

The train to London was packed full and I loved it, everything about it. The slamming doors, the guard shouting, the shrill whistle, the chug chug and the chuff chuff, the taste of the smoke, the swaying about and the noise in the dark tunnel, the clattering of the rails and the screech of the brakes as we came into a station, and more guards shouting. Then it would all happen all over again and again.

A lady passenger was asked if she would not mind taking me along to the toilet. It was ever so posh in there. The wash hand basin had warm water, soap and a towel. The lady was very kind and cared for me very well. Later my friend had to get out his big white hanky to wipe away soot smudges from my face.

When we got off the train, I asked if we were in London yet. My friend said, "Not quite. We have to catch a bus." The bus we caught was not going where we were going, but the conductor thought it would be ok. The bus would slow down at the corner of the road that we needed. His passengers often jumped off there.

So we were standing ready on the platform, when the conductor threw my suitcase onto the road. My friend jumped off the bus, then I was picked up, collar and seat fashion and swung like a coal scuttle, backwards and forwards and up, and up into the sky and I flew over a great arch. The wind was warm on my face. There was a happy sound in my ears. I was airborne, and I had come alive. What a way to get to London!

My feet touched the ground just at the same time that my friend grabbed for the raincoat. We were crouching down together in the road. "I never thought," he said. "You wouldn't know to put your arms out for me to catch you. Good old mam, for tying your belt up like that." I could almost hear my mammy laughing and saying, "Oh boy, oh boy."

I was carried to the coursey and put down, and told to wait there while my friend fetched my suitcase. For the first time in my life, I thought I had been treated like a normal kid.

I thought about Daddy's London song, so I got down on my hands and knees to see if the street was really made of gold, and I saw a golden glow. I had been on the lookout for shining gold, but I was on my way to school because I could not see, I told myself. My friend said, "I've heard about kissing the ground, but..." He took my hand. We walked along the coursey in the sunshine, with the buildings on our left, and the motor cars pap-papping beside me.

Then I knew that I had been here before. Daddy had called it 'Up smoke'. There were thousands of living sounds, all making one big beautiful rumble. It made me laugh as I skipped along beside my friend. He said, "I never thought it'd be this easy."

Daddy's London song said that there were gangs of folks digging up the streets. I asked my friend about it. He said, "They dig 'em up at night in London." That's what the song said.

At the corner there were railings round the edge of the coursey. I thought, that's good, it'll stop folk from falling off. A gentleman standing there had a box that made music and I was picked up to put pennies in the slot. I thought that was what made it work, but the gentleman showed me how it was he who made the music with the box. He had to stretch it out and press the buttons. It opened like a fan. My mammy could make me fans from the papers that wrapped up the little tea parcels.

I was told that this gentleman was blind. Something happened inside my tummy. This was the first time I had met a blind person. I thought, is this what life is like for all blind kids when they grow up?

We turned left, and on the next corner, we came to a market stall, just one stall. Not like our market place at home. My friend bought me something, but I would not eat it, because I thought it was dusty. He told me that was the skin, and I was meant to eat it. But then he told me it was a peach, and then I ate it. That was in Daddy's London song. The song was right; the peach was ripe, and the juices all came off on my cheek. It was the best thing I had ever eaten. Out came the white hanky again, and a clean spot had to be found to wipe my chin.

On the train to take me to school, we had the compartment to ourselves, so my friend took me along the corridor to the toilet. He came in with me, and put my hands on everything I needed to find in there, and he put warm water in the wash hand basin. He said, "You've been before, so now you know what to do." And he left me to manage by myself, and waited outside in the corridor. I *did* manage by myself, but I got my sleeves a bit wet. It was warm on the train, and I asked to have my coat taken off. My friend said, "You must keep it on, because you must be clean when I get you to school."

He opened my suitcase to get out my sandwiches. We had both brought the same sort of sandwiches. That is how you know when your friend is a real friend. In between bites, he told me, "I've got to take a little boy to school tomorrow, and he's got to wear that raincoat. He's littler than you are, and I don't know what he's going to look like in it. It's too big for you."

When we had finished our sandwiches, he tried to wipe the front of the raincoat with his big white hanky. “Oh, just look at it,” he said. “I don’t know how anybody can get this clean.”

My friend was as happy as I was. He told me the story of Goldilocks and the three bears, and he knew the story of the three little pigs. I learned to sing, ‘Old MacDonald had a Farm’, and we played, ‘Fly away Peter, fly away Paul’. I could not see that game, but I did try to join in, and my new friend could pull off his thumb, and put it back on again.

We stood in the corridor to get some fresh air and look out of the window. My friend told me what he could see. There were little cottages and cows down by the water. He was sad that all I could see was green. I was happy. I had never been so happy!

“Can you see the green hills?” I asked.

He said, “Yes. They’re farther on.”

“Have they got walls?” I asked.

He said, “I can’t see them clearly, they’re so far away.”

I was so happy I thought I was going to cry. I did not want my friend to see. It might upset him. So I went back into the compartment and climbed on the settee. Seat, he called it. I leaned back in the warm golden sunshine. If the green hills were farther on, we would not be getting off the train just yet. I would have to sit and wait.

I traced the plush patterns of the seat with my fingers, and let myself be rocked with the trumbling train, and listened as it said, ‘far away, far away, far away, far away.’